EUROPEAN STUDIES

An Interdisciplinary Series in European Culture, History
and Politics

Executive Editor

Menno Spiering, University of Amsterdam
m.e.spiering@uva.nl

Series Editors

Robert Harmsen, The Queen's University of Belfast
Joep Leerssen, University of Amsterdam
Menno Spiering, University of Amsterdam
Thomas M. Wilson, Binghamton University,
State University of New York

EUROPEAN STUDIES

An Interdisciplinary Series in European Culture, History
and Politics

20

EUROSCEPTICISM:
PARTY POLITICS, NATIONAL IDENTITY AND
EUROPEAN INTEGRATION

Edited by

Robert Harmsen
and
Menno Spiering

Amsterdam, New York, NY 2004

Cover Photo: © ANP/AFP, 2005

Cover design: Pier Post

Le papier sur lequel le présent ouvrage est imprimé remplit les prescriptions
de 'ISO 9706: 1994, Information et documentation – Papier pour documents –
Prescriptions pour la permanence'.

The paper on which this book is printed meets the requirements of 'ISO 9706:
1994, Information and documentation – Paper for documents – Requirements
for permanence'.

ISBN: 90-420-1168-8 Bound
©Editions Rodopi B.V., Amsterdam - New York, NY 2004
Printed in The Netherlands

PREFACE TO THE PAPERBACK EDITION:
EUROSCEPTICISM AND THE 'NO' TO THE EUROPEAN
CONSTITUTIONAL TREATY

Since the publication of the hardback edition of this volume in the
European Studies series in early 2004, the phenomenon of what is con-
ventionally termed 'Euroscepticism' has continued to gain prominence
across the continent. The June 2004 elections to the European Parliament saw major gains made by Eurosceptic movements across many of
the now twenty-five member states of the enlarged European Union.
More dramatically, in the spring of 2005, referendums on the European Union Constitutional Treaty in two of the Union's founding
member states produced negative results. Within the space of four
days, voters in France and then the Netherlands appeared ready to put
the brakes on the further progress of a European integration project in
which their nations had, from the outset, played leading roles.

The verdict of the voters in the two national referendums was delivered with unmistakable strength. If European Parliament elections
have long suffered from low levels of public interest, the two national
referendum debates, on the contrary, captured the public's imagination. A highly charged campaign in France concluded with the vote on
29 May 2005, in which 54.7% of French voters rejected the Treaty on a
69.4% turn-out. Although the Dutch campaign lacked the intensity of
its French counterpart, it too, by its final stages, saw the kindling of a
national debate on European integration of a type not previously
witnessed in the country. The 1 June 2005 poll in the Netherlands
further produced a still more emphatic 'No', as 61.5% of the Dutch
voted against the Treaty on a 63.3% turn-out.

Yet, these more recent developments should not be viewed in isolation, nor as representing a uniform or one-dimensional rejection of

European integration. Rather, they form part of longer-term trends, detailed in the present volume, whereby the progressive evolution of European integration has inevitably produced new patterns of politics and reformulations of identities. The emergence and growing prominence of Euroscepticisms thus remain integrally linked to wider processes of Europeanisation, as both political actors and ordinary citizens seek to situate themselves within the complex – and potentially disorienting – landscape of Europe's evolving practices of multilevel governance.

The full significance of the verdicts delivered by the French and Dutch voters in 2005 may, indeed, be fully understood only against the background of both longer-term, cross-national trends and the more specific dynamics which have structured national European debates. The strongest trend to appear across the two countries was that of a marked 'anti-establishment' vote. In both cases, this anti-establishment vote may, in part, be reduced to a more narrowly based protest vote against unpopular centre-right governments. This factor remained, however, of limited importance. More striking was the broader desire expressed by the two electorates to sanction the entire national 'political class' or 'political establishment'. Here, the referendums served as something of a microcosm for the broader partisan construction of the European issue – and the problems of legitimation which this may create. As discussed in the introduction to the present volume, more radical forms of opposition to European integration are largely associated with parties otherwise on the periphery of national party systems, for whom it may serve as a further means to distinguish themselves from governmental or 'cartel' parties. Consequently, a debate concerning the fundamentals of the integration project itself will tend to fall along a fault line, in most European democracies, separating mainstream or governmental parties on the one hand from 'protest' parties (of the far left or the far right) on the other. While this line of division will largely be subsumed in most electoral contests by the need for voters to engage with a range of issues, it is given centre stage by a referendum concerned with the future of the integration project itself.

The referendum, in effect, frames the European issue in a manner which tends to put the 'centre' and the 'periphery' of national party systems on an equal footing. Particular problems, as such, arise for mainstream parties – for those in currently in government, but perhaps even more for those in opposition but with governmental aspirations. If pro-integration, mainstream parties fully engage with their opponents, they risk legitimating what otherwise would tend to be minority positions associated with the relative margins of the political system. Yet, conversely, not to engage such a debate is to risk the accusation of an absence of real democratic choice and accountability – voters, in effect, being given the sense that they have a choice only between a 'Yes' and a 'Yes'. In both countries, it is clear that the main national parties were unable to square these circles. In the Dutch case, attempts by senior governmental figures to delegitimate the 'No' – warning of dire consequences for peace and prosperity – were unmistakably counterproductive, undermining the credibility of the Treaty supporters themselves. Similarly, in the French case, the main governmental parties were unable effectively to counter the perception of a 'conspiracy of the elites'. Tellingly, perhaps the most memorable image of the French campaign was that of a *Paris Match* cover photograph for which the main party leaders of the right and the left, Nicholas Sarkozy of the *Union pour un Mouvement populaire* (UMP) and François Hollande of the *Parti socialiste* (PS), had posed together. The photograph, intended as a show of solidarity for the 'Yes', was, instead, extensively exploited in the campaign literature produced by their opponents as emblematic of a unified political elite which had collectively lost touch with the underlying interests of their electorates.[1]

The two results must further be situated relative to their specific national contexts. The referendums form part of a historical process whereby distinctive national European debates are structured. As demonstrated throughout the present volume, the tenor and content of these debates varies considerably, reflecting both different constellations of interests and different political cultures. This was also evident in the two campaigns, which were shaped by diverse senses of national identity and contrasting mental maps of the relationship between the national and the European levels.

---

[1] This image was most effectively exploited by the 'anti-globalisation' (*altermondialiste*) group ATTAC. The cover of one of its widely circulated anti-Treaty books featured an image of Hollande and Sarkozy, skating arm in arm towards a map of Europe, under the title '*Constitution européenne: Ils se sont dit Oui*' (Paris: Librairie Mille et Une Nuits, 2005).

The French referendum campaign was significantly shaped by the distinctive Euroscepticisms of the right and the left detailed in the two French chapters in this volume. On the right, the picture which emerged during the course of the 2005 campaign marked an interesting evolution relative to that documented by Paul Hainsworth, Carolyn O'Brien and Paul Mitchell in their chapter. Euroscepticism of the right, as it emerged in France during and after the 1992 referendum on the Maastricht Treaty, encompassed three distinctive strands: a dissident Gaullism within the mainstream right; a more traditional conservative and *souverainiste* position, most prominently associated with Philippe de Villiers; and a populist opposition to European integration espoused by the *Front national*. Strikingly, in the current campaign, the traditional Gaullist opposition to European integration was largely muted. In contrast to 1992, when around two-thirds of Gaullist voters opposed the Maastricht treaty, polling data suggests that UMP supporters voted by a three to one margin in favour of the Constitutional Treaty – and the government position – in 2005. The mainstream right also lacked the heavyweight leadership in 2005 which it enjoyed in 1992, when Charles Pasqua and, perhaps even more, Philippe Séguin were able to impose themselves as the most prominent figures in the 'No' camp. Moreover, while the *Front national* again marked its virulent opposition to the European project, Jean-Marie Le Pen himself was unable, in part due to health reasons, to occupy as prominent a place as he had in past European debates. French Euroscepticism of the right thus came, to a large extent, to be embodied by Philippe de Villiers, whose otherwise diminishing political fortunes have been given a clear boost by the results. It remains to be seen, however, whether he will prove to be more successful on this occasion than in the past at translating this European success into a more central presence in the national political arena.

While both a populist and a *souverainiste* Euroscepticism of the right thus formed part of the basis for the French 'No', the key explanation for the result nevertheless lies in the decisive majority which emerged against the Constitutional Treaty on the left of the political spectrum. The referendum campaign saw the clear emergence of the type of oppositional politics foreseen by Susan Milner in her chapter on the French left. Distancing itself from an established mainstream consensus which spanned both the centre-right and the centre-left, this oppositional politics sought to defend a distinctive 'European social model' and to define the basis for an 'alternative Europe'. Specifically, the 'No' campaign on the left focused on a rejection of what it termed the Treaty's 'constitutionalisation' of an 'Anglo-Saxon' liberal model of capitalism. This 'anti-liberal' discourse served as a unifying theme for a broad coalition, bringing together a majority of *Parti socialiste* supporters (despite the party's official support for the Constitutional Treaty) with a wide spectrum of parties and movements further to the left.[2] It was, moreover, this theme which served more generally to structure the terms of debate in France. Fuelled by a controversy surrounding the so-called 'Bolkestein directive' on the liberalisation of the internal market in services, the referendum campaign appeared to give form and voice to deeper French anxieties concerning both the destabilising impact of globalisation and the country's declining influence on the European stage. The Treaty's supporters, both in the Socialist Party and in the government, were thus put squarely on the back foot. Much of the 'Yes' campaign came to be focused on a refutation of criticisms concerning the Treaty's alleged 'ultra-liberal' or 'anti-social' character, rather than in making a positive case for the project itself.

The Dutch referendum campaign lacked a correspondingly sharp focus. The Dutch rejection of the Treaty appears, instead, to be the product of a rather diffuse amalgam of anxieties, criticisms and oppositions – amplifying that which Robert Harmsen, in the present volume, termed the 'stirrings of dissent' on European questions which have been visible in Dutch politics for now well over a decade. To judge by exit polling, concerns over the size of the net Dutch budget contribution to the European Union ultimately topped the list of reasons for a 'No' vote.[3] These concerns, however, were also joined by a host of other issues, including lingering doubts over the adoption of the euro (focusing particularly on the exchange rate at which the guil-

---

[2] TNS-Sofres/Unilog exit polling data published by *Le Monde* in its edition of 31 May 2005 indicated that 67% of voters identifying with the left, and 59% of Socialist Party supporters, opposed the Treaty.

[3] Interview-NSS exit poll data, as reported in the *NRC Handelsblad*, 2 June 2005. In a multiple response poll, 62% of 'No' voters cited 'the Netherlands paying too much' as a reason for their vote. The following three reasons were: 'the Netherlands is losing control over its own affairs' (*'Nederland minder baas in eigen land'*) (56%); 'Too little influence compared to other countries' (55%); and 'the Netherlands is losing its own identity' (53%).

der was merged into the single currency) and anxieties over both past and future enlargements of the European Union. Insofar as an overarching theme may be discerned, it is that of a generalised sense that the European Union had simply gone 'too far, too fast'.

As such, doubts surfaced as to the 'limits of Europe' – not only the geographical boundaries of the continent, but more directly the extent of its policy competence and the real or perceived threats which this might pose to Dutch national identity. On the right, the populist *Groep Wilders* sought to exploit this sentiment by way of a campaign which alleged that a 'Yes' vote would see the Netherlands lose control over its immigration policy. On the left, adoption of the Constitutional Treaty was portrayed as posing a threat to the 'crown jewels' of distinctive Dutch social policy choices in areas such as euthanasia, gay marriage, and the regulation of soft drugs. While the role played by such particular issues should not be overemphasized, they nevertheless formed part of the more general climate of opinion which took hold during the referendum campaign. This generalised, if partially unarticulated sentiment of qualified doubt was perhaps best captured in the anti-Treaty campaign of the left-wing *Socialistische Partij* (SP). The SP, in probably the most effective image of the Dutch media campaign, confronted voters with a map of Europe extending beyond the present-day boundaries of the Union, but from which the Netherlands itself had – literally – disappeared into the ocean. The accompanying slogan, 'the Netherlands off the map' ('*Nederland van de kaart*'), captured an underlying sense of anxiety about the weight of a relatively small country in a much enlarged Union and its ability, correspondingly, to preserve the distinctive attributes of its national identity.

At the time of writing, the ultimate fate of the European Constitutional Treaty, either as a package or as a potential source for more modest reforms, has not yet been determined. It is clear, however, that the French and Dutch 'No' votes of 2005 are likely to mark an important juncture in the process of European integration – at least on a par with the turning-point marked in 1992 by the first Danish 'No' vote and the French '*petit Oui*' as regards the Maastricht Treaty. As the Danish and French votes on Maastricht served to underline the end of a model of integration based on tacit consensus, the more recent negative verdicts point even more emphatically to the continued existence of a potentially worrying gap between national elites and wider public opinions. This is not to say that European integration will be 'derailed'. As argued above, the common use of such linear metaphors itself belies a certain misunderstanding of the nature and complexity of the process. In many respects, the growth of Euroscepticism appears less as a sign of a fundamental rejection of the European project, than as the result of its many successes. One might, indeed, be tempted to argue that the more moderate forms of Euroscepticism are significantly defined by the search for meaningful forms of politics which connect to Europe's already well-established supranational structures of governance.

It is against the background of this varied and changing landscape that we are pleased to publish the paperback edition of this collection. The volume, reflecting the extensive expertise of our multi-national and interdisciplinary team of collaborators, provides an exceptional survey of contemporary Euroscepticism, which has only gained in relevance and timeliness since its first publication.

The Editors
Amsterdam and Belfast
June 2005

NOTE FOR CONTRIBUTORS

European Studies is published several times a year. Each issue is dedicated to a specific theme falling within the broad scope of European Studies. Contributors approach the theme from a wide range of disciplinary and, particularly, interdisciplinary perspectives. Past issues have focused on such topics as Britain and Europe, France and Europe, National Identity, Middle and Eastern Europe, Nation Building and Literary History, and Europeanisation.

The Editorial board welcomes suggestions for other future projects to be produced by guest editors. In particular, *European Studies* may provide a vehicle for the publication of thematically focused conference and colloquium proceedings. Editorial enquiries may be directed to the series executive editor.

Subscription details and a list of back issues are available from the publisher's web site: www.rodopi.nl.

CONTENTS

EUROPEAN STUDIES 20 (2004): 13-35

INTRODUCTION:
EUROSCEPTICISM AND THE EVOLUTION OF EUROPEAN POLITICAL DEBATE

Robert Harmsen and Menno Spiering

Euroscepticism initially appeared as a distinctively English phenomenon, further contributing to a sense of the country's 'awkwardness' or 'otherness' in relation to a Continental European project of political and economic integration. Yet, at least since the early 1990s, a variety of forms of Euroscepticism have assumed an increasingly prominent place in Continental European political debate as well. The intensity of such Euroscepticisms, ranging from fundamental rejections of European integration in its present form through to mild reformist critiques, markedly varies from country to country. The general trend towards a more critical perception of European integration is, nevertheless, inescapable. Indeed, the integration process may be seen as a victim of its success. The European Union's progressively expanding policy competence has, correspondingly, multiplied the potential sources of friction which may give rise to forms of Euroscepticism. Equally, the EU's particular propensity for 'existential' political debate, regularly revising its founding treaties in the midst of discussions as to its finalities and purpose, has perhaps also served to fuel a commensurate questioning of that purpose.

The growth of political Euroscepticism has been accompanied by a growing literature on the subject. Noteworthy collections of Eurosceptic texts have appeared on the market, which, respectively, seek to assemble the Eurosceptic case (Holmes 1996; 2002) or to present a critical counterpoint for use in courses on contemporary Europe (Tiersky 2001). A burgeoning literature on Euroscepticism and the party politics of Euro-

pean integration has also emerged. Many of the principal contributions to
this literature are discussed in the pages which follow. It is, however,
apposite at this point to note the particular contribution of the 'European
Parties, Elections and Referendums Network' (EPERN), founded in June
2000 as the 'Opposing Europe Research Network' (OERN).[1] This international network, based at the University of Sussex in the UK, represents
the most comprehensive grouping of scholars to date concerned with
both Euroscepticism and broader questions pertaining to the impact of
Europe on national party systems.

It is against this background that the present number of *European
Studies* was conceived. Its basic intent is a modest, but important one – to
provide a single-volume comparative treatment of Euroscepticism across
a range of national cases. To this end, the present volume brings together
an international team of collaborators who examine the forms and dynamics of Euroscepticism across ten countries in twelve chapters. Within
the inevitable limits of a single-volume study, this allows for a representative group of countries to be analysed in depth. Much of the strength of
the present volume lies in this empirical richness, drawing on the recognised national expertise of our collaborators.

Specifically, the range of cases included in the present volume allow
for the analysis of a spectrum of experiences of European integration,
taking into account the successive enlargements of the European Com-
munity/European Union. The first four chapters of the volume thus look
at the experiences of founding member states. Separate chapters on the
French right (by Paul Hainsworth, Carolyn O'Brien and Paul Mitchell)
and on the French left (by Susan Milner) allow for a detailed examination
of the variants of Euroscepticism which have appeared across the political spectrum in France. The following two chapters, on Germany (by
Klaus Busch and Wilhelm Knelangen) and the Netherlands (by Robert
Harmsen) round out this grouping, in both cases noting the growth of
critical voices in countries long known for their steadfast support of
European integration.

The next three chapters look at the experiences of countries which
joined the EEC at the time of its first enlargement, in the 1970s. The
roots of British Euroscepticism are examined both in terms of the general nature of the polity and society (by Menno Spiering) and with spe-

---

[1] The network, convened by Paul Taggart and Aleks Szczerbiak, maintains an
extensive web site at www.sussex.ac.uk/Units/SEI/oern/index.html.

cific reference to the UK's notoriously Eurosceptic press (by Peter Anderson). This contrasts with the experience of the Irish Republic, where (as Karin Gilland shows) a long-established 'pro-European' consensus has only recently shown signs of fraying at the edges.

Attention then turns to more recent processes of enlargement. Chapters on Sweden (by Milena Sunnus) and Austria (by Anton Pelinka) analyse the experiences of two West European 'neturals' which joined the EU only in 1995. This is followed by chapters on the Czech Republic (by Petr Kopecký) and on Poland (by Aleks Szczerbiak) which look at the growth of Euroscepticism in countries poised to join the Union in 2004, after an extended and markedly asymmetrical process of entry negotiations. Finally, an account of Swiss Euroscepticism (by Clive Church) closes the volume from the viewpoint of a longstanding 'outsider'.

The following pages seek to draw out some of the major themes which emerge across the various case studies – in essence, presenting the comparative findings of this collaborative project. An opening section looks at the differing usages of the terms 'Euroscepticism' itself, both as these arise in the present volume and against the background of the wider literature. The next two sections then present the major conclusions of this book as regards the (non-) impact of European integration on national party politics and the evolution of European political debate. Here, a crucial paradox emerges, as parties are shown to have increasingly invested in European issues, despite the persistingly low levels of electoral salience which attach to such questions. The final section addresses this paradox, suggesting a research agenda which may 'solve the puzzle'. The suggested research agenda situates a predominant concern with the party politics of Euroscepticism relative to the need for a wider, interdisciplinary framework, giving due attention to the cultural contexts within which discourses of Euroscepticism are embedded.

Defining Euroscepticism

The term Euroscepticism appears to have entered the British political and journalistic lexicon in the mid-1980s. The *Oxford English Dictionary*, which defines a 'Euro-sceptic' as 'a person who is not enthusiastic about increasing the powers of the European Union', provides a citation from a June 1986 article in *The Times* as its earliest reference to the usage of the term. Yet, as Menno Spiering notes in the present volume, instances of somewhat earlier usage may also be found. In *The Times* itself, the word had already been used some months earlier, in a November 1985 article.

Tellingly, in this 1985 article, the word was used interchangeably with the older term 'anti-marketeer'. As Spiering demonstrates, this association of the word with a basic opposition to British participation in the European integration project has since been maintained. The most common British usages of the term 'Eurosceptic' are thus 'harder' than that suggested by the *OED* definition, implying an opposition to UK membership of the European Union and its antecedents, rather than a milder lack of enthusiasm for the project.

The early uses of the term must also be understood as more generally embedded within the specific British political and historical context. Most obviously, the term Euroscepticism attaches to the 'anti-integrationist' *prises de position* which have, to varying degrees, found expression in both the Conservative and Labour Parties throughout the post-war period (Forster 2002), even if the word itself is of more recent vintage. Yet, Euroscepticism, in the British case, also refers to a rather broader phenomenon. This is, in part, captured by Stephen George's (2000) reference to Britain as a 'Eurosceptic state', pointing to a complex series of political, economic, and cultural factors which may be seen as distinguishing Britain from its Continental neighbours. British Euroscepticism, at its core, is not simply an opposition to the particular institutional forms which have been assumed by European integration. It is rooted in a deeper sense of a (Franco-German dominated) Continent as 'the Other', which finds expression not only through party politics, but in a rich vein of literary and cultural commentary as well (see Spiering 1997). This abiding sense of alterity was perhaps best captured by Sir Anthony Eden's often cited remark, made in a 1952 speech at Columbia University in New York, that British membership of a 'federation on the continent of Europe' was something 'we know in our bones we cannot do' (Cited in Young 1998, 73-74).

The sense of alterity as regards the Continental 'Other' is often further linked to a converse feeling of solidarity with a wider community of English-speaking nations. A primary attachment either to the 'Transatlantic Alliance' (understood in terms of the 'special relationship' with the United States) or to the 'Anglosphere' (see Tiersky 2001, 299-300) is posited as a mutually exclusive alternative to sustained involvement in the process of European integration. It is in this light that Peter Anderson, in the present volume, demonstrates the existence of a discourse of 'co-exclusive nationalism' in the British press. Anderson defines this as 'a form of nationalism which will accept one or just a very few other forms of nationalism as equal or superior, but which regards all other nationalisms as inferior, subsidiary or servile'. A discourse particularly prevalent on the Eurosceptic right of the Conservative Party,[2] such co-exclusive nationalism often assumes particular prominence through its fierce defence of the North Atlantic Treaty Organisation against the EU's incursions into the security field, which are perceived as dangerous and illegitimate. As illustrated by Anderson with reference to the press coverage of the proposals for the creation of an EU Rapid Reaction Force, this discourse remains rooted in an underlying scepticism as to the reliability of 'the Europeans' as allies, in contrast to a core faith in the solidity of the time-tested partnership with the United States.[3]

Though initially cultivated in English soil, the term Euroscepticism has progressively taken root elsewhere. Particularly with the growth of a more critical European discourse during the debates over the ratification of the Maastricht Treaty in the early 1990s, increasingly frequent references to 'Euroscepticism' – or analogous terms such as the French *'souverainisme'*[4] – may be catalogued in many countries. One must, however, be careful to contextualise these 'transplanted' usages of the term. Where the term 'Euroscepticism' is adopted in the context of distinctively articulated national political debates, it assumes a meaning which must be understood relative to the different national political traditions and expe-

---

[2] The late Peter Shore, a prominent Labour Eurosceptic, placed a comparable emphasis on the UK remaining 'inescapably committed to and involved with strong English-speaking nations in three of the six continents of the world' (Shore 2000, 158).

[3] A topic worthy of further research in this regard is the external impact of this particular form of Euroscepticism. As the 'pro-American, anti-European' right of the Conservative Party in the UK has strong affinities with conservative political circles in the US, one might well question the extent to which the current Bush administration's view of European integration may be shaped by a Eurosceptic understanding of the EU. See, for example, 'Les craintes européennes de Washington', *Libération*, 20 June 2003.

[4] The term *souverainiste* is applied in the French context, as well as *eurosceptique*, to those holding views which are (strongly) critical of the current course of European integration. *Souverainistes*, as the word suggests, seek to preserve the sovereignty of the French state against what are deemed to be the excessive incursions of the European institutions. The epithet, applied to politicians of both the left and the right, is usually associated with a strong defence of 'Republican values'. The nation, in this view, is held to derive a unique legitimacy as the only viable contemporary embodiment of the principles of both democratic governance and social solidarity. See Joly (2001) for an activist's exposition of *'souverainiste'* doctrine, as well as Benoit (1997) for an analysis of what he terms the doctrine of 'Social-Nationalism'. Interestingly, the term is shared with Québécois *souverainistes*, who advocate the creation of a sovereign (independent) Quebec state.

riences of European integration which frame those debates. In all of the cases dealt with in the present volume, the attendant 'scepticisms' appear to be of a narrower variety than their British etymological progenitor. All Euroscepticisms are marked by a doubt or an opposition as regards the particular *political* forms which have been assumed by European integration. Beyond the British case, however, the scepticisms dealt with in the present volume do not generally exhibit the wider *cultural* feelings of alterity which characterise much British Euroscepticism. This is not to assert that European integration does not raise significant issues of identity in a number of countries. Clearly, as Milenna Sunnus' discussion of 'Nordic superiority' in the Swedish case or Clive Church's analysis of the *Sonderfall Schweiz* highlight, European integration elicits strong, identity-based reactions well beyond Britain. It is, however, to underline that only in the British case does a sense of belonging to Europe, rather than 'Europe', appear to raise politically significant questions. As Spiering puts it, Britain remains distinctively marked by 'a tradition of literal *Euro*-scepticism, a long-established wariness not just of European integration, but of all things European'.

As noted in the opening section of this chapter, the growing political importance of Euroscepticism has prompted a growth in the scholarly literature on the subject. This literature has been significantly concerned with questions of definition, seeking both a better understanding and a more precise delimitation of the phenomenon. One of the first major efforts in this direction was a 1998 article by Paul Taggart, which presented a comparative analysis of Euroscepticism in the national party systems of the EU's fifteen member states and Norway. In this piece, Euroscepticism was defined as 'an encompassing term', which 'expresses the idea of contingent or qualified opposition, as well as incorporating outright and unqualified opposition to the process of European integration' (Taggart 1998, 366). In later comparative work, Taggart together with Aleks Szczerbiak extended the range of analysis to encompass the new democracies of Central and Eastern Europe as well as the established democracies of Western Europe (Taggart and Szczerbiak 2001; 2002). This later work also refined the initial definition of the term, suggesting a clearer distinction between 'hard' and 'soft' forms of Euroscepticism. Following Taggart and Szczerbiak (2002, 7), hard Euroscepticism is defined as a situation 'where there is a principled opposition to the EU and European integration'. This may take the form of a direct advocacy of withdrawal from the EU in the case of existing member states, or of opposition to membership as regards candidate states. It may also take the form of 'policies towards the EU [which] are tantamount to being opposed to the whole project of European integration as it is currently conceived'. Soft Euroscepticism, conversely, refers to a situation in which there is not a principled objection to membership, but in which concerns or criticisms are expressed as regards EU policies which amount to a 'qualified opposition'. This may take the form of 'a sense that [the] "national interest" is currently at odds with the EU's trajectory' (Taggart and Szczerbiak 2002, 7).

Petr Kopecký and Cas Mudde (Kopecký and Mudde 2002; see also Kopecký in this volume) have put forward an alternative categorisation to that of Taggart and Szczerbiak. Kopecký and Mudde distinguish between *specific* support for the European Union on the one hand and *diffuse* support for European integration in general on the other. This produces a two by two matrix of possible party positions on European integration (reproduced on p. 231 of the present volume) structured along an EU pessimist/optimist axis and a Europhobe/Europhile axis. Four general types of party position correspondingly emerge. Euroenthusiasts are those who are both supportive of the broad project of European integration and optimistic as regards the actual trajectory of the European Union's development. Europragmatists are not supportive of the broad project of European integration, but nevertheless are positive about the current EU insofar as it is deemed to serve particular national or sectoral interests. Eurosceptics, conversely, hold a positive view of the broad project of European integration, but are critical of the actual development of the EU. Finally, Eurorejects reject both the general idea of European integration and the specific form which it has taken in the European Union. Within this model, the term Eurosceptic itself is thus of more restricted scope than in most common usages, referring to only a specific category of critics of the European Union.[5]

Finally, Chris Flood (2002, 5) has recently suggested a six-point continuum along which broad party positions towards the EU may be situated. This continuum runs from a 'rejectionist' position at one end (im-

---

[5] Although the basic logic of the categorisation has remained consistent, Kopecký and Mudde (2001) applied a somewhat different set of names to the categories in an earlier, widely cited version of the paper. Most notably, in this earlier categorisation, the term 'Eurosceptic' was reserved for what, above, is described as a 'Euroreject' position – i.e. an outright opposition to both the EU and European integration more generally.

plying either opposition to EU membership or to participation in some particular EU institution or policy) to a 'maximalist' position at the other end of the spectrum (associated with a strong positive advocacy of further integration, as regards either the overall project or some particular aspect thereof). The four intermediate positions are identified as 'revisionist' (seeking a return to the situation which existed prior to a major treaty reform); 'minimalist' (an acceptance of the status quo, but resisting further integration); 'gradualist' (accepting further integration, but only at a slow, prudent pace) and 'reformist' (a position of 'constructive engagement', seeking to improve existing arrangements). In all cases, the categories encompass support for or opposition to particular policies or institutions, as well as positions concerning the overall trajectory of the integration project. The framework is intended to be 'value-neutral', allowing for a descriptive categorisation of positions, without initially seeking to determine the underlying ideological or strategic motivations for those positions.

As this brief survey of the literature demonstrates, there is clearly no single, accepted usage of the term 'Euroscepticism'. This plurality of usages is reflected in the present volume, in which authors have determined the appropriate definition and scope of the term as it relates to their particular subject area. Across the contributions, the most common distinction is that between a 'hard' and a 'soft' Euroscepticism. Yet, the latter category, as Taggart and Szczerbiak (2002, 37) themselves have noted, appears to require further narrowing. In effect, the term 'soft Euroscepticism' is often used to designate trends which might be better conceptualised in terms of the 'Europeanisation' of political debate, as parties and other actors critically engage with different policy choices over a growing range of areas at the European level. These problems of definition have not been a significant impediment to the development of the literature. Indeed, quite the opposite appears to be true. The debates surrounding questions of definition are largely the reflection of an increasingly vigorous scholarly interest in the nature, origins and prospects of Euroscepticism.

'Europe' and national party systems

There is a strong consensus in the literature that European integration has not acted as a realigning issue at the level of national party systems. Peter Mair (2000), for example, compellingly argues that questions of European integration have not had a significant impact as regards either the format or the mechanics of national party systems. As regards format, most simply equated with the number of parties, Mair notes that parties which define themselves principally with reference to a pro- or anti-integration cleavage have not emerged as electorally important within the domestic arena in any member state. While 'anti-European movements' have occasionally been able to exploit the particular dynamics of European Parliament elections in order to make electoral inroads (see below), these successes have not 'spilled back' into national political arenas. In terms of mechanics, concerned with the pattern of relationships between the (main) parties in a system, Europe again does not appear to have figured with any prominence. The terms of party competition have not been altered by European integration; a pro- / anti- integration cleavage shows no signs of superseding the existing national-level patterns of politically relevant cleavages most obviously structured around left-right, territorial, and confessional axes (see further Marks and Wilson 2000).

The national case studies in the present volume largely confirm the limited impact consensus in the literature. There is little evidence of either existing parties substantially redefining themselves in terms of European integration or of new parties principally concerned with European issues making major breakthroughs at the national level. Pre-existing national patterns of politically salient cleavages, if not 'frozen', nevertheless appear largely undisturbed by a potentially disruptive European dimension.

The persistence of pre-existing patterns of cleavage finds confirmation in, for example, the relative failure of Jean-Pierre Chevènement's candidacy in the 2002 French presidential election. As detailed by Susan Milner in her chapter on the French left, Chevènement's candidacy sought to cut across the traditional left-right divide in French politics. He attempted to create a broad cross-party alliance around a 'Republican platform', which included a significant Eurosceptic element. Briefly, it appeared that he might succeed, emerging as the 'third man' in the presidential race relative to incumbent President Jacques Chirac and incumbent Prime Minister Lionel Jospin. Revealingly, however, Chevènement was ultimately able to win only a little over 5% of the vote and finished in a disappointing sixth place on the first ballot of a presidential election marked by strong protest votes for parties of both the extreme right and the extreme left. Following the presidential election, Chevènement's *Mouvement des Citoyens* turned in an equally poor performance in the ensuing legislative elections. This 'disastrous showing', as Milner argues, 'casts doubts on the appeal of an ultra-Gaullist line on European integration shorn of its social base, that is, of its distinctive left or right-wing elements'.

Only the case of Switzerland appears as a partial exception to the general limited impact thesis. In the Swiss case, Clive Church argues that 'the European issue has helped to revitalise the Right'. The European issue, more so than themes such as immigration, has 'increasingly dominated' the discourse of Christoph Blocher and the *Schweizerische Volks-partei* (SVP), playing an important role in its major electoral gains of recent years. Europe, in effect, has been something of a *fer de lance* for the SVP, allowing it to introduce a more confrontational tone and oppositional logic to Swiss politics. This Swiss exception must, however, be placed within the specific national context from which it arises. In part, the European issue sits on a much wider cleavage line concerning the country's position in the world. This line marks a division between 'an open, outward looking mainly urban Switzerland' on the one hand, and a 'closed, inward looking and mainly rural Switzerland' on the other. The SVP's success in exploiting the European issue must also be understood relative to the unique characteristics of the country's political system. In part, as Church details, one must account for the strong Swiss tradition of direct democracy and the frequent holding of referenda on European issues. The SVP forms only part of the wider 'anti-European' movement which has been able to coalesce as a campaigning force over the course of these numerous *votations*. The unique character of the Swiss executive and the SVP's position in the government must further be factored into the equation. The junior partner in the four-party permanent coalition which governs the country (holding a single seat under the so-called 'Magic Formula' which determines the distribution of seats in the seven-member Federal Council), the SVP has simultaneously been able to play a role in governmental decision-making and assume a more oppositional posture in the country at large. The comparatively greater prominence of the European issue thus appears the product of both the country's unique geopolitical situation and the distinctive characteristics of a political system which departs in a number of major respects from a more classic parliamentary model.

In this latter regard the Swiss case corresponds to a more general phenomenon, which has been the subject of a growing interest in the literature. Studies of the impact of European integration on national party systems have increasingly focused on the institutional dynamics which may create or limit possibilities for inter- or intra- party divisions to emerge on European issues in particular national settings (see, for example, Aspinwall 2000; Lees 2002). Such factors as the nature of national electoral systems, the characteristics of national policy-making procedures and the (non-) existence of important sub-national political arenas have thus been examined by scholars as potentially shaping the manner and the extent to which Eurosceptic opinions may establish a presence in a party system. In the present volume, this institutional dimension is, for example, highlighted by Menno Spiering in his discussion of British Euroscepticism. Spiering, drawing on a substantial literature suggestive of the 'awkwardness' of the British state in European terms, notes such factors as the impact of the British 'first-past-the-post' electoral system on the handling of European issues. As he argues, this 'winner take all' system has tended to have a polarising effect, with the major parties having to cater to dissident (sceptic) opinion to a disproportionate extent in order to maintain their internal cohesion. This is argued to stand in contrast to proportional representation electoral systems used elsewhere, which facilitate government 'from the centre'.

The opportunity structures which allow for the emergence of Eurosceptic movements also receive extended attention in the chapter on the French right by Paul Hainsworth, Carolyn O'Brien and Paul Mitchell. Within the framework of a survey of Euroscepticism on both the mainstream and the extreme right in France, the chapter puts forward an extended analysis of the opportunity structure which allowed for the emergence, and accounts for the limitations, of Villierism as a political movement. Philippe de Villiers' Eurosceptic *Autre Europe* list achieved a major electoral breakthrough in the 1994 European Parliament election, when it won 12% of the vote. This breakthrough is explicable with reference to what Reif and Schmitter (1980) have described as the 'second order' character of European Parliament elections. Such elections, which are not decisive for the exercise of political power at the national level, may be viewed by the electorate as an opportunity to express discontent with the current government or with governmental (mainstream) parties more generally. As such, these contests are frequently marked by the emergence or success of smaller parties, often with distinctive agendas. Moreover, the higher profile given to European issues by EP elections further tends to make these elections particularly attractive arenas for political movements focused on European integration, particularly if paradoxically, Eurosceptic parties. The success of Villierism in 1994 clearly fits this wider pattern. The opportunity structure which allowed for the movement's success cannot, however, be understood only in terms of the structural opportunity created by EP elections for the expression of dissent. Equally, as Hainsworth et al. demonstrate, one must look at the specific configuration of the main political forces in place and the manner in which this facilitated mobilisation around a strong Eurosceptic discourse. It is this detailed analysis of opportunity structures which allows one to understand the movement's later failures. While a joint list under the leadership of de Villiers and the prominent Gaullist Eurosceptic Charles Pasqua repeated the success of 1994 in the 1999 EP election, these European electoral gains have never been parlayed into a successful implantation in the domestic political arena. In keeping with more general patterns, 'Europe' has not emerged as a salient issue in 'first order' presidential or parliamentary elections, and has, as such, not served as an effective vehicle for national political ambitions.

The handling of questions concerned with European integration has thus largely been shaped by the established dynamics of national party systems and the broader institutional contexts in which they are embedded. Although an occasional source of intra-party turbulence (as in the case of the British Conservative Party), European integration has been absorbed within – or at least has shown no signs of displacing – pre-existing patterns of cleavage in contemporary European democracies. The issue remains of low electoral salience, with occasional Eurosceptic successes in EP elections not spilling over into domestic political arenas.

Yet, this affirmation of the limited impact of European issues at the level of national party systems tells only part of the story. National debates on European integration have not remained static. One may, for instance, point to substantial changes in party positions on 'Europe' over the years. Such an evolution is, for example, detailed by Anton Pelinka as regards the case of Austria in the present volume. As Pelinka documents, Austrian Euroscepticism has undergone a long-term evolution from the left to the right. While sceptical or critical attitudes towards Austrian participation in the EU and its antecedents were historically stronger on the left, it is now the populist far right *Freiheitliche Partei Österreichs* (FPÖ) which stands alone among the main Austrian parties in espousing a Eurosceptic position. Indeed, as Pelinka shows, the positioning of the main Austrian parties on the European issue has come almost full circle, insofar as in the late 1950s the FPÖ had also stood alone, but at that time in its support for Austrian membership of the EEC.

More generally, one may further point to a notable evolution as regards the typical contours of national debates on European integration. Despite the limited electoral salience of European integration per se, the growing importance for national policy-making of the European Union has increasingly led parties to engage – critically – with European issues. As such, there has been a marked increase in the prominence of the European dimension within most national political arenas, as both the broad trajectory of the integration project and individual policy choices made at the European level come under closer national scrutiny. 'Europe' has become something of a staple of national political discourse, in terms detailed in the following section.

The evolution of European political debate

As noted at the outset of this chapter, European integration took a 'critical turn' in the early 1990s. This critical turn largely coincided with the negotiation and ratification of the Treaty on European Union (TEU) or Maastricht treaty. Maastricht marked a major, substantive advance in the integration process, eliciting a much stronger critical engagement on the part of national public opinions. Both the initial Danish 'No' vote in the country's June 1992 referendum on the treaty and the French *'petit oui'* which followed in September of that year sent clear signals of the erosion of the 'permissive consensus' which had long prevailed. Proponents of the integration process could no longer confidently rely upon a climate of diffuse support for European integration coupled with public deference to elite choices. From Maastricht onwards, those choices were subject to both an increasing level of public scrutiny and a much greater proclivity for the expression of dissent. Susan Milner, in her introduction to a special issue of the *Journal of European Integration* on Euroscepticism, speaks in this regard of a post-Maastricht Euroscepticism which provided a 'salutary shock', as it marked 'a shift in emphasis away from elites and towards public concerns' (Milner 2000, 3). Bruno Cautrès (1998), on the basis of Eurobarometer polls, similarly notes not only a growth in critical or negative opinions about European integration after Maastricht, but also a clear 'structuring' or 'crystallisation' of national public opinions on questions related to European integration. In other words, from the early 1990s onwards, there is evidence of 'Europe' increasingly becoming a 'normal' political issue, subject to debate along relatively stable and clearly articulated lines of division.

This critical turn in public opinion finds expression in three ways in the present volume. First, in the case of a number of EU member states, one may detect a 'discursive shift' in recent years as regards European integration. This refers to a situation in which a markedly more critical European discourse has come to characterise mainstream political debate in countries with historically low levels of Euroscepticism, but without 'Europe' having become an electorally salient issue. Among the countries covered in the present volume, Germany, the Netherlands, and Ireland all display such a discursive shift. Second, in the EU candidate countries of Central and Eastern Europe, a rather different trajectory may be seen, which corresponds to the political dynamics created by the accession process itself. Here, an initial and somewhat uncritical perception of European integration, linked to a 'return to Europe' (or to 'the West'), progressively gave way to a more nuanced, interest-based European politics. This, in particular, can be seen as the reflection of an essentially asymmetrical negotiation process, in which the opposition of the day could (all too) easily gain political mileage by criticising the concessions inevitably made by the government of the day. Both of the prospective member states dealt with in this volume, the Czech Republic and Poland, displayed this trajectory. Finally, across the full range of cases dealt with in the present volume, one may detect the more general growth of an increasingly critical European discourse. This discourse centres on a defence of national interests and identities, as well expressing a heightened concern with institutional and policy choices at the European level itself. These trends are examined in more detail below, with reference to the relevant national cases.

The German case offers clear evidence of the erosion of a long-established 'permissive consensus'. As documented by Klaus Busch and Wilhelm Knelangen, there has been a notable change in prevailing German perceptions of European integration since the early 1990s. Although party-based Euroscepticism remains a marginal phenomenon in Germany, public opinion has shown itself to be increasingly sceptical of the integration project. Historically above-average levels of public support for European integration, as measured by Eurobarometer polls, have dropped to only average or, on occasion, below average levels. This drop in public support may, moreover, be linked to key policy choices. Busch and Knelangen demonstrate that the cumulative effects of the completion of the single market, the adoption of the single currency and EU enlargement have stoked fears that German employment, wage and social standards are being threatened by the present trajectory of European integration. German Euroscepticism thus engages broader discussions concerning the further development of a European Social Model, as well as attendant debates over competing models of capitalism.

A similar growth of critical sentiment may be seen in the case of the Netherlands. Robert Harmsen, in his chapter on Dutch Euroscepticism, focuses on these 'stirrings of dissent', which mark a break with a well-entrenched 'pro-European' consensus in the country's politics. As in the German case, 'objective' root causes may be found for the growth of Dutch unease with the integration project. The emergence of a more critical Dutch European discourse coincided with the country becoming a net (and progressively heavier) contributor to the Community budget in the early 1990s. More recently, concerns over the impact of enlargement on both the EU budget and the credibility of the Union's institutions have fuelled political debate. Against this background, Harmsen documents the manner in which a more explicitly articulated notion of national interest has become a staple of mainstream Dutch European discourse. Initially associated in the early to mid-1990s with Frits Bolkestein, at the time leader of the free market liberal *Vollkspartij voor Vrijheid en Democratie* (VVD), this newly assertive insistence on the need to 'fight the national corner' in European negotiations has found echoes across the political spectrum. Notably, mainstream Dutch Eurocriticism has been further amplified by the unparalleled electoral success in 2002 and 2003 of movements whose broader 'protest' agendas included clear Eurosceptic elements (the *Lijst Pim Fortuyn* and the *Socialistische Partij*). Thus, though 'Europe' remains of low electoral salience in the Netherlands (as elsewhere), a discursive shift has nevertheless clearly taken place in which a critical engagement with European issues has increasingly figured on the Dutch political stage.

Irish European discourse has displayed a comparable shift. Here, one must carefully contextualise the most dramatic development to date, the No vote in the June 2001 referendum on the Treaty of Nice. As Karin Gilland argues, the first Nice result 'should not be automatically read as a sign of Euroscepticism taking hold in Ireland'. In fact, there were actually fewer No voters in 2001 (529,478) than there had been in the 1998 referendum which approved the Treaty of Amsterdam (when 578,070 No votes were recorded). Yet, though the widely reported 'shock' of the first Irish Nice vote cannot be read as a sign that the Irish Republic is becoming a 'Eurosceptic state', more nuanced changes in public opinion and political debate may be discerned. A number of prominent Irish politicians have, in recent years, struck dissonant notes in what had previously been an almost uniformly 'pro-European' chorus. Among other recent developments, Gilland highlights the 'Boston-Berlin' and 'budget row' controversies. The Boston-Berlin debate was initially prompted by a speech given by the Táiniste (Deputy Prime Minister), Mary Harney, in July 2000. In this speech, Harney expressed her admiration for American social and economic models in contrast to their European counterparts, suggesting that Ireland was 'spiritually a lot closer to Boston than Berlin'. The budget row refers to a very public spat between the Irish Minister of Finance Charlie McCreevy and the EU Economic and Monetary Affairs Commissioner Pedro Solbes, triggered by the latter's criticism of the Irish government's December 2000 budget with reference to the disciplines required by Economic and Monetary Union. One may thus detect a growing willingness on the part of mainstream politicians to give a public airing to instances in which they feel there to be a discordance between the national interest and the direction of European policy. As in the Dutch case, a Eurocritical discourse has thus entered mainstream political debate, even as the principal parties continue to hold to strongly 'pro-European' programmes in general. Interestingly, also corresponding to the Dutch case, this growth in mainstream Eurocriticism has been further accompanied by the growing electoral success of parties whose programmes include clear Eurosceptic elements. As Gilland notes, both the Green Party and Sinn Féin made significant gains in the May 2002 Dáil election.

The evolution of European debate in the accession states of Central and Eastern Europe has, as previously noted, followed a rather different trajectory. In these countries as well, there are signs of the generalised growth of a more critical European discourse. Yet, inevitably, this discursive evolution principally reflects the experience of a protracted, asymmetrical negotiation process. It is this pattern which, for example, Petr Kopecký details as regards the Czech Republic in the present volume. Kopecký notes that, initially, the issue of European integration had 'very little salience in Czech political discourse'; the issue of Czech EU membership was 'subject to a positive, if only romantic and illusory, consensus among the political elites and the public alike to become part of Europe'. Nevertheless, as the negotiations proceeded and concessions progressively mounted on sensitive issues, critical voices were increasingly heard both from the interests affected and from opposition parties quick to exploit the opportunity to criticise the government's supposed 'weakness' in defending national interests. As Kopecký illustrates, 'the abstract and broad geopolitical terms' of the initial consensus on European integration thus progressively gave way to a 'more nuanced, concrete, and most importantly, somewhat more salient debate about what EU membership actually entails'. The growth of Eurocritical and Eurosceptical opinion has not, of course, impeded Czech entry into the EU. The June 2003 Czech accession referendum saw a 77% Yes vote on a 55% turn-out. The pattern of pre-accession politics is likely, however, to leave its mark on post-accession European political debate in the Czech Republic. The country, in Kopecký's turn of phrase, may well prove itself a notably 'awkward newcomer'.

Aleks Szczerbiak highlights a similar evolution of political debate and public opinion in the Polish case. Until the late 1990s, Polish EU membership was subject to 'an overwhelming political elite consensus', as well as enjoying 'extremely high levels of public support'. As in the Czech case, however, this consensus 'was couched in very abstract and broad geopolitical or historical terms'. The intensification of the accession negotiations thus predictably brought to the fore an increasingly acute sense of divergent interests. The profile of European issues was raised in Polish political debate, but in a manner which very largely focused on the concessions which the country was having to make as part of its bid for entry. As Szczerbiak stresses, 'Brussels' thus came to be 'viewed increasingly as a focus for conflict and hostility'. If a strong nationalist discourse largely failed to resonate in Polish public opinion, a marked growth in both Eurocritical and Eurosceptic attitudes may be tracked in relation to identifiable socio-economic interests. Again, this growth of more critical sentiment has not impeded Polish accession. Despite fears of a low turn-out, almost 59% of the Polish electorate turned out in the June 2003 referendum which approved accession by a margin of 77% to 23%. Equally, however, one can assume that this pattern of pre-accession politics will leave its mark on post-accession Polish European policy and discourse.

Across a range of cases encompassing both current and prospective EU member states, one may thus point to a clear evolution of European political discourse in a manner which confirms both the increasing prominence of European issues and the commensurate affirmation of a more critical discourse. Much of this critical discourse has taken the form of a progressively stronger articulation of notions of 'national interest', usually linked to prevailing national socio-economic interests. Yet, more generally, the place assumed by 'identity' should not be minimised. In particular, as Milena Sunnus demonstrates in her chapter on Sweden, issues of 'interest' and 'identity' may be tightly intertwined. The defence of 'Nordic Values', which underpins much Swedish Euroscepticism, encompasses both specific policy choices (in fields such as gender equality, environmental protection and alcohol abuse) and a broader model of polity and society (the *'folkhem'*) within which these choices are embedded. As Sunnus illustrates, the politics of European integration – and Euroscepticism – may thus also be conceptualised in terms of 'cultural flows' from the 'centre' to the 'periphery' and back again. In essence, national models of polity, policy and society both seek to shape and are shaped by emerging European models.

The picture which emerges of national-level political debates on European issues is thus a rather 'healthier' one than that painted in much of the literature. Clear signs are present of a politics which meshes questions of interest and identity, substantive policy choice and jurisdiction, in a manner which will be familiar to students of many federal or multicultural polities. There are, undoubtedly, legitimate concerns over both the gaps in accountability and the low level of transparency which characterise Europe's emerging system of multi-level governance. Yet, it is equally clear that forms of national political debate are emerging which both reflect and respond to this unique and uniquely complex system of governance. With a delightful irony, the strongest trend to emerge from the study of Euroscepticism is that of the 'Europeanisation' of national political debate.

An emerging research agenda

The two strands of analysis discussed above point to the existence of an interesting and potentially important paradox. In essence, the findings of this volume, within the framework of a wider literature, confirm both the increasing level of party engagement with European issues and the continuingly low electoral salience of those issues. The question thus arises as to why parties have increasingly invested themselves in an arena which promises little in the way of direct returns. The answer demands, in the first instance, that we move beyond the prevailing focus on electoral politics in the study of Euroscepticism. A full understanding of Euroscepticism requires a fully articulated conceptualisation of the multiple roles assumed by political parties in contemporary European democracies, including their role as governmental actors. This, in turn, leads one to the consideration of a wider research agenda, which sees the emergence of differing forms of Euroscepticism as an aspect of the multiform proceses of Europeanisation which are reshaping European polities and societies.

At the level of party politics, the concept of a 'cartel party', developed by Richard Katz and Peter Mair, offers a particularly useful point of departure for understanding the dynamics suggested above. Katz and Mair, in a widely cited 1995 article, argue that a new model of party has emerged in West European democracies over the past quarter-century. In contrast to previous models of party, such as the 'mass party' (rooted in civil society) or the 'catch-all party' (acting as a broker between civil society and the state), the 'cartel party' is itself an agent of the state. A symbiotic relationship has developed between party and state, in which the principal governmental parties are able to form a permanent 'cartel' excluding rival formations. These parties, in particular, have benefited from substantially increased levels of state funding, which allow them to conduct essentially media-based campaigns. The traditional party militant is replaced by a mixture of professional cadres and a broader, but less engaged base of supporters. Elections largely cease to be contests between competing programmes, but rather are primarily fought 'on the basis of competing claims to efficient and effective management' (Katz and Mair 1995, 19). This model has been subject to a number of criticisms, concerning both its conceptualisation and the empirical evidence on which it rests (see, for example, Koole 1996). Yet, it remains highly apposite in the present context as one of a number of 'heuristically convenient polar types, to which individual parties may approximate more or less closely at any given time' (Katz and Mair 1995, 19).

The idea of a 'party cartel' is perhaps most readily applicable in understanding Euroscepticism as a form of anti-establishment protest. As Paul Taggart (1998) has convincingly demonstrated, a 'hard Euroscepticism' has generally been a 'touchstone of dissent' in West European party systems; an 'anti-European' stance has formed part of the more general 'anti-system' discourse of parties on the periphery of national party systems. 'Europe', in other words, emerges as one of several elements which differentiate 'protest' parties from the 'mainstream' or 'cartel' parties which, in alternation, exercise governmental responsibility. This general argument is further confirmed by the case studies in the present volume. Here, as in Taggart's study, 'hard Euroscepticism' appears confined to

movements which are otherwise on the margins of national party systems.

The converse question has, however, received little attention in the
literature. If harder forms of Euroscepticism may be understood in terms
of strategic or ideological reactions to the 'pro-European' orientation of
the governing 'cartel', one is still left with the question of how the cartel
parties themselves handle European issues. The cartel party model, as
articulated by Katz and Mair, appears to offer part of the answer. The
handling of European issues has clearly been infused with a strong managerial ethos, which may be seen as restricting debate and rendering illegitimate alternative agendas. In this vein, the handling of European issues is
consistent with a model of cartelisation, in which the actors concerned
seek to preserve their collective monopoly and exclude those outside as
being 'unfit for government' (lacking the qualities of a *Regierungsfähige*
party in the telling German epithet). Yet, this equally clearly is not the full
story. Mainstream European discourse has shifted in a markedly more
critical direction, in ways which cannot simply be ascribed to a 'defensive'
posture seeking to preserve existing 'cartels'. Governmental parties themselves have increasingly given voice to Eurocritical sentiments, particularly on specific, policy-based grounds. This points, in part, to the limits
of the cartel party model, insofar as governmental parties continue to
assume the brokerage role between civil society and the state ascribed by
Katz and Mair to catch-all parties. It further points to the need for a
fuller articulation of the role of parties as 'agents of the state' within the
cartel party model, looking beyond questions of resource dependency.
One might, for example, examine the extent to which the much discussed
'professionalisation' of political parties (see, for example, Panebianco
1988) has intersected with a comparable 'professionalisation' of European questions in which a distinct cadre of 'European experts' is emerging (Georgakakis 2002). Beyond an interesting exercise in socio-political
mapping, this might give one an indication of the extent to which political parties are embedding themselves within a 'technocratic elite', rather
than, as is more commonly assumed, being displaced by it. Further questions might concern such issues as the 'management of public opinion' by
governmental parties and the extent to which the handling of European
questions corresponds to or departs from more general national patterns.
It is clear that the questions elicited by Euroscepticism and the evolution
of European political debate centrally engage much deeper questions

concerning the nature of contemporary political parties and the roles which they play in the political process.

The study of Euroscepticism also, inevitably, leads one to a consideration of broader processes of 'Europeanisation'. It is beyond the scope of the present exercise to examine the multiple uses of the term Europeanisation which have entered the scholarly literature, across a range of social science disciplines, in recent years. Drawing on an earlier volume in the *European Studies* series (Harmsen and Wilson 2000), a distinction might, nonetheless, be made between a wider scholarly agenda associated with Europeanisation and the more conventional uses of the term European integration. Following Harmsen and Wilson, it may be suggested that the concept of Europeanisation, relative to that of European integration, more fully encompasses a simultaneous concern with developments at the European and national levels, as well as more explicitly focusing on the interrelationship between institutions and identities. The study of Euroscepticism readily fits within this wider interdisciplinary framework. It is necessarily situated at the intersection between the national and European levels, mapping national responses to the integration process. The form assumed by these responses, however, takes one beyond the narrow confines of the political system, to broader understandings of national cultures and identities. Simply put, '*n'est pas eurosceptique qui veut*'. Eurosceptic discourses, if they are to resonate as mobilising themes, must normally be consonant with the perceived core values of national polities and societies. This is all the more true insofar as most strong Euroscepticisms are, in essence, 'particularist' reactions to the 'cosmopolitan project' of European integration.[6] As such, much Eurosceptic discourse seeks to vaunt the particular merits of distinctive national practices and values, seen as threatened by a 'homogenising' European influence. As with Europeanisation, the understanding of Euroscepticism must, in short, be placed within the framework of a vigorously interdisciplinary European Studies. While Euroscepticisms are principally played out in the arena of party politics, one must not lose sight of the fact that these arenas are themselves embedded in wider cultural contexts.

---

[6] The 'internationalist' discourse of the far left is a notable exception in this regard. One might, however, argue that both the particular forms assumed by internationalist discourses and the relative receptivity to them remain conditioned by national political cultures.

References

Benoit, Bertrand. 1997. *Social-Nationalism: An Anatomy of French Euroscepticism.* Aldershot: Ashgate.

Cautrès, Bruno. 1998. Les attitudes vis-à-vis de l'Europe. In *Les enquêtes Euro-baromètres: Analyse comparée des données socio-politiques,* eds. Pierre Bréchon and Bruno Cautrès, 91-114. Paris: L'Harmattan.

Flood, Chris. 2002. Euroscepticism: A Problematic Concept. Paper presented to the University Association for Contemporary European Studies research conference. Queen's University of Belfast. 2-4 September.

Forster, Anthony. 2002. *Euroscepticism in Contemporary British Politics: Opposition to Europe in the British Conservative and Labour Parties since 1945.* London: Routledge.

Georgakakis, Didier, ed. 2002. *Les métiers de l'Europe politique: Acteurs et professionalisations de l'Union européenne.* Strasbourg: Presses Universitaires de Strasbourg.

George, Stephen. 2000. Britain: Anatomy of a Eurosceptic State. *Journal of European Integration* 22, no. 1: 15-33.

Harmsen, Robert and Thomas Wilson, eds. 2000. *Europeanization: Institutions, Identities and Citizenship. Yearbook of European Studies* no. 14. Amsterdam: Editions Rodopi.

Holmes, Martin, ed. 1996. *The Eurosceptical Reader.* Basingstoke: MacMillan.

Holmes, Martin, ed. 2002. *The Eurosceptical Reader 2.* Basingstoke: Palgrave.

Joly, Marc. 2001. *Le souverainisme: Pour comprendre l'impasse européenne.* Paris: François-Xavier de Guibert.

Katz, Richard S. and Peter Mair. 1995. Changing Models of Party Organization and Party Democracy: The Emergence of the Cartel Party. *Party Politics* 1, no. 1: 5-28.

Koole, Ruud. 1996. Cadre, Catch-All or Cartel?: A Comment on the Notion of Cartel Party. *Party Politics* 2, no. 4: 507-523.

Kopecký, Petr and Cas Mudde. 2001. Empty Words or Irreducible Core?: Euroscepticism in East Central Europe. Paper presented to the annual meeting of the American Political Science Association. San Francisco. 30 August - 4 September.

Kopecký, Petr and Cas Mudde. 2002. The Two Sides of Euroscepticism: Party Positions on European Integration in East Central Europe. *European Union Politics* 3, no. 3: 297-326.

Mair, Peter. 2000. The Limited Impact of Europe on National Party Systems. *West European Politics* 23, no. 4: 27-51.

Marks, Gary and Carole J. Wilson. 2000. The Past in the Present: A Cleavage Theory of Party Response to European Integration. *British Journal of Political Science* 30: 433-459.

Milner, Susan. 2000. Introduction: A Healthy Scepticism? *Journal of European Integration* 22, no. 1: 1-14.

Panebianco, Angelo. 1988. *Political Parties: Organization and Power.* Cambridge: Cambridge University Press.

Reif, Karlheinz and Hermann Schmitt. 1980. Nine Second-Order National Elections: A Conceptual Framework for the Analysis of European Election Results. *European Journal of Political Research* 8, no. 1: 3-44.

Shore, Peter. 2000. *Separate Ways: The Heart of Europe.* London: Duckworth.

Spiering, Menno. 1997. Novel Attack by Historian: The Euro-sceptic Vision of Andrew Roberts' *The Aachen Memorandum. Theoretische Geschiedenis* 24, no. 2: 97-112.

Taggart, Paul. 1998. A Touchstone of Dissent: Euroscepticism in Contemporary West European Party Systems. *European Journal of Political Research* 33, no. 3: 363-388.

Taggart, Paul and Aleks Szczerbiak. 2001. Parties, Positions and Europe: Euroscepticism in the EU Candidate States of Central and Eastern Europe. Sussex European Institute Working paper no. 46. Brighton: Sussex European Institute. www.sussex.ac.uk/Units/SEI/pdfs/wp46.pdf

Taggart, Paul and Aleks Szczerbiak. 2002. The Party Politics of Euroscepticism in EU Member and Candidate States. Sussex European Institute Working Paper no. 51. Brighton: Sussex European Institute. www.sussex.ac.uk/Units/SEI/pdfs/wp51.pdf.

Tiersky, Ronald, ed. 2001. *Euro-skepticism: A Reader.* Lanham, MD: Rowman and Littlefield.

Young, Hugo. 1998. *This Blessed Plot: Britain and Europe from Churchill to Blair.* London: Macmillan.

EUROPEAN STUDIES 20 (2004): 37-58

DEFENDING THE NATION:
THE POLITICS OF EUROSCEPTICISM
ON THE FRENCH RIGHT

Paul Hainsworth, Carolyn O'Brien and Paul Mitchell

Abstract

France is a founder member of the European Community (EC) and it is difficult to envisage European integration having seen the light of day without the initial French presence and leadership. But equally, as a country with strong nationalist sentiments, a long history of nation-state construction and an assimilationist-minded imperialism, it is perhaps not surprising to find that pro-integrationist attitudes towards Europe have had to coexist with significant Eurosceptic feelings. This was apparent from the beginning, but the reality of differences over Europe was particularly apparent in more recent times in the 1992 referendum on the Maastricht Treaty. The 1992 campaign and results revealed a France divided in two, with forces on the political right (and, for that matter, the left) lined up in both Euro-camps simultaneously. This article focuses on the Euroscepticism of the right, as illustrated by the main party political strands which campaigned in the 1992 referendum for a 'no' vote: namely a distinct form of Gaullist nationalism, championed by political heavyweights such as Philippe Séguin and Charles Pasqua; national-populism, in the form of Jean-Marie Le Pen's *Front National* (FN); and – somewhere in between these two forces – Villierism, a maverick political force that made some impact in the 1990s, but whose political future now rests in doubt.

Gaullist Euroscepticism: the evolution of the national ideal

The neo-Gaullist *Rassemblement pour la République* (RPR) has been the most divided of the mainstream parties on the question of Europe – perhaps unsurprisingly given its historical position on the primacy of the nation-state and national independence. The Gaullist party has always been a 'national' movement (if not party), 'claiming the ability to speak for all French people across historic divides' (Hanley 2001, 309). The nation-state, then, is the 'natural arena' for action. In the European domain, the traditional Gaullist stress on national sovereignty, unity and grandeur is illustrated in a deep distrust of supranational structures and institutions, and opposition to the idea of a federal Europe. Indeed, the RPR's 2000 Manifesto, for instance, situated the nation *'au premier rang'* as regards Gaullist values (RPR 2000). The incorporation of the RPR into the umbrella right-wing grouping of the *Union pour un Mouvement Populaire* in 2002 has not lessened the tensions inherent in the Gaullist approach to European integration.

The original Gaullist approach to European integration was characterised by hostility: Gaullists voted against the proposed European Defence Community in 1954 and then against EEC and Euratom membership in 1957. However, opposition turned to 'pragmatic acceptance' of French membership of the EC following de Gaulle's accession to power (Guyomarch, Machin and Ritchie 1998, 84). This revised approach was underpinned by a realist view that French-led European integration, coupled with a strong Franco-German alliance, was the best way to strengthen France's political and economic position in the Cold War environment. Despite underlying contradictions between European integration and Gaullism's fundamental principles, the party broadly supported the Cold War development of the Community (EC) as furthering the national interest. The tensions inherent in this approach came to the fore in the post-Cold War 1990s, as the European Union (EU) developed and deepened (Guyomarch, Machin and Ritchie 1998, 94-102). The Maastricht Treaty on European Union (TEU) resulted in major difficulties for traditional Gaullists who feared the loss of nation-state sovereignty and identity. Intra-party rifts on the question of Europe and its relationship to the nation-state emerged, centred on three related, but conceptually distinct, themes: sovereignty, identity and the socio-economic consequences of European integration.

De Gaulle himself brought a specifically confederal vision to the European integration project, based on the belief that the nation-states of Europe were the indispensable and central building blocks of a European and global order. At the core of his approach to Europe was a 'certain idea of France' stressing national independence, grandeur and unity, and incorporating anti-federalist and anti-Atlanticist positions (Petitfils 1977;

Fysh 1993). He promoted a 'Europe of States' (de Gaulle 1970a, 406-407) and referred to European integration as a 'process of evolution that might lead to (...) confederation' (1970b, 182).[1] His vision held that French independence was not to be compromised, and that France was destined to lead any emerging European confederal organisation. Knapp (1994, 422) identifies the underlying tension in de Gaulle's 'European equation': a Europe that would support France's leading global role while not compromising French sovereignty.

The *leitmotif* of national sovereignty and its preservation within a European system appears throughout de Gaulle's speeches and writings. Accordingly, his favoured *modus operandi* for European cooperation was determinedly intergovernmental. This could be seen in two separate developments: first, in his (failed) proposal for a common foreign and defence policy outside of the Community framework – the Fouchet Plan – followed by a choice to deepen the bilateral Franco-German relationship; and second, in the 'Empty Chair' crisis of 1965-66 which established a national right of veto in the so-called 'Luxembourg compromise' (Prate 1993, 199-209). Seen as a victory for an intergovernmental, rather than supranational, community, the compromise continued to be referenced by French policy-makers and politicians into the 1990s (*Le Figaro*, 22 February 1996).[2]

However, the evolution of the Gaullist movement following de Gaulle's departure saw some major – and contested – shifts in the 1980s and 1990s which were to affect its approach to European integration (Fysh 1993, 1996; Derville 1994). Some have referred to a 'degaullising' of the party as it moved away from the defence of national sovereignty and a *dirigiste* approach to the economy (Hanley 2001). Knapp (1994, 419) comments that leader Jacques Chirac's and his RPR party's position on Europe 'changed practically out of recognition' in the early 1980s. In 1984 Chirac agreed to a joint list with the pro-European UDF (Union for

---

[1] The phrase '*Europe des patries*' is often attributed to de Gaulle. De Gaulle more commonly referred to a Europe of States. '*Europe des patries*' is a phrase now commonly used by the FN.

[2] *Le Figaro* reported on the internal governmnent document which guided the French representatives during the 1996 IGC negotiations. These government guidelines stated that 'concerning the first (Community) pillar and decision-making in Council ... France takes the view that any Member State should still be able to invoke, where necessary, the existence of a significant national interest, thus justifying postponement of the vote and the continuation of negotiations along the lines of the "Luxembourg compromise"'.

French Democracy) for the European elections, and by 1986, the party had agreed to the Single Internal Market (and the neo-liberal economics implied therein) and the introduction of Qualified Majority Voting – the antithesis of de Gaulle's 'veto' stance and his staunch insistence on the preservation of national sovereignty. Indeed, the FN (see below) has been skilful in taking on the partly discarded Gaullist rhetoric and using the language of sovereignty to lead its nationalistic and xenophobic anti-EU campaigns. All but eight RPR deputies voted for the Single European Act in 1987 (Knapp 1994, 357-358).

The decisions taken to meet stringent economic and monetary union (EMU) convergence criteria following Chirac's 1995 French presidential success suggest that, despite the national rhetoric, there has been a move towards a tacit acceptance of the 'pooling' of sovereignty. Once a central pole of Gaullist philosophy, the RPR pragmatically shifted from an un-compromising defence of the sovereign nation-state. Yet this reality remains tempered by continuing Gaullist rhetoric on the primacy of the nation-state. In election campaign mode, Chirac asserted that he would 'not accept that Europe transforms itself into a European super-state (...) It is perfectly legitimate to defend in Europe our national identities, our language, our view of cultural diversity or public service, our agriculture and our overseas territories' (*Financial Times*, 7 March 2002).

Although the party continued to proclaim its central value as 'the nation', this was situated within a European context: its manifesto of values asserted that 'because we have confidence in the future of the nation-state we are attached to the construction of Europe'. The (concept of) the nation is not that of conservatives and those nostalgic for the past – 'a refuge and a fixed reference'; rather, it is the privileged domain of 'democracy, liberty and solidarity', and acts in the general interest (RPR 2000). Nonetheless, this is somewhat ambiguous: if democracy and na-tionhood remain centrally linked, it is not clear how this may be recon-ciled with a supranational approach, in particular in sensitive areas where national sovereignty has been sacrosanct.

Dissident Gaullist Euroscepticism

The RPR might officially have been European 'by reason', if not by con-viction, but the party – and its supporter base – is divided.[3] It was the

---

[3] Although the RPR was often described as split between 'nationalist' Eurosceptics and pro-Europeans, Gueldry usefully distinguished three currents within the RPR:

TEU in particular that drew attention to the inherent tensions in the Gaullist – and indeed the French – approach to integration. As François Furet commented: 'The French, almost since the beginning and in any case since de Gaulle, have been caught in the contradiction of wanting both a strong Europe and weak shared institutions.' The TEU brought this contradiction into the open, as the 1992 referendum resulted in 'the first great public discussion in France of the organisation of Europe' (Furet 1995, 86-87).

The TEU ratification process gave impetus to an overt dissident Eurosceptic strand within the RPR, but also pointed up mainstream Gaullist ambivalence. More than six months passed after the signing of the treaty before a single major RPR figure came out in support: Nicolas Sarkozy, followed by Alain Juppé, followed by Chirac (Knapp 1994, 421). Chirac's actions typified Gaullist ambiguity. He refused to take the podium during the National Assembly debates on ratification (Stone 1993, 76), and although he voted for the treaty, despite misgivings and reported 'personal reluctance', he did so not as Chairman of the RPR but as a 'personal choice' (Gueldry 2001, 7).

However almost half of the 126 RPR deputies (58) supported Philippe Séguin's move to reject the ratification of the TEU and declare it unconstitutional (Fysh 1996, 183). The subsequent referendum, called unexpectedly by Socialist president François Mitterrand, gave leading dissident Gaullists, notably Séguin and Charles Pasqua, the opportunity to mount a well organised and dynamic 'no' campaign. Séguin and Pasqua formed an alternative 'rally': the *'Rassemblement pour le Non'*. This was by no means a case of a maverick breakaway grouping. The former RPR president and the former interior minister were joined by three past Gaullist prime ministers: Debré, Messmer, and Couve de Murville. In the referendum a majority of RPR voters (67 per cent) voted against the treaty – a majority not found in the other mainstream parties (*Le Monde*, 25 September 1992).

The Gaullist 'no' campaigners claimed that they were not 'anti-Europe', but 'anti-TEU'. At issue was the type of Europe being constructed and its impact on the nation-state. The central theme comprised the defence of national sovereignty: the 'traditional Gaullist fetish of the nation-state and of French exceptionalism was unexpectedly revived' in

Europeans 'by conviction' (e.g. Juppé), 'by reason' (e.g. Chirac), and Eurosceptics (e.g. Pasqua). Gueldry 2001, 186.

the referendum process, according to one analyst (Stone 1993, 86). Yet this might have been expected given the far-reaching impact of the treaty on the nation-state, in particular the transfer of powers from the national to the European level. Séguin published two books reaffirming the importance of the bounded nation-state as a basis for democracy (Séguin 1992; Garaud and Séguin 1992; Berger 1995, 206-207). He set out a vision of 'another Europe' based on an association of free peoples (including the eastern European countries), not an imposed technocratic federation. What was at stake was the future existence of France as a sovereign nation (*Le Nouvel Observateur*, 11-17 June 1992). These concerns were allied with a more general preoccupation with French national identity, as the 'no' campaign also incorporated more populist themes, including debate on the EU's proposed powers in immigration (Guyomarch, Machin and Ritchie 1998, 87).

The '*petit oui*' of the French electorate in the September 1992 referendum did not extinguish the dissident Gaullist strand. Séguin and Pasqua's *souverainiste* faction within the party, 'Tomorrow France' (*Demain la France*), campaigned against the government's *franc fort* policy in the 1993 election campaign (Knapp 1994, 131-135). Calling for '*une autre politique*', its concerns extended to unemployment and the lack of social cohesion. This 'reflection group' also opposed the 1997 Amsterdam Treaty, describing it as 'the death knell for France's sovereignty and independence' (*The Economist*, 13 February 1999, 29).[4] In the 1999 European election campaign, Pasqua broke with the RPR to set up a separate *souverainiste* list with de Villiers, and they subsequently established the *Rassemblement pour la France et l'Indépendance de l'Europe* (RPF-IE) (see below). This party continues today under Pasqua's leadership, with de Villiers resigning in 2000.

The 1999 European Parliament (EP) election results epitomised the Gaullist 'problem' with Europe and the continuing attraction of arguments based on national sovereignty and solidarity. The Pasqua-de Villiers list gained more votes than that of the RPR and, with thirteen seats, formed the largest grouping on the French right in the European

---

[4] Séguin has since changed his line on Europe, taking a more pragmatic approach and arguing that France 'has no future without Europe'. See *The Economist*, 'France, Divided by Europe', 13 February 1999, 29. Once a champion of a *dirigiste* approach to the economy, Séguin also now argues that an open liberal economic model is the key to France's economic growth.

Parliament.[5] Its 13.1 per cent share compared with the RPR's 12.8 per cent and the UDF's 9.3 per cent. It may have benefited from the split in the FN prior to the elections, indicating that both parties promote similar themes, if with differing national and European visions. However the RPF is at pains to differentiate itself from Le Pen's party, and position itself within Gaullist and Republican traditions, notably that of the Republican nation-state based on Renan's idea of the nation (RPF 2002a).

The RPF's primary reference is Gaullism: according to its charter, established at its 20-21 November 1999 founding congress in Paris, it appeals to 'patriotic Republicans loyal to the teachings of de Gaulle'. Having established its Gaullist credentials, it sets out the party's fundamental principles: to defend first, national sovereignty; second, stable institutions; and third, national solidarity (RPF 1999). Three major themes permeate its discourse and policies: Europe, globalisation, and the Republican nation-state.

The concept of national sovereignty lies at the core of these issues and its anti-EU stance. Statute 2.2 of the party states that 'the principal and fundamental aim of the RPF is the reestablishment of the sovereignty of France and of the French people' (RPF 1999). According to the RPF, sovereignty is threatened by the dual phenomena of supranational integration and globalisation. The party, then, aims for a renewal of the Republic and the restoration of an 'independent and sovereign France' (RPF 1999).

This continues the major theme of Pasqua's 1999 EP campaign, which centred on the technocratic EU as a danger to sovereignty: 'Every people, every nation is being asked to give up its sovereignty and its liberty for the benefit of technocrats in Brussels' (*European Voice*, 14-20 January 1999). The nation-state is the best guarantor of democracy. The programme fiercely rejects globalisation and free trade, and situates European integration within that process, which, it argues, serves to promote US domination (RPF 1999). There is overlap here with the discourse of the anti-EU Republican left led by (the 2002 French presidential candidate) Jean-Pierre Chevènement (see Milner in this volume), a fact not lost on either the RPR or the RPF (*Le Monde*, 24 October 2001). Indeed, ex-

[5] For a listing of all French MEPs, and their European party groups, see the EP web site at www.europarl.eu.int. With de Villiers' resignation from the RPF, three MEPs remain in the 21-member 'Union for a Europe of Nations' led by Pasqua, while those associated with de Villiers' *Mouvement pour la France* are non-affiliated.

Pasqua stalwart William Abitbol (who switched to Chevènement's *Pôle Républicain*) asserts that both leaders 'say more or less the same thing' on the major issues of Europe, globalisation and the Republic (*Le Monde*, 5 September 2001).

The programme also harks back to another Gaullist tradition, that of the strong state, and the need for the state to promote national solidarity. This has attraction as France struggles with the problems of *la fracture sociale* and *insécurité*. In 1992, Séguin attacked the Maastricht Treaty as an attempt to transfer the 'social contract' from the national to the European level (Stone 1993, 76). Such democratic concerns remain, but the party also stresses the need for socio-economic reform. The neo-liberal direction of the EU and the economic constraints imposed by the requirements of the Stability Pact have arguably lessened the ability of the nation-state to moderate inequality and alleviate poverty. All parties have the tendency to use the EU as an 'easy target' and blame the EU for its inability to keep campaign promises. The RPF takes this further and calls for the renegotiation of EU treaties to enable the state to promote national solidarity (RPF 1999, 2002b).

Overall, the Eurosceptic strand of dissident Gaullism bases its position on an uncompromising reading of Gaullist traditions. The EU should not be allowed to spell the end of the indivisible and sovereign French Republic (an argument also heard on the left), nor mark the end of French exceptionalism. It is also, then, an argument based on the contested issue of identity, which is echoed in the rhetoric of the far right. The constant references to national sovereignty – a contested and qualified concept – simplifies a complex European and global reality. As Stanley Hoffmann notes, there are two conceptions of sovereignty at play: a rigid, absolutist and indivisible reading versus a more open, pragmatic and flexible interpretation (Hoffmann 1993, 72). The RPR's admittedly ambivalent approach to the EU allowed for a more nuanced approach, as well as drawing on the argument that France can best defend its national interests as an influential member of a powerful regional entity. However this has been problematic for the party, as 'much of its electorate is still sentimentally attached to a more traditional vision of sovereignty' (Hanley 2001, 309). These issues and questions are likely to preoccupy the new right-wing umbrella political force (including the RPR), the *Union pour la Majorité présidentielle*, that was created in 2002 (and then re-named the *Union pour un Mouvement populaire*) to support Chirac's French presidential re-election and majority.

The Front National: France first

European integration has provided an important platform for the FN, notably by enabling the party to exploit proportional representation (PR) voting to win seats in the European Parliament (EP) and thus be in a position to offer encouragement and Euro-leadership to other like-minded parties across Europe. The acquisition of seats at Strasbourg has also served as a compensation for the dearth of French National Assembly seats, which a PR system would have delivered to the FN (as briefly happened in 1986-1988). In fact, the Euro-election of 1984 (along with the 1983 municipal elections in France) has widely been seen as marking the FN's breakthrough on to the national political stage (10%, 11 seats). The Euro-elections provided Le Pen with an opportunity to flaunt his Europeanism. As he wrote in the midst of the 1984 campaign, 'We must start by recognising that we are first and foremost Europeans, and that we should be proud of this. For ours is the most extraordinary civilisation in the world, with all its inestimable rich legacy.' Le Pen went on to call for 'a European patriotism' (cited in Fieschi, Shields and Woods 1996, 238, 239). FN primary sources in the mid-1980s – such as programmes and manifestos – claimed to support a coherent European project, that included support for a common European defence and nuclear strategy, a common foreign and security policy, common immigration controls, a common currency and a 'European preference' (to parallel and extend the party's touchstone concept of a 'national preference' in terms of jobs, housing, benefits and the like) (Hainsworth, 2000).

Yet, these *apparent* flashes of pro-Europeanism should not disguise the fact that, despite Le Pen's claim to have successfully reconciled a strong nation-state and a strong Europe, the party has had difficulty in marrying these two entities. Overwhelmingly, the national has been preferred to the European. The cries of 'France first' and 'France for the French' have been put forward consciously as the FN's most potent and identifiable slogans. Again, as Fieschi, Shields and Woods (1996, 239) point out:

> In passing from ideology to practical politics, from the rarefied conception of Europe as 'a common fund of civilisation' to the concrete realities of the EU as a political and economic entity, the FN's vision undergoes a radical transformation. The party's appeals to Europeanism turn out, under scrutiny, to be little more than a rhetorical strategy deployed in the service of a discriminatory ideology, an amplified 'nationalism' projected on a European stage.

In the 1989 European elections the party campaigned – true to its values – under the banner of *Europe et patrie*, for a Europe of nation-states. The choice at stake, according to Le Pen, was one between 'a geographically, politically and culturally defined Europe' or 'a cosmopolitan and multi-racial Europe', 'a resolutely patriotic' or 'a Socialist, *mondialiste*, utopian adventure' (Hainsworth 1989, 138). In fact, as suggested above, with the ongoing movement of mainstream Gaullism towards a more accommo-dating than hitherto Euro-perspective, the FN increasingly posed as the best exponent of old-style Gaullist values vis-à-vis European integration (Hainsworth 1989; Fysh 1993). Arguably, this posture was enhanced in 1989 by the recruitment of ex-Gaullist politician Yvan Blot to the FN's Euro-list, for Blot was the initiator of the French Committee for a Eu-rope of Fatherlands, inspired by Margaret Thatcher's famous Bruges speech and by de Gaulle's anti-supranationalism. Le Pen too was sympa-thetic to Thatcher's famous speech and in particular her rejection of a European social dimension (Le Pen 1989, 89-90).

In the 1990s, the FN's status as a Eurosceptic party was enhanced by two simultaneous processes. These were the push for deeper European integration, as personified by European Commission president Jacques Delors and as ushered in by the 1992 Maastricht Treaty and, on a wider front, the emergent New World Order that became manifest in the Soviet Union's collapse and the concomitant strengthening of US hegemony. The latter process has been discussed elsewhere (Hainsworth 1996) and it involves the FN's critique of European nation-states succumbing to American domination in the military, foreign policy, economic, cultural and other spheres.

The FN took a resolutely anti-Maastricht stance and campaigned strongly on it. The party's opposition to the TEU was a natural extension of the FN's defence of French identity and sovereignty within a confede-ral Europe of nation-states. Maastricht was seen simply as 'the end of France, the French people, its language and its culture' (Le Pen, in Front National 1993, 366-367). When, in June 1992, President Mitterrand an-nounced the referendum on Maastricht, the FN could look forward at least to the prospect of campaigning on their own ideological agenda: nationalism, sovereignty, anti-bureaucracy and identity. In short, the Maastricht issue was tailor-made for the FN to play its national and Eurosceptic card: '*La France contre les Maastricheurs*' (a play on the French word for traitor) (*La Lettre de Jean-Marie Le Pen*, no. 160, July 1992, 2). Maastricht was seen as an irreversible step towards a federal Europe – 'a

Europe of federasts' (another obvious FN play on words) – under the authority of the Brussels Commission. According to Le Pen: 'The death of nations is being plotted at Maastricht' (*National Hebdo*, 12 December 1991). The TEU was thus tantamount to 'an organised suicide' for nation-states (*National Hebdo*, 24 August 1992).

Le Pen aspired to lead the Eurosceptic campaign against Maastricht in 1992, but (as noted above) the fact that Gaullist heavyweights Philippe Séguin and Charles Pasqua broke ranks with their Gaullist pro-Maastricht colleagues enabled these two individuals to emerge as the leading voices in the 'no' campaign (see *Libération*, 9 and 12 September 1992). The effect of the Séguin-Pasqua campaign was to prevent Le Pen from appropriating the Gaullist Eurosceptic discourse. Le Pen tried nonetheless to put his party centre-stage with the assertion that 'only the National Front is clearly and unanimously against Maastricht', whereas other fellow-travellers (i.e. Pasqua and Séguin) remained basically attached to the 'yes' forces (*La Lettre de Jean-Marie Le Pen*, no. 160, July 1992).

The anti-TEU stance was a key FN theme throughout the 1990s and served to enhance the party's Eurosceptic credentials. The FN's 2001 programme *Pour un avenir français: Le programme de gouvernement du Front National* provided an extensive summary of FN policy stances for the twenty-first century. Europe figures prominently here, not only in a dedicated chapter, but also in Le Pen's introduction and in sections on sovereignty, foreign policy, and culture. Significantly, there are no references in the 2001 programme to European patriotism or preference, or even to any declared aspiration to reform the EU. The concept of 'European citizenship' (*à la Maastricht*) is seen to be anti-national and therefore not acceptable. Instead, the FN calls for a restoration of French sovereignty and independence and for the exit of France from the EU (2001, 160-161). Le Pen's introduction to the document is to the point: 'Let's liberate France'. One of the principal forces seen to be oppressing France is 'the Brussels bureaucracy': 'the Europe of Brussels is a prison for its people'. Everything allegedly has been sacrificed to Europe: liberties, money, agriculture, fishing, much of French industry, sovereignty and identity. Against this 'programmed death' (2001, 145), the FN puts forward a Gaullist-style Europe of nation-states and fatherlands, and co-operation with other European nation-states outside the trappings of the EU. The FN sees a federal, supranational state emerging in Europe as a prelude to the creation of a world government.

Pursuing themes that were to the fore in the FN's 1993 programme and in Le Pen's 1995 French presidential campaign, the 2001 document sees global forces such as the World Trade Organisation (WTO), the General Agreement on Tariffs and Trade (GATT), the USA, the dollar and unbridled free trade as behind the movement towards this world government. Europe is deemed to have become 'an ultra-liberalised economy under the influence of the United States, which works for the profit of anonymous financial powers' (2001, 147-148). Here the anti-big business tone of the FN's Eurosceptic discourse mirrors that of the French Communist Party (PCF). This is unsurprising since both parties have been fishing for support in the same 'popular quarters' since the emergence of the FN as a serious electoral force (and the PCF has in the past also been associated with national-populist and anti-EU themes, see further Milner in this volume). Economically, and again there are similarities with the PCF, the FN sees global institutions biased towards the United States as putting undue pressure on European nation-states, including on their cultures: '*L'Europe, c'est la submersion par la culture d'Hollywood*' (2001, 151). The FN portrays global and Atlanticicist pressures as conspiring with Brussels, in effect, to undermine the nation-state.

The 2001 programme foreshadowed many of the FN themes that were to emerge in the 2002 French presidential and parliamentary elections. In April 2002, for instance, Le Pen called for a referendum to bring back the French franc and to take France out of the EU. In June 2002, the FN manifesto supported the primacy of French over European law and the withdrawal of France from NATO (dominated by the US) and from the EU's Eurocorps forces. Whilst the FN's rivals attacked Le Pen for putting simplistic would-be solutions before the electorate, the FN leader was nonetheless able to attract protest (and policy driven) voters against the ruling parties and elites and to trade on popular disillusionment with enhanced European integration. As Nicholas Startin (2002, 14) has pointed out, whilst the Gaullist RPF grouping (see above) was created to exploit the Eurosceptic vote in the 1999 Euro-elections, 'by the 2002 presidential, however, right-wing Eurosceptic voters were positioning their support behind Le Pen.' In this light, a significant feature of the 1999 Euro-elections and the 2001 municipal elections in France had been the inclusion of one of Charles de Gaulle's grandsons on the FN lists.

In 2002, Le Pen took his presidential campaign to the heart of Europe when, on 23 March, he visited the European Parliament in Brussels. European Commissioner Chris Patten added his voice to the anti-Le Pen protestors that day: 'I have the impression that one of the least pleasant aspects of European civilisation is in the process of manifesting itself at the door' (*Le Point*, 7 May 2002). However, Le Pen's spectacular 17% (4.8 million voters) made him the talking point across Europe. This vote placed him just ahead of the Socialist candidate (the outgoing prime minister, Lionel Jospin) on the first ballot and thus into the second ballot run-off against the outgoing president, Chirac. To some extent, as Miguet (2002, 208) contends, Le Pen's success was due to the FN leader's polishing of his image, although the 'favourite demagogic themes remained immigration, insecurity and europhobic, xenophobic rhetoric'. Whilst 'Europe' never figured as a leading issue in the campaign, post-electoral polls significantly revealed that 59 % of Le Pen's electorate confessed to 'a negative opinion of Europe' (*Le Point*, 3 May 2002). Certainly, Le Pen's nostalgia for the franc against the euro was a persuasive factor with Eurosceptic voters (Mayer 2002, 356) and the FN leader, if elected, also promised promptly to withdraw France from the EU. However, only 45% of Le Pen's own electorate, and much less of the electorate as a whole (16%), supported this particular move. In fact, Le Pen's supporters found this to be the least attractive policy item in his programme (Mayer 2002, 377-379). The significant doubts *within* the party towards this proposal and the massive rejection of it *without* illustrate the reticence across the French electorate towards an FN-sponsored Euroscepticism carried to extremes.

Villierism: man and movement

The maverick right-wing politician Philippe de Villiers has also been a prominent exponent of French Euroscepticism. A staunch (and staunchly aristocratic) conservative, de Villiers resigned as a deputy prefect in protest at the election of Socialist president François Mitterrand in 1981. In 1986, he was named junior minister at the Department of Culture and Communication by prime minister Chirac. However, de Villiers found the period of left-right 'cohabitation' unbearable. His visceral distate at sharing power with a president of the left, compounded by a near total breakdown in his relationship with his superior at the Culture Ministry, François Léotard, led de Villiers to resign from government in 1987. De Villiers was able to become a *député* for the Vendée in the same year, and in 1988 he was elected president of the Vendéen *conseil général*, a position he has held ever since.

Ambitious for a return to national politics, de Villiers saw his chance in the 1990s, launching *Combat pour les Valeurs* (CPV), an organisation designed ostensibly to mobilise the public and political class against the seemingly endless series of political and financial scandals, by instilling a sense of propriety and 'values' into political life. The launch of CPV coincided with the 1992 referendum on the Maastricht Treaty. Convinced that it represented a serious threat to the future of the nation-state, de Villiers campaigned against the Treaty, alongside (as noted above) Charles Pasqua and Philippe Séguin.

Emboldened by the narrow defeat of the anti-Treaty lobby in the referendum, de Villiers incurred the wrath of his largely pro-European *Union pour la Démocratie Française* (UDF) colleagues by running in the 1994 European Parliament election as head of the Eurosceptic *Majorité pour l'Autre Europe* list. The list received 12.3 % of the poll, 2.4 million votes and 13 seats. Like Le Pen a decade earlier, de Villiers was the surprise of the European election. This success was repeated in the 1999 EP election when the *Rassemblement pour la France* list, bringing together de Villiers with Charles Pasqua, won 13% of the vote and again 13 seats.

However, de Villiers's attempts to replicate this success in national elections, with a right-wing, low taxation, anti-immigration manifesto, have failed to gain popular currency. Setting up his *Mouvement pour la France* (MPF) in November 1994, de Villiers ran for the French presidency in 1995, but failed to capitalise on his 1994 success, winning less than 5% of the vote. Since then, de Villiers's fortunes in national elections have failed to improve. In the 1997 National Assembly elections, the MPF received less than 3% of the vote. In the 1998 regional elections, the MPF won just 14 out of almost 1800 seats. Whilst the 1999 European elections signified an upturn in de Villiers's fortunes, it did not herald a national breakthrough, with the MPF receiving 0.92% in the 2002 Assembly elections. De Villiers, the party's only personality of note, is also the MPF's only *député*, seemingly secure in his Vendéen bastion.

In terms of policy, Villierism can best be understood by recalling his party's 1997 election manifesto (*Mouvement pour la France* 1997). According to the views set out here, the European Union should be transformed into a Confederation of Sovereign States. The Council of Ministers, in which all member states would enjoy a national veto, would be the sole executive body. The Commission would play a purely administrative role. There would be a common, but not a single currency. National border controls would be reinstated, while tariffs and quotas would be increased on imports into Europe in order to protect European business and jobs. Immigration into France would be tightened up, with stricter controls on the entry and residency of non-EU nationals. There would be a firm clampdown on illegal immigration and a revision of the nationality code requiring would-be French citizens to declare their allegiance to France and to prove their desire to assimilate into French life.

De Villiers's Euroscepticism is not merely couched in terms of opposition to, for example, the euro currency or the Commission. Rather, it is situated within a larger worldview that defines moves towards European integration as part of a wider international conspiracy to dismantle the nation-state. Prior to his 1994 success, de Villiers had expressed concern that Europe was being threatened by de-stabilising forces, notably by Socialism and free-tradeism (*libre-échangisme*). Socialism, de Villiers argues, is bureaucratic, undemocratic, corrupt, morally bankrupt and pro-immigration; it is not merely internationalist, but supranationalist, with European Socialists deemed to be responsible for the Maastricht Treaty and moves towards a European 'super-state'. Indeed, de Villiers maintains that, prior to the collapse of the Soviet Union, Socialists *everywhere* looked to Moscow as the 'central brain' (de Villiers 1989, 30). Now that the USSR is extinct, Socialists allegedly have found a new 'central brain' in Brussels and the European Commission.

Free-tradeism, de Villiers holds, is also unpatriotic: it has no respect for national economic considerations, and is orientated solely towards commercial profit, irrespective of the harm done to the economic, political and social infrastructure of a nation. De Villiers sees Socialism and free-tradeism as effectively working in tandem, as two sides of the same coin. In his opinion, they have the same supranationalist goal of denuding nations of their political and economic sovereignty. In mock honour of the former head of the European Commission, Jacques Delors, de Villiers calls this hybrid creed 'Delorism' and maintains that it has been imposed on France by an international technocratic elite, armed with a disregard for democracy and a politically correct mentality of 'there is no alternative'. Moreover, de Villiers considers the RPR-UDF as 'contaminated' by their periods of cohabitation with the Socialists, having effectively coalesced with Delorism.

According to de Villiers, Delorism has destroyed France because it has destroyed 'the values of initiative, and responsibility, patriotic and national values, moral and civic values, values of mutual aid (*entraide*), aesthetic and ethical values' (de Villiers 1991). But this need not be the case, he argues, if values can be instilled at the national and political level. For those who doubt that this can be achieved, he claims that Communism in eastern Europe fell because it could not withstand the values of the people: if values can bring down Communism, they also can bring down Delorism in France and western Europe.

Villierism and the opportunity structure of right-wing Euroscepticism

Given his political discourse, it is perhaps not surprising that many have been quick to decry de Villiers as a fellow traveller of the extreme right-wing *Front National*. For example, Bernard Tapie, the maverick Socialist and former government minister, branded de Villiers as 'Le Pen in his Sunday best' (*Le Monde*, 2 June 1994). A leading anti FN campaigner, Jean-Christophe Cambedélis, similarly accused the aristocratic de Villiers of being a disseminator of '*lepénisme* in silk stockings' (*Minute*, 24 June 1992). Even the FN has felt tempted to claim de Villiers as one of its own. Speaking in 1994, the then de facto deputy leader of the FN, Bruno Mégret, congratulated de Villiers on his political discourse, stating, 'Thank-you M. de Villiers! You are working in the right direction' (*Le Parisien*, 7 June 1994).

Irrespective of what claims are made by others as to de Villiers's relationship with the FN, de Villiers himself has constantly directed his political message towards those voters of the traditional mainstream right who were disenchanted with, in particular, the pro-EU policies of the RPR and UDF. Indeed, analysis of de Villiers's electorate during the 1994 European election shows that, across a range of socio-economic factors (age, occupation, religion, and so on), those who voted for de Villiers's *Autre Europe* list were considerably more aligned to the electorate of the RPR-UDF list, than to those who voted for the FN (*Le Monde*, 19 November 1994). In short, the electorate of the RPR-UDF and *Autre Europe* tend to be older, more bourgeois, more Catholic and more mainstream, than the younger, more working class, agnostic and extreme right FN electorate.

Yet the proximity between the electorate of de Villiers's list and that of the RPR-UDF does not, in itself, explain the size of the de Villiers's 1994 vote. There were three main factors behind the size and scale of de Villiers's breakthrough. Firstly, the European election was a 'second order election' (Reif and Schmitt 1980, 3-44), in which there is 'less at stake' than in more important 'first order elections', such as national parliamentary or presidential elections. Such second order contests should, in theory, encourage voters to look beyond the traditionally dominant parties. They are also characterised by the 'specific arena dimension' argument, which maintains that parties with a clear agenda on a specific area of policy (e.g. de Villiers's undoubted Euroscepticism) will benefit if other parties remain divided or ambiguous. Following this logic, the uneasy alliance between the avowedly pro-EU UDF and the officially pro-EU, but hardly enthusiastic RPR played right into de Villiers's hands (see Gaffney 1996, 96 for a discussion of the tension within the RPR-UDF alliance at this election).

Secondly, de Villiers's success in 1994 may be understood in terms of the opening up of a 'political opportunity structure' on the issue of Europe. Kitschelt (1995) argues that, in order for such an opportunity structure to develop, the mainstream parties need to cluster around the centre, leading to the creation of an opening in the political spectrum. According to Gaffney (1996, 96), a televised debate between the leader of the RPR-UDF list, Dominique Baudis, and the leader of the PS list, Michel Rocard, 'demonstrated the near-impossibility of defining a difference in the outlook of the two main blocs'. De Villiers was thus able to exploit this Eurosceptic void in mainstream politics, claiming that 'there is no left-right debate on Europe as the programme (of the RPR-UDF) is a Siamese twin of that of the *Parti Socialiste*' (*Le Monde*, 13 April 1994). Therefore, by adopting a Eurosceptic agenda, which appealed to many RPR-UDF voters who could not bring themselves to vote for the FN, de Villiers was able to exploit an apparent space on the French right between traditional mainstream and extreme positions.

Kitschelt's analysis of political opportunity structures is developed further by Eatwell (1998, 143-155), who claims that the notion of space, whilst important, is not enough for a political party to make a breakthrough. Following Eatwell, a party further needs 'legitimisation', which in de Villiers' case points to the third reason for his breakthrough: the 'Pasqua factor'. Although he stood against the UDF for the 1994 European election, de Villiers still belonged to the party. Not surprisingly, the UDF sought to distance itself as much as possible from this renegade member. Whilst the leadership of the RPR tried to follow suit, the Gaullist 'conscience' of the party found it difficult to reconcile itself with the officially pro-EU stance of the RPR-UDF list, thus making de Villiers's Eurosceptic manifesto highly attractive to many disaffected Gaullists. But what elevated de Villiers's list in the last few days of campaigning, from a respectable 8% in the polls to a dramatic 12% in the actual ballot, was the intervention of Charles Pasqua. Four days before the vote, Pasqua, the then Minister of the Interior and former associate of de Villiers from the 1992 anti-Maastricht referendum campaign, made a speech in which he all but gave his seal of approval to de Villiers:

> A dissident list has been presented for which a certain number of the electors of the (parliamentary) majority is prepared to vote. We can only regret it, but are we going to eject or expel its voters? No! For me, it is quite clear, the majority is that which was elected in 1993 (*Le Monde*, 10 June 1994).

As de Villiers was elected as a UDF *député* in 1993, Pasqua was clearly saying that de Villiers was from the same family as the RPR-UDF and thus the latter's electorate should have few qualms in voting for the *Autre Europe* list. Pasqua's intervention is crucial in understanding the performance of de Villiers's list in this election. The near total acceptance of the Europe of Maastricht by the leaders of the RPR-UDF opened up a political opportunity structure for de Villiers to exploit, but Pasqua's blessing 'legitimised' de Villiers's campaign and increased *Autre Europe*'s vote to over 12%.

Nevertheless, second order elections tend to have a sting in the tail for new parties and for ambitious politicians. It comes in that the electorate, 'liberated' by the nature of the 'less important' second order contest, is not prepared to gamble with their vote in subsequent first order elections. Hence, whilst an ambitious politician might bask in the glory of success in a second order election, he or she may underestimate the scale of the task ahead in holding on to their newfound electorate. This is the fate that befell de Villiers. In standing for the French presidency in 1995, de Villiers failed to realise that his 1994 electorate was really that of the RPR-UDF. While these voters had temporarily gone over to de Villiers's camp in the EP election, they were not prepared to abandon their traditional party allegiance for the first order presidential election. Nor were they prepared to switch allegiance for the National Assembly elections in 1997 and 2002. Furthermore, in all subsequent first order elections, de Villiers has been shorn of the crucial 'legitimisation' of Charles Pasqua.

Yet Pasqua has still played an important role in the post 1994 career of de Villiers. In the run up to the 1999 European election, opinion polls were suggesting that a de Villiers led list was heading for electoral disaster. A BVA poll put de Villiers's rating at 3%; another for SOFRES put him on 5% (*L'Humanité*, 20 February 1999 and *Libération*, 24 February

1999). But the decision by Pasqua to acquiesce to de Villiers's pleas for help led to the two men forming the Eurosceptic *Rassemblement pour la France et pour l'Indépendance de l'Europe* list for the election, with Pasqua as president and de Villiers as his deputy. This list, as previously noted, achieved 13% of the vote and 13 seats. Once again, Pasqua had both 'legitimised' de Villiers and saved him from electoral failure. Yet, those who hoped that the de Pasqua-de Villiers tandem would break the mould of French politics were to be disappointed. Personal rivalry led to the break-up of the partnership, with de Villiers returning to the MPF banner and Pasqua becoming leader of the *Rassemblement pour la France*.

Since the 1999 election, de Villiers's electoral fortunes have not improved. Perhaps wisely, he chose not to stand in the 2002 presidential election. In the National Assembly elections of the same year, his party's mere 230,000 votes (0.92%), placed the MPF behind Bruno Mégret's FN splinter party, the *Mouvement National Républicain* (MNR). De Villiers can perhaps take some consolation from the fact that he was elected to the Assembly on the first ballot, with 67.15% of the vote, in his Vendéen fiefdom.

Despite recent losses, de Villiers has, for the the best part of a decade, been able to capitalise upon the unease of many within the electorate of the traditional mainstream right towards European integration. The future, however, does not look bright. He may be able to continue as the voice of the disaffected Eurosceptic mainstream right, but the chances of his party making a breakthrough in national politics appear slim. Indeed, now that he has broken with Pasqua, there is no guarantee that de Villiers will receive the required 'legitimisation' should he choose to stand again in the 2004 European election. It could well be that de Villiers might become the lost leader, bereft of a party of consequence or audience, gesticulating from the sidelines.

Conclusion

Euroscepticism is a characteristic of French politics. This article has assessed the nature of this phenomenon on the French right, as exemplified by (elements of) Gaullism, the *Front National* and Villierism. For reasons of space, we have not been able to cover the whole of the Eurosceptic right. A fuller picture would, notably, have included the minority forces ranged behind FN breakaway dissident Bruno Mégret and his MNR. Also, it is worth emphasising that Euroscepticism is not simply confined to the right – but, again, to pursue this particular theme any further is beyond the scope of this study (see Flood 2002 and, on the French left, Milner in this volume).

What undoubtedly gives French Euroscepticism a certain pedigree and legitimacy is its association with the key figure in twentieth century French politics, Charles de Gaulle. In this context, historic Gaullist reservations about European integration provide contemporary French Eurosceptics with a marker, a reference point that can be utilised to some extent against others on the *mainstream* right and against Brussels. Thus, as we have seen, the anti-Maastricht campaign and the second order nature of Euro-elections have served as occasions for the Eurosceptics to flex their beliefs – centered around concepts such as identity, anti-supranationalism, sovereignty and national independence.   However, the forces of Euroscepticism 'have flattered to deceive' when it has come to first order elections, deemed to be of more importance to French politicians and electors. In short, when Europe or the European Parliament has been centre-stage in the referendum or electoral campaigns, then Euroscepticism has performed strongly; but, in French presidential and parliamentary elections, Euroscepticism has neither carried over, nor impacted significantly. This is not to say that Le Pen has not performed well on these occasions – not least in 2002 – but, as Mayer (2002) has illustrated, Europe did not emerge as a decisive vote-winning issue here. All in all, then, these observations illustrate both the strengths and the weaknesses of French Euroscepticism. As a force in French right-wing politics its potency should not be exaggerated. Yet, married especially to anti-globalisation and anti-Atlanticist sentiments, it nonetheless retains a capacity for mobilisation and remains a source of tension and division on the French right, notably between the mainstream and the marginalised streams.

References

Berger, Suzanne. 1995. Trade and Identity: The Coming Protectionism?. In *Remaking the Hexagon: The New France in the New Europe*, ed. Gregory Flynn, 195-210. Boulder, Co.: Westview.

Derville, Jacques. 1994. Les partis gaullistes: fidélité aux principes et évolutions doctrinales. In *Le Discours politique en France*, ed. Pierre Bréchon, 37-58. Paris: La documentation française.

Eatwell, Roger. 1998. Britain: The BNP and the Problem of Legitimacy. In *The New Politics of the Right: Neo-Populist Parties and Movements in Established Democracies*, eds. Hans-Georg Betz and Stefan Immerfall, 143-155. London: Macmillan.

European Parliament. 2002. Members of the European Parliament. www. europarl.eu.int/.

Fieschi, Catherine, James Shields and Roger Woods. 1996. Extreme Right-wing Parties and the European Union. In *Political Parties and the European Union*, ed. John Gaffney, 235-253. London: Routledge.

Flood, Chris. 2002. The Challenge of Euroscepticism. *The European Union Handbook*, ed. Jackie Gower, 73-84. London/Chicago: Fitzroy Dearborn.

Furet, François. 1995. Europe after Utopianism. *Journal of Democracy* 6, no. 1: 75-89.

Fysh, Peter. 1993. Gaullism Today. *Parliamentary Affairs* 46, no. 3: 399-414.

Fysh, Peter. 1996. Gaullism and the New World Order. In *France: From the Cold War to the New World Order*, eds. Tony Chafer and Brian Jenkins, 181-192. Basingstoke: Macmillan.

Gaffney, John. 1996. France. In *The 1994 Election to the European Parliament*, ed. Juliet Lodge, 84-106. London: Pinter.

Garaud, Marie-France and Philippe Séguin. 1992. *De l'Europe en général et de la France en particulier*. Paris: Le Pré aux Clercs.

de Gaulle, Charles. 1970a. *Discours et Messages*, vol. III. Paris: Plon.

de Gaulle, Charles. 1970b. *Mémoires d'espoir: Le renouveau 1958-1962*. Paris: Plon.

Gueldry, Michel. 2001. *France and European Integration: Towards a Transnational Polity?*. Westport, Conn.: Praeger.

Guyomarch, Alain, Howard Machin and Ellen Ritchie. 1998. *France in the European Union*. Basingstoke: Macmillan.

Front National. 1993. *300 mesures pour la renaissance de la France: Front National programme de gouvernement*. Paris: Editions Nationales.

Front National. 2001. *Pour un avenir français: Le programme de gouvernement du Front National*. Paris: Editions Godefroy de Bouillon.

Hainsworth, Paul. 1989. The Triumph of the Outsider: Jean-Marie Le Pen and the 1988 Presidential Election. In *Contemporary France: A Review of Interdisciplinary Studies*, eds. Jolyon Howorth and George Ross, vol. 3, 160-172. London: Pinter.

Hainsworth, Paul. 1996. The Front National and the New World Order. In *France: From the Cold War to the New World Order*, eds. Tony Chafer and Brian Jenkins, 193-206. Basingstoke: Macmillan.

Hainsworth, Paul. 2000. The Front National: From Ascendancy to Fragmentation on the French Extreme Right. In *The Politics of the Extreme Right: From the Margins to the Mainstream*, ed. Paul Hainsworth, 18-32. London: Pinter.

Hanley, David. 2001. French Political Parties, Globalisation and Europe. *Modern and Contemporary France* 9, no. 3: 301-312.

Hoffmann, Stanley. 1993. Thoughts on the French Nation Today. *Daedalus* 122, no. 3: 63-80.

Kitschelt, Herbert. 1995. *The Radical Right in Western Europe: A Comparative Analysis*. Ann Arbour: University of Michigan Press.

Knapp, Andrew. 1994. *Gaullism since de Gaulle*. Aldershot: Dartmouth.

Le Pen, Jean-Marie. 1989. *L'Espoir*. Paris: Editions Albatros.

Lord, Christopher. 1998. The Untidy Right in the European Parliament. In *Transnational Parties in the European Union*, eds. David Bell and Christopher Lord, 118-131. Aldershot: Ashgate.

Mayer, Nonna. 2002. *Ces français qui votent Le Pen*. Paris: Flammarion.

Miguet, Arnauld. 2002. The French Elections of 2002: After the Earthquake, the Deluge. *West European Politics* 24, no.4 : 207-220.

Mouvement pour la France. 1997. *Programme pour une autre majorité*.

Petitfils, Jean-Christian. 1977. *Le Gaullisme*. Paris: Seuil.

Prate, Alain. 1993. La Ve République et l'Europe. In *La Vie politique en France*, ed. Dominique Chagnollaud, 199-219. Paris: Seuil.

Rassemblement pour la France. 1999. *La Charte du RPF*. www.rpfie.org/charte.html.

Rassemblement pour la France. 2002a. *Ce qui nous oppose au Front National*. www.legislatives.rpf.org/.

Rassemblement pour la France. 2002b. *Le Programme du RPF en 18 points pour les élections législatives de juin 2002*. www.legislatives.rpf.org/.

Rassemblement pour la République. 2000. *Manifesto of Gaullist Values*. www.rpr.org/.

Reif, Karlheinz and Hermann Schmitt. 1980. Nine Second-Order National Elections: A Conceptual Framework for the Analysis of European Election Results. *European Journal of Political Research* 8, no.1: 3-44.

Séguin, Philippe. 1992. *Discours pour la France*. Paris: Grasset.

Startin, Nicholas. 2002. *Parties et Patries: The Troubled Evolution of Europe and the French Right*. Thrity-Second University Association for Contemporary European Studies Annual Conference, Queen's University Belfast (September).

Stone, Alec. 1993. Ratifying Maastricht: France Debates European Union. *French Politics and Society* 11, no. 1: 70-88.

Uterwedde, Henrik. 1998. Mitterrand's Economic and Social Policy in Perspective. In *The Mitterrand Years*, ed. Mairi MacLean, 133-150. Basingstoke: Macmillan.

de Villiers, Philippe. 1989. *La Chienne qui miaule*. Paris: Albin Michel.

de Villiers, Philippe. 1991. *La Lettre de Philippe de Villiers* (April).

EUROPEAN STUDIES 20 (2004): 59-81

FOR AN ALTERNATIVE EUROPE:
EUROSCEPTICISM AND THE FRENCH LEFT SINCE THE MAASTRICHT TREATY[1]

Susan Milner

> Among the great powers, there is a French exceptionalism in Europe, which lies in the promotion of human rights, a heritage of values and social radicalism, and a certain view of public services, of secularism, of sovereignty combined with openness to the world, and of the United Nations.
>
> Daniel Cirera, Communist Party international affairs spokesperson (cited in Boniface 2002).

Abstract

This article reviews the position of the main French left groupings in relation to European integration since the early 1990s. The views of the more pro-European Socialist Party (*Parti Socialiste*) are contrasted with those of the *Mouvement des Citoyens* and the far left. The radical left view is anti-elitist and critical of the lack of direct citizens' input, opposing deregulation, privatisation and liberalisation. The electoral fortune of these groups has fluctuated, with the far left making significant gains in the late 1990s. The success of the Trotskyist left coincides with the growth of anti-globalisation movements and defensive mobilisation by trade unions at the end of the 1990s. The Chevènementists' shift away from left-right positioning has not paid off electorally. This suggests the persistence of a left-wing Euroscepticism – in the sense of a radically different vision of European integration from that currently advocated by heads of state and government – with its roots in popular mistrust of political elites and fear of neo-liberal policies.

[1] The author would like to thank Laurent Binet, and members of the University Association for Contemporary European Studies working group on France and Europe, particularly Helen Drake, for comments on the first draft of this article.

Euroscepticism – in the general sense of doubts and criticisms about the present state of European integration – flourished on the left in France at the end of the 1990s and at the beginning of the twenty-first century. Yet it remained controlled within the party system, largely because of the disciplining effects of the electoral system, but also because of the electoral risks involved in campaigning on an anti-EU platform when most polls showed that European issues did not figure among voters' prime (avowed) concerns. As a result, the far left parties which campaigned on a sceptical platform in the 1999 European Parliament elections garnered only around twelve per cent of the total vote, less than the Greens whose campaign led by MEP Daniel Cohn-Bendit had been uncompromisingly supportive of monetary union. Left-wing parties' campaigning against the pace and direction of European integration appeared to have died down at the end of the twentieth century, and Europe was 'barely present' in the electoral campaigns of 2002 (Ysmal 2002; see also Drake forthcoming), even if latent hostility to European integration formed part of left-wing voters' response to other issues, notably employment and living conditions.

However, mobilisation around European issues increased as trade unions and associations linked European policies with employment. Whereas demonstrations against the Maastricht and Amsterdam treaties had managed to mobilise only small numbers of mainly right-wing 'sovereignists', the Nice summit in December 2000 marked the beginning of a broader grassroots movement which brought significant sections of the left into a more overtly critical stance on European integration, within the context of an increasingly popular 'anti-globalisation' movement. This mobilisation had been prepared by earlier demonstrations against unemployment, mainly within the national context, but sometimes explicitly aimed at European institutions and policy-makers. Demonstrations against Renault's announcement of factory closures in Belgium (Vilvoorde) in 1996 directly targeted EU decision-makers and focused on demands for tighter regulation of the activities of multinational companies, following the 1993 demonstrations against the transfer of Hoover's production from France to Scotland. The success of the Vilvoorde demonstrations forced the left government elected in 1997 to promise regulation of redundancies in France and to seek European regulations against social dumping. In 2001, the much publicised Marks and Spencer redundancies further fuelled criticism of the inadequacies of 'social Europe' and linked protests against EU summits with wider critiques of global capitalism.

The transition to monetary union also focused economic and social policy-making more directly on the EU. From the early 1990s, the strong franc policy pursued by the French treasury under governments of both right and left had been criticised by left-wing economists and by trade unionists as destructive of jobs. The move towards full monetary union allowed proponents of a more expansionary macroeconomic policy to transfer their arguments to a European level, but also diffused their criticisms to some extent because of the technocratic mode of governance of European monetary policy. Thus, the transfer and diffusion of responsibility for decision-making both fuelled Eurosceptism and led to greater uncertainty about the appropriate locus of mobilisation. This uncertainty undoubtedly contributed to the crisis of the Socialist Party (*Parti Socialiste*, PS) in 2002.

The constraining effects of the French electoral system, particularly for the left, have been noted elsewhere (Milner 2000; see also Usherwood 2001). In the period 1997-2002, these constraints found expression in the 'plural left' coalition in government. In the 1999 European Parliament elections, the PS managed to form an alliance with Jean-Pierre Chevène-ment's *Mouvement des Citoyens*, which had been the principal focus of the left Eurosceptic vote in the 1994 EP elections. Their ambiguous joint slogan, '*Construisons notre Europe*' ('Let's build our Europe'),[2] did little to hide fundamental disagreements and demonstrated the uneasiness of the alliance, from which Chevènement soon broke free. However, as we shall see below, Chevènement's sovereignist ideology, which led him to break away from the left and seek 'Republican' alliances across the party spectrum, failed miserably in the 2002 elections. The failure of free-floating 'social-nationalism' (Benoit 1997) would seem to confirm the argument, made by Colette Ysmal (2002), that in a political culture profoundly marked by the left-right divide, there are distinctive left-wing and right-wing variants of Euroscepticism in France, closely linked to sociological factors. In 2002, as in earlier elections and as notably in the 1992 referendum on the Maastricht treaty, anti-European attitudes are found mainly

---

[2] This is an ambiguous wording. '*Notre Europe*' is the title of the pro-European, but not quite federalist (see the discussion on 'a federation of nation-states' in this article) think-tank led by Jacques Delors, who continues to supply the Socialists with many of their ideas on Europe. The term, however, also implies an alternative vision of Europe to that currently operating.

among those with lower levels of income and educational qualifications. Left-wing Euroscepticism is concentrated among blue-collar workers and lower-level white-collar workers. The endurance of the left-right divide in voters' attitudes towards European integration is also noted by Jocelyn Evans (2000; see also Andersen and Evans 2002) in his analysis of exit poll data from the 1990s.

The hardest core of anti-European sentiment, found in disproportionately high levels among voters of the far left and far right parties, is termed 'Europhobe' by Ysmal (in opposition to 'Europhile'), although the term is used synonymously with 'Eurosceptic'. All of the political parties scrupulously avoid the term 'Eurosceptic', but the left-wing critics of the EU have devised an ingenious set of adjectives to describe their stance, all beginning with the 'Euro' prefix. Thus, the Communist Party (*Parti Communiste Français*, PCF) has variously used the terms 'Eurocritical' and 'Eurorealist' (a label also adopted by Lionel Jospin in 1996-1997), whilst in 2002 Chevènement preferred the adjective 'Euroambitious'. The use of such terms in preference to the starker 'Euroscepticism' denotes the parties' reluctance to make European integration a primary focus of campaigning.

In this article we will look briefly at the European policies of the main left party, the PS, before focusing on the main Eurosceptic party groupings and finally considering the positions of the main trade union confederations, which have mobilised against EU summits with increasing success.[3] Together, the 'left sceptic' candidates in the 2002 presidential elections (Chevènement, the PCF general secretary Robert Hue, and the Trotskyist candidates Arlette Laguiller and Olivier Besancenot) garnered almost twenty per cent of the first-round vote. It could be argued, then, that the party discipline of the 'plural left' has led to a dispersal, rather than a suppression, of left-wing Euroscepticism.

The Socialist Party: in search of an alternative vision?
The policies of the main left party form an important part of the context for party-based Euroscepticism, particularly as the main party of government in the 1997-2002 period. The party's official policy since 1999 has been based on the notion of a 'federation of nation-states'. The term,

---

[3] The Greens are not discussed in this article since their policy is officially pro-European, even if they call for more attention to social Europe and have taken an active part in the 'anti-globalisation' movements.

invented by Jacques Delors, is the object of political consensus on the centre-left and mainstream right: broadly, what could be described as the pro-European mainstream of French politics. It implies acceptance of the mixed form of European governance currently in operation, but proposes a European constitution and greater co-legislation powers for the European Parliament, as well as a European Commission formed from the parliamentary majority. Criticism of the PS's project from within the party and from other sections of the left focus not so much on the institutional implications of a federation, but on the ambiguities surrounding the effective capacities of the national state and also the adequacy of a mixed form of governance to address the 'democratic deficit'. Instead, the more radical view emphasises the need for direct input from citizens (see Herzog 1999).

For the Socialists adherence to the ideal of European integration can be taken for granted, yet problems of reconciling market and welfare state were amplified in the 1990s, as the fall of the Berlin Wall appeared to open up the way for the clear establishment of the hegemony of the neo-liberal economic model (Baumel 1999). The strike movement of 1995 led the party to express more openly its reservations on the austerity policies imposed by the eurozone stability pact.[4] Hence one sees the references to the European social model which, alongside the idea of Europe as a power (that is, a rival to the United States of America), often appear from the outside as typically French obsessions. The central contradiction between 'an emphasis on belt-tightening neo-liberal economic policies and expansive social policies' (Schmidt 2001, 254) was heightened by the commitment to the strong franc and to monetary union. In response, the idea of 'economic government' was coined by one of Prime Minister Bérégovoy's advisers in 1988 and formed the basis of the 1997 Socialist manifesto (see Clift 2001).[5] The PS itself is of course notoriously divided, although the power of the factions has been diluted by the demands of presidentialism and governmental discipline. The party programme adopted under great pressure in late 1996, which formed the basis of the 1997 manifesto, advocated a 'Eurorealist' line which assumed transition to the euro under the conditions of the Maastricht treaty (Trea-

---

[4] The Socialist minister for European affairs acknowledged the impact of the strike movement on party policy in his 1999 book. See Moscovici 1999, 20-21.

[5] For a recent exposition of the case for economic government (although he prefers to use the term 'economic governance'), see Strauss-Kahn 2002.

ty on European Union, TEU) but also advocated political oversight of monetary policy (economic government). However, alternative texts were also put forward, including a proposal by the '*Gauche Socialiste*' for renegotiation of the TEU. Opposition to the current working of the European Union also formed part of the platform of the new faction created on the left of the party (including the former *Gauche Socialiste* faction) in September 2002, whose leaders Henri Emmanuelli and Jean-Luc Mélenchon argued that enlargement could not proceed without fundamental change to the EU's institutions and policies.

Appeals for stronger social regulation, the protection of public services and economic government form part of a general unease about the dominant paradigm of European integration which reflects common elements of French political culture, but which increases in intensity as one moves leftwards along the political spectrum.

The Chevènementists: all about sovereignty?

The formation of the *Mouvement des Citoyens* (MDC) as a separate party in 1991 (rather than as previously a faction within the PS) by Jean-Pierre Chevènement and his allies was triggered principally by opposition to the Treaty on European Union and to the Gulf War. Rather than opposing European integration outright, it campaigned consistently on the theme of an alternative vision of European integration, with the slogan '*Pour une autre Europe*' ('For an alternative Europe') in 1994 and later '*Construire une autre Europe*' ('Build an alternative Europe'). The alternative vision rested on a distinctive 'third-worldist' and anti-US foreign policy, articulated in the idea of a 'multipolar world', as well as in a rejection of federalism and an insistence on intergovernmentalist modes of decision-making. The MDC has also defined itself by its hostility towards monetary integration and a preference for a John Major-style 'soft currency' option, while also supporting common infrastructure projects and a generous Common Agricultural Policy. In the economic and social sphere, the Chevènmentists have advocated the tighter regulation of the activities of multinational corporations, a coordinated employment policy and strict measures to curb social dumping. These themes have remained constant and featured in the MDC's 1999 EP election campaign.

The MDC's argument in 1999 was based on the idea that the nature of European integration had changed since 1991. In particular, the construction of a Common Foreign and Security Policy (operating on an intergovernmental basis) had opened the way for autonomous European action which could challenge US hegemony and contribute to the development of a 'multipolar world', with priority given to dialogue with Russia and the southern hemisphere. Moreover, the possibility of closer cooperation on immigration policy also offered the chance for a renewed debate on citizenship, which would not only enhance decision-making powers, but would also help to restore the Republican ideal (Naïr 1999). The MDC was responding to a changed situation regarding European governance, but also following a logic of influence in the European institutions.

What should be noted here is that the MDC's position on European integration does not stand in outright opposition to the official French line, but rather constitutes a hardened version of traditional mainstream French policy. This policy has long been marked by support for Europe as a power, particularly in opposition to US dominance (*'l'Europe-puissance'*), and by support for joint projects which enhance prestige and pool costs without jeopardising national sovereignty (*'l'Europe des projets'*). At the same time, it is also marked by a rejection of a federalist vision of Europe (Cohen-Tanugi 1995).

The formula which allowed the PS and MDC to campaign on a joint platform in 1999 was 'a Europe of nation-states', but the MDC conveniently omitted any reference to the term 'federation' in its own declarations. Indeed, the MDC attacked the idea of a 'federation of nation-states', claiming that Chirac and Jospin espoused the concept because they thought its ambiguity rendered it harmless. Instead, the MDC argued, 'The French people aren't taken in. They want a Europe of projects and exchanges. They reject a Europe conceived as a paralysing accumulation of administrative procedures, which is just the continental version of neo-liberal globalisation' (Sarre 2001). Chevènement returned to the charge in response to the conclusions of the Laeken summit of December 2001 (which had decided to set up a constitutional convention), claiming that the use of the 'oxymoron' federation of nation-states 'stifles public debate and feeds the indifference of citizens' (Chevènement 2001). Instead of a federalist Europe, which he described as a German plan to model Europe in its own image, Chevènement called explicitly for *'une Europe des projets'* designed to rehabilitate the role of nations as the main spaces of democracy.

Chevènment returned to the idea of the nation as the repository of sovereignty in his well-publicised June 2000 debate with German foreign

minister and Green leader Joschka Fischer. Fischer, on the eve of the
French presidency of the EU in the summer of 2000, had stolen France's
thunder with his speech outlining proposals for a federal Europe.
Chevènement's riposte attributed Germany's advocacy of 'constitutional
patriotism' to a failure to come to terms with the country's Nazi past, and
likened a federal Europe to the Germanic Holy Roman Empire. The
outspokenness of the subsequent debate between the two protagonists
broke the political silence around the troubled past of Franco-German
relations and exposed Chevènement's deep-seated fear of Germany, as a
native of the eastern territory of Belfort close to the German border. As
well as revealing deep pessimism concerning the EU institutions' ability
and desire to control multinational capital, his response to Fischer's proposals highlighted a fundamental difference of approach. Whilst Fischer
assumed a post-national consensus in Europe and sought to match institutions to the perceived need for policy cohesion, Chevènement insisted
that popular consent had to come first. This is the essence of the
sovereignist argument, although Chevènement himself rejected the label
in the Fischer debate, adding: 'But I believe that, naturally, the people is
the repository of sovereignty' (*Le Monde*, 21 June 2000).

The MDC as a separate list has never performed particularly well in
national elections. Even in European elections it has always been a minority party, garnering only 2.49% of the total vote in 1994. Partnership
in the 'plural left' government after 1997 placed the MDC in an awkward
position, but as minister of the interior Chevènement continued to claim
a distinctive place in French politics. He remained very much in the public eye through his well-publicised spats with other ministers over crime
and public order (promoting a repressive line on juvenile offenders,
against justice minister Elisabeth Guigou's preventive approach) and over
local government (where as a defender of Republican redistribution he
stepped on the environment minister's toes). He also disrupted the government by resigning for the third time in his career, this time over a plan
to grant more autonomy to Corsica.

Chevènement's image as a man of principle made him so popular that
in early 2002 he appeared as the 'third man' in the presidential contest
and was even forecast by some pundits to come in second place behind
Jacques Chirac. However, this essentially negative support (a rejection of
political cohabitation and the ideological blandness in mainstream politics) did not necessarily mean endorsement of the MDC's policy positions or of a cross-party 'Republican' platform. In the end, Chevènement

was able to win only a little over five per cent of the vote on the first ballot of the 2002 presidential election, placing him a distant sixth.

Although always present in his discourse on Europe, Chevènement's appeal to Gaullist nationalism had previously been downplayed in favour of specific policy priorities (foreign policy, monetary policy and social policy). This had placed Chevènement and the MDC clearly on the left. Changed circumstances since 1999, in particular German determination to push forward a federalist agenda and the post-Nice moves towards a European constitution, had contributed to a hardening of the Chevènementists' stance in 2002. However, the legislative campaign, which saw the MDC field a motley array of candidates who were often refugees from the left and from the neo-Gaullist *Rassemblement pour la République*, failed to make any significant impact on voters. Chevènement himself lost the seat which he had held for over thirty years, and the MDC held onto only one of its eight seats in the National Assembly (which had been saved through an alliance with other left parties including the PCF).

The MDC's disastrous showing in the 2002 legislative elections casts doubts on the appeal of an ultra-Gaullist line on European integration shorn of its social base, that is, of its distinctive left or right-wing elements. Above all, it highlights the MDC's problems of political positioning in an unstable but still bipolar electoral system. Yet, it would be wrong to read too much into the legislative elections results, given the exceptional circumstances of the 2002 vote, which effectively excluded all the left parties. The MDC cannot simply be dismissed as a spent force. Its future depends to a large extent on the possibilities of realignment on the left in the context of the PS's renewal strategy. Opposition to the existing form of European integration will continue to dominate the MDC's ideology not only because it has been an integral component since the party's inception, but for tactical reasons as well. European Parliament elections continue to offer the MDC the best platform to mobilise and to measure electoral support.

The Communist Party: an uncomfortable 'Euroconstructive' approach

In terms of policy and institutional proposals, the Communists' position on European integration closely resembles that of the Chevènementists, although their discourse is markedly less Republican and more 'social'. Their Marxist framework of reference leads them to emphasise social conflict and economic crisis, as in a speech by party general secretary Robert Hue during a visit to Poland in July 2000:

> The current crisis of Europe is above all the crisis of the ultra-liberal model, which gives priority to the free movement of capital and the creation of a single market. But today, how can we think of successfully enlarging the European Union, without publicly posing the question of a new direction for reforms, turning our back on the ultra-liberal choices which are at the root of the current problems and which are increasingly contested? (Hue 2000)

Like the MDC, the PCF refers to national sovereignty. For Hue, the alternative vision of European integration consists primarily of '[a] social Europe. A Europe which values sovereignties and does not stamp them out' (Hue 2000). In its 1999 EP election manifesto, the party similarly insisted on the maintenance of national vetoes in EU decision-making, arguing that 'sovereignty, as the freedom of each people to choose its destiny, is inalienable' (see Guillou et al. 1999). As far as the overall vision of integration is concerned, the term used to denote the Communists' alternative construction is 'a Union of Nations of Europe', an amalgam of United Nations and the ambiguous 'federation of nation-states'.[6] In the PCF view, as in that of the MDC, this constitutes an ambitious approach to integration because it goes beyond the existing order, which is seen as a simple economic project conceived 'in the sole interest of the financial markets'.

The PCF also has a distinctive approach to eastward enlargement. It adopts the cautious approach advocated by Mitterrand in the early 1990s, preferring to draw the former eastern bloc countries into partnership with the EU rather than inviting them into full membership.

With public opinion increasingly receptive to campaigns against unemployment, insecurity and the deterioration of public services, the PCF has developed a mobilising strategy of opposition to the European Union on these socio-economic themes. This also allows it to connect European issues with the movement against global capitalism. It participated in the Nice and Barcelona counter-summits (alongside the Communist or former Communist parties of the other member states in a 'transformatory left' grouping), which it linked with the Seattle and Doha anti-World Trade Organisation demonstrations and the Porto Alegre counter-sum-

---

[6] Note that the term Union does not have the explicitly federalist connotations in French that it does in German, being closer to 'alliance'.

mit. The party's response to the Barcelona summit in March 2002 echoed the same themes. The party was particularly critical of the decision taken at Barcelona to raise the retirement age and the summit's resolution to push forward the liberalisation of energy provision. The PCF representative of the United Left grouping within the European Parliament denounced the (conservative) Spanish presidency of the EU for having defined the summit's philosophy in terms of 'liberalisation, privatisation [and] competition', which may be 'a businessman's or a share-holder's dream come true', but was out of step with the interests of the majority of the Union's citizens (Wurtz 2002).

However, the party has been unable to translate grassroots mobilisation into electoral support. As with the MDC, EP elections give the PCF an electoral platform and access to networks organised in the European Parliament. But the PCF's share of the EP vote declined sharply from the 1980s, in line with its overall electoral performance. Its share of the vote dropped from 20.42% in 1979 to 11.20% in 1984, then to 8.12% in 1989, 6.88% in 1994 and 6.78% in 1999 (Milner 2000, 57). The electoral 'dividend' for the PCF of the European elections has thus been reduced to one or two percentage points above its national election score. The 1999 performance was particularly disappointing for the PCF since it had worked hard on a high-profile campaign (*'Bouge l'Europe!'* or 'Get moving Europe!'), featuring a broad-based coalition of 'star' supporters from the cultural, sporting and associative worlds. Proximity to political power consistently works against the PCF electorally, and the 1999 elections proved to be no exception. If anything, the appeal to a youthful and fashion-conscious audience outside its traditional grassroots exacerbated this problem by confusing the party's image and offending traditional supporters. The PCF for its part attributed its poor showing in 1999 (an election marked by a historically low turnout in France, as elsewhere) to the European Union's failure to involve citizens and to develop a coherent social project. Party general secretary Robert Hue (1999) claimed that the publication of the Blair-Schröder manifesto just before the election had shown contempt for the proponents of a social Europe, who had stayed away from the polls in response. The party organ, *L'Humanité*, analysed the results in a similar manner, arguing that both the results in general and the high abstention rate in particular revealed popular 'distrust' in national politicians and in the current state of European integration: 'Europe accumulates all the handicaps of power which is too far removed from citizens' (Laurent 1999).

Also evident in the PCF's response to the 1999 election results was unease about its own position on European integration whilst a member of the 'plural left' government, which other far left parties (notably *Lutte Ouvrière*) were criticising openly and with increasing electoral success. The PCF's 'Eurorealist' discourse during this period stayed largely in step with the official PS line on the need for economic government, although the presentation of a separate list at the EP elections allowed the Communists to question whether the Socialists' proposals to include the objective of job creation in the European Central Bank's statutes aimed high enough: 'Is a little reference to employment really adequate in a Europe which is still dominated by the needs of the financial markets?' (Guillou et al. 1999). A 'Euroconstructive' approach – that is, a willingness to seek influence in Brussels through participation in national government, in order to promote its European agenda – evidently constrained the party by preventing it from adopting its classic oppositional stance. At the same time, this also betrayed the PCF's lack of concrete proposals distinct from those of the PS.

The PCF itself has all but dwindled into electoral insignificance and to its embarrassment was overtaken by the Trotskyist left in national elections in 2002. Despite some internal reform attempts, it has not produced any lasting answer to long-term electoral decline. As noted above, it has undoubtedly been adversely affected by coalition partnership with the Socialists. Yet, even freed from governmental constraints, it is unlikely to become a major political player again. Its significance lies mainly in the localised counter-culture which can still be mobilised through the new transnational networks of the movement against global capitalism. The party still has close ties with the *Confédération Générale du Travail* (CGT) union and is one of the few parties to quote trade unionists' views on social Europe. It therefore retains an ability to tap into public discontent about the social effects of 'neo-liberal' Europe, particularly if – as the Communists have warned – eastward enlargement proves problematic.

The Trotskyist left: the people's struggle against the 'rich men's club'

The Trotskyist left, electorally reliant on a negative message of rejection of mainstream politics, has traditionally been less concerned with reorienting European integration and more concerned with its outright denunciation. It has therefore been able to benefit from the twin 'distrust' of European integration and national politics noted by the PCF in 1999 (see above). Electoral space has been opened up by the PCF's decline and its apparent move into the centre under the constraints of 'plural left' government. As Arlette Laguiller (2002a) recognised explicitly in her presidential election campaign declaration: 'My aim is not to reduce the PCF's vote, it is to defend the programme that the PCF has abandoned.'[7] More recently, parts of the Trotskyist left have developed more specific European policy recommendations, in tune with the growing protest movement targeting EU decision-making fora.

France, one of the strongholds of the Fourth International, is home to no fewer than nineteen Trotskyist organizations. Three of these are dominant in electoral or membership terms: the *Ligue Communiste Révolutionnaire* (LCR); the *Union Communiste Internationale* (UCI), which is usually known under the name of its journal, *Lutte Ouvrière*; and the *Parti des Travailleurs* (Bourseiller 2002). Together these three groups have a reported membership of around 6,000, with *Lutte Ouvrière* weakest in membership terms but strongest electorally thanks to its indefatigable presidential candidate Arlette Laguiller. The far left, particularly *Lutte Ouvrière* and the LCR, gained considerable ground in the 1990s as the mainstream left during its periods in government became associated with unemployment and a climate of economic insecurity. The turning point was the 1995 presidential election, where 'Arlette' polled over five per cent of the first-round vote for the first time. This level of support has been maintained ever since. At the 1999 EP elections, the joint LO-LCR list led by Laguiller came close to the PCF's score, with 5.84% of the vote, and secured five MEPs. In the working-class areas just north of Paris, the joint list overtook the PCF (François 1999).

The EP elections do not seem to have given the LO-LCR list a particular advantage relative to national elections, apart from the advantage of the party list electoral system. Other 'second-order' elections in the late 1990s produced similar results: a combined score of 4.35% of the vote in the regional elections of 1998, and a high score in the municipal elections of March 2001, which brought 31 municipal councillors for LO, 25 for the LCR and 12 for the *Parti des Travailleurs*. The far left's success in the municipal elections was widely attributed to voter disillusionment with the 'plural left' government, then in power for nearly four years. The 1999 EP elections, on the other hand, were unique in bringing LO and

---

[7] See also Laguiller's speech (2002b) to her campaign rally at the Zénith (Paris, 14 April 2002), which identified the PCF leader Robert Hue as the main target.

the LCR together on a joint platform. Tactical differences prevented a similar alliance in subsequent elections, including the legislative elections of 2002, since the more hardline LO refused to contemplate instructing its voters to select mainstream left candidates in the second round as the LCR was willing to do.

The two leading Trotskyist parties also differ increasingly in their programmatic response to European integration. Traditionally, the workerist and internationalist far left has tended to see European elections as the chance to attack the domestic government. The 1999 EP elections were consequently presented as a chance to mobilise on mainly domestic issues such as mass redundancies and the *sans-papiers* movement in support of illegal immigrants (Célin 1999). European integration as such has not been a focus of analysis or campaigning. However, as it developed a broader ecologist and 'social movement' programme, and as a new generation of spokespeople like the young 2002 presidential candidate Olivier Besancenot came to the fore, the LCR began to elaborate a series of demands for a European regulatory space and a more detailed critique of the EU's policies and institutional workings. The LCR emphasises both the importance of the European Union as the locus of decision-making and the potential for change via grassroots mobilisation (through trade unions and associations).

Thus, the LCR's analysis of the Nice summit laid the blame for the EU's neo-liberal ethos at the door of national governments (noting the tactical and ideological agreement between Chirac and Jospin), the institutional framework which encouraged heads of state and government to behave like 'vulgar carpet sellers', and the structural imbalance between the different national partners which reflected economic and financial power relations (Aguirre 2000). Instead of the Charter of Fundamental Rights which had been adopted at Nice, the LCR proposed that a new charter should be drafted by trade unions and the associational movement. Following the Barcelona summit, the LCR's publication *Rouge* argued that the heads of state and government had acted at the behest of multinational capital in privatising public services ('the European Union is a real Trojan horse for globalisation') and noted that 'the Commission is simply executing the choices made by member states' (Auzende 2002). In response, action by trade unions and progressive organisations at both national and European level could force the decision-makers to change course. Specifically, the LCR called for an extensive series of European-level measures. Its broad agenda encompassed: a European law prohibiting redundancies by profitable companies; European-level guarantees on the maintenance of pay-as-you-go pensions and high levels of social protection; upward harmonisation of labour law and collective agreements; the establishment of a European minimum wage of 1,500 euros a month; taxation of capital movements and the removal of tax havens; environmental protection laws; sustainable infrastructure programmes in transport, energy and water; support for an Israeli-Palestinian peace plan; greater access to the EU for African and South American goods; the cancellation of Third-World debt; denuclearisation and disarmament programmes; and more flexible partnership and association agreements with eastern and southern European countries.

The LCR's critique of the EU allows it to specify the links between domestic government and the broader context of economic globalisation, whilst calling for protest at all levels. As Besancenot argues: 'The fight against liberal Europe is first and foremost a rejection of sovereignism or nationalism. We need to bring all the struggles and all the social and political forces together, to thwart the advocates of liberalism and the market' (Auzende 2002). The Trotskyist left's message since the mid-1990s has thus chimed with growing public dissatisfaction with domestic leaders and fears about globalisation.[8] At the same time, the broad 'anti-globalisation' movement opened up a new space for ideas into which the LCR has moved, particularly around the review *Contretemps* launched in 2001.

The trade unions and the 'social movement': regulation or contestation?

From the 1980s, at a time of employer exit from centralised bargaining and/or loosening of national regulatory frameworks, trade unions across Europe have increasingly tended to look towards the European level as a regulatory space, particularly as a protection against multinational corporations and the liberalising agenda of international institutions. This is especially true in France of the reformist *Confédération Française Démocratique du Travail* (CFDT), which sees the European social dialogue as one of the principal 'levers' for action in the globalised era (see Milner forthcoming). Allegiance to the European Trade Union Confederation also

---

[8] This is, for example, evidenced by a 2001 poll in which 76% of those interviewed expressed the view that the economy was insufficiently regulated, 58% declared that multinational companies had too much influence on the world economy, and 63% supported the 'anti-globalisation' movement (SOFRES 2001)

drew national unions into the orbit of European institutions through the social dialogue and the ETUC's support for the Commission's social policy initiatives. However, the desire to present a positive image of 'social Europe' has increasingly clashed with the trade unions' disappointment at the achievements of European social regulation, whilst in the late 1990s and early twenty-first century the growing protest movement around the EU opened up a new space for contestation.

Yet, ambivalence about the European project was evident from the start. Of the three leading confederations, the CFDT has consistently been the most pro-European, and has invested heavily in the European social dialogue despite the meagre achievements of the latter. Within the ETUC, it continues to press for the transfer of competencies (bargaining and decision-making mandates) to the European organisation, unlike the other French members. As Jean-Marie Pernot argues (Pernot 2001), the Europeanisation of the CFDT's programme and strategy accompanied its more general 'recentring'. This recentring has seen the Confederation move away from its association with the Socialist Party and towards collective bargaining at all levels, while assuming a deliberately reformist stance on social policy and industrial relations. The CFDT, particularly under its general secretary Nicole Notat (who left office in June 2002), defended the modest achievements of 'social Europe' by arguing that progress takes place in small steps (see Notat 2000). After the Nice summit, Notat expressed satisfaction with the outcome, but disappointment with the maintenance of the British veto on social policy, in contrast with the other confederations' more outspoken criticisms.

After Nice, however, the Confederation's calls for a stronger social dimension to European integration led it to harden its criticism of the EU, particularly at the Barcelona summit. Increasingly, the CFDT and the CGT have come together in organised demonstrations to call for an alternative Europe. Alongside the CGT and *Force Ouvrière* (FO), the CFDT took part in the 'Eurodemonstrations' organised by the ETUC at the Porto, Brussels, Nice and Barcelona summits. In an interview on the eve of the Nice counter-summit, Notat made it clear that despite the Confederation's support for European integration 'in small steps' she did not trust governments to make the right decisions. Trade unions needed to be present to defend Europe's 'social space'. As she put it '[the Europe] of monetary integration, of free circulation of goods and people, is not enough. It's time that each citizen had rights which did not vary from one country to another' (Notat 2000). The Barcelona summit brought more explicit criticism of the EU's privatisation drive and its inadequate attention to social policy, particularly employment and equality between men and women (CGT-CFDT-UNSA-CFTC-CFE-CGC 2002).

The Confédération Générale du Travail, close to the Communist party and at the time committed to Soviet-controlled international organisations, was originally deeply sceptical about the European integration project. The CGT has, however, increasingly Europeanised its framework of reference over the years, particularly since it was finally admitted to the ETUC in 1999. Of the three main confederations, the CGT was the most vocal in its criticism of the Single European Act and the Maastricht treaty, denouncing 'the Europe of money, where the multinationals would reign supreme' and the 'law of the jungle' (see Milner 1992). Like the PCF, the CGT argues that Europe faces a major crisis unless it strengthens its regulatory capacity, develops mechanisms of solidarity and institutes new means of direct citizen participation in decision-making (Braibant 2002). In line with its traditional theme of grassroots struggle, the CGT has embraced the 'Eurodemonstrations' which allow it to express strong opposition to the EU whilst remaining within the European trade union structures. This has also, as already noted, encouraged *rapprochement* with the CFDT.

Force Ouvrière stands apart from the other trade unions not so much because of disagreement about their criticism of the direction of European integration, but because it has always made a point of emphasising its independence. FO refused to take part in the public consultation exercise on the future of Europe, on the grounds that the debate belonged to the political sphere. However, it has been active in the protest movement and has regularly participated in the 'Eurodemonstrations' since 2000. A mainly public sector union, FO has campaigned hard on protection of public services and published angry denunciations of the Barcelona summit.

The EU summits of 2000-2002 thus provided the trade unions and actors of 'civil society' with a contestatory space which in turn is linked with the broader 'anti-globalisation' movement. This contestatory space is also home to other groupings within the left, including intellectuals working individually or collectively. One of these is the group around *Le Monde Diplomatique*, which at the time of the 1999 EP elections published an appeal by Pierre Bourdieu for a renewed trade union mobilisation in favour of social Europe. Earlier that year it had published a detailed critique of the institutional workings of the EU. This critique attributed the adoption of regressive economic policies to the Union's democratic deficit, highlighting the inadequacy of parliamentary control and the absence of public debate. Instead of these policies, 'the European Union constitutes one of the rare international levers which could be used to oppose liberal globalisation, which is in the process of making the market, blind and destructive as it is, the supreme master of the planet' (Robert 1999). Similar arguments can be found among other groups within the broad 'anti-globalisation' movement, including anti-McDonald's protester José Bové. Bové has denounced the EU in its present form, but called for 'more Europe' with a stronger social dimension and a tighter control of the activities of multinational companies.

Conclusion

This brief survey locates Euroscepticism within the traditional left-right ideological positioning of political parties. Left scepticism typically focuses on the lack of citizen involvement in decision-making at EU level and on the subordination of social policy to macroeconomic objectives. Calls for a referendum on treaty reform are a common demand. It is not opposed to European integration as such, but promotes an alternative view in which the EU serves as a regulatory space protecting member states from global (read US) capitalism. A further element is a third-worldist (MDC) or one-worldist (LO-LCR) foreign policy, coupled with deep reservations about eastward enlargement. Finally, in line with its critique of the democratic deficit, left scepticism aligns itself with non-governmental organisations as part of a wider anti-capitalist movement, but has increasingly fastened on the EU as a 'lever' or regulatory space. The contestatory space has grown as trade unions and other non-governmental actors have become more adept at organising at European level, and as unpopular decisions have increasingly been concentrated at key EU summits. However, as table 1 below shows, differences appear between the different parties which are both ideological and tactical.

Table 1: French parties of the left: a summary of their positions on European integration.

Party	Salience of sovereignty	Mode of action	Policy position
MDC	High	Elections	Maximalist (social policy) Reformist (macroeconomic policy) Alternative (foreign policy; immigration policy) Anti-elitist
PCF	High	Protest movement; elections	Maximalist (social policy). Reformist (macroeconomic policy) Alternative (foreign policy; immigration policy) Anti-elitist
LO/LCR	Rejection of sovereignty argument	Protest movement	Rejectionist (LO) Maximalist (social policy; environmental policy – LCR) Alternative (foreign policy – LCR) Anti-elitist

Thus, to use Paul Taggart and Aleks Szczerbiak's (2002) definition, left scepticism in France is 'soft' rather than 'hard'; it is a skepticism of qualified opposition based on concerns about specific policy areas, rather than principled opposition to European integration itself. If we take Chris Flood's more detailed categorisation of Eurosceptic positions (Flood 2002), left sceptic parties may be described as 'reformist', insofar as they constructively engage with the problems of existing policies and institutions, or even 'maximalist' in their desire for tighter regulation of economic activity and upward coordination of social policy. What needs to be emphasised is that, beyond specific policy proposals, the left parties present an alternative vision of Europe which is coherent in its own terms and congruent with their overall ideological position.

Our overview of left scepticism in France also confirms the argument, put forward by Paul Taggart (1998) and recently developed in the Scandinavian case by Nick Sitter (2001), that Euroscepticism is best understood as the 'politics of opposition'. The smaller Trostkyist parties in particular have benefited electorally from their status as 'outsiders' in the political system and this is reflected in their ideological position on European integration. As a specifically European contestatory space has opened up, the LCR in particular has moved from a rejectionist to a more constructive but still oppositional position on European integration. The PCF on the other hand suffered from its proximity to government during the 1997-2002 period when its left Euroscepticism became blurred. In this respect the parties reflect the attitudes of their electorates. Dissatisfaction with the present state of European integration is greater among voters who locate themselves 'very much on the left' or 'very much on the right', in France as elsewhere (Courtois 1999).

At the same time, we have suggested that specific elements of domestic political culture act as further factors framing the government-opposition dynamic. In the French case, there is an enduring resistance to European federalism, but receptiveness to political leaders' calls to further European integration in the name of defending French values and ways of doing politics. If anything, the climate in the early twenty-first century hardened this specificity, with a centrist consensus around the concept of a 'federation of nation-states'. Pro-European centre-left politicians like ex-prime minister Michel Rocard articulated this view in forthright terms:

> To protect our values, are we going to isolate ourselves from Europe and the world, emphasise our differences, decrease our contacts and influences from outside because they contaminate us, and defend to the death our institutions and procedures instead of the values which produce them? Or are we going to immerse ourselves in the movement of Europe and the world, even though we do not know where it is leading us, in order to put forward a corpus of values in which we believe so strongly because we feel they are the best?' (Rocard 2002)

The problem for the mainstream left was how to reconcile this view with support for an explicitly liberalising agenda of the EU after the Lisbon summit. This helps to explain why, as Helen Drake argues (forthcoming), the discomfort of the mainstream left regarding Europe was confirmed in the 2002 elections. The societal pressures that brought the Socialists back to power in 1997 – for the preservation of high levels of social spending, public ownership of key services and public investment programmes – worked against them as the party of government in 2002.

On the other hand, if as Frank (2002) and others argue, fears about national sovereignty constitute a major element of the French response to European integration, they are not dominant on the left, at least in terms of explicit discourse. The reference to national sovereignty appears principally in the demand for 'economic government' and the relaxation of the macroeconomic convergence criteria (hence the significance of Maastricht as the high-point of Euroscepticism), but it is a product of particular policy preferences and it is mitigated by an internationalist framework of reference.

The idea of Euroscepticism as the politics of opposition would lead us to conclude that the end of the left's period of office in 2002 will alter the dynamics of Euroscepticism in France in the short term. It is reasonable to assume that the Socialists will be able to develop more explicitly oppositional policies on European integration, while the PCF, freed of the constraints of ministerial discipline, will move further into the contestatory space. This, in turn, will affect the tactics of the Trotskyist left. Although Frank (2002) argues that popular Euroscepticism in France is cyclical in nature and that the post-Maastricht period of pessimism is reaching an end, there remains a strong potential for grassroots mobilisation around social anti-Europeanism. This may prove more durable than abstract and distant issues of constitutionalism and EU institutions, and responds to a different (economic) cycle currently entering a downturn.

References

Aguirre, Léonce. 2000. Europe libérale contre Europe sociale. *Rouge*. 14 December.

Andersen, Robert and Evans, Jocelyn A.J. 2002. Is Three a Crowd? Values, Cleavages and Party Choice in France, 1988-1995. Unpublished paper.

Auzende, Patrick. 2002. Pour une autre Europe. Démocratique, sociale et solidaire. *Rouge*, 4 April. Interview with Olivier Besancenot.

Baumel, Laurent. 1999. De la nation à la fédération d'États-nations. *La Revue Socialiste* 2 (October).

Benoît, Bertrand. 1997. *Social-Nationalism: An Anatomy of French Euroscepticism*, Aldershot: Ashgate Publishing.

Boniface, Pascal. 2002. Un nouvel internationalisme comme alternative au néolibéralisme. Interview with Daniel Cirera. *La Revue Internationale et Stratégique* 45. www.pcf.fr/docs/telecharger/276DC.IR.doc.

Bourdieu, Pierre. 1999. Pour un mouvement social européen. *Le Monde Diplomatique*. 1 June.

Bourseiller, Christophe. 2002. De Trotsky à Jospin... La mosaïque trotskiste. *L'Histoire* 263: 50-55.

Braibant, Guy. 2002. *Ensemble, dessinons l'Europe. Rapport du groupe 'Débat sur l'avenir de l'Europe'*. Paris: La Documentation française.

Célin, Barnabé. 1999. 5,2%... et après? *Rouge*. 24 June. Interview with Alain Krivine.

CGT-CFDT-UNSA-CFE-CGC. 2002. Les syndicats réaffirment leur attachement à l'objectif de plein-emploi de qualité. Joint Declaration of French Trade Unions on the Barcelona Summit. 15-16 March.

Chevènement, Jean-Pierre. 2001. La démocratie en péril à Laeken. *Le Monde*. 14 December.

Clift, Ben. 2001. The French Socialists and the Troubled Europeanisation of Employment Policy. Paper presented to the annual conference of the Association for the Study of Modern and Contemporary France. University of Portsmouth. September.

Cohen-Tanugi, Laurent. 1995. Le débat sur l'Europe. *Regards sur l'actualité*, March-April: 3-12.

Courtois, Gérard. 1999. Les Européens veulent plus d'Europe et une autre Europe. *Le Monde*. 1 June.

Drake, Helen. forthcoming. 'Europe' in the 2002 French Elections. In *The French Presidential Elections of 2002*, ed. John Gaffney. Aldershot: Ashgate.

Evans, Jocelyn A.J. 2000. Contrasting Attitudinal Bases to Euroscepticism amongst the French Electorate. *Electoral Studies* 19: 539-561.

Flood, Chris. 2002. Euroscepticism: A Problematic Concept. Paper presented to the University Association for Contemporary European Studies research conference. Queen's University of Belfast. 2-4 September.

François, Pierre. 1999. Cinq élus LO-LCR au Parlement européen. *Rouge*, 17 June.

Frank, Robert. 2002. La France de 2002 est-elle eurofrileuse? *Revue Politique et Parlementaire* 1017-1018: 190-199.

Guillou, Lin et al. 1999. Europe: les véritables projets des candidats. *L'Humanité*. 5 June.

Herzog, Philippe. 1999. L'Union politique passe par la démocratie participative. *Regards*, 46. www.regards.fr/archives/1999/199905/199905cit02.html.

Hue, Robert. 1999. La declaration de Robert Hue. 13 June. www.pcf.fr/Elections_europeennes/resultats/declarations.html.

Hue, Robert. 2000. Déclaration de Robert Hue lors de sa visite en Pologne. 6 July. www.pcf.fr/documents/RH/000706pologne.htm.

Laguiller, Arlette. 2002a. La profession de foi d'Arlette Laguiller. www.lutte-ouvriere.org/elc2002/pre/txt/pre-prf.html#top.

Laguiller, Arlette. 2002b. Extraits du discours d'Arlette Laguiller au Zénith, le 14 avril. www.lutte-ouvriere.org/elc2002/pre/txt/al-szen.html.

Laurent, Pierre. 1999. L'effet révélateur du scrutin européen. *L'Humanité*. 16 June.

Milner, Susan. 1992. French Trade Unions and the Single European Market. *Modern and Contemporary France* 51, no. 3: 11-21.

Milner, Susan. 2000. Euroscepticism in France and Changing State-Society Relations. *Journal of European Integration*, 22, no. 1: 35-58.

Milner, Susan. forthcoming. Le discours syndical sur la mondialisation en France et au Royaume-Uni. In *Recompositions syndicales. Fragments en hommage à René Mouriaux*, ed. Sophie Béroud. Paris: Syllepse.

Moscovici, Pierre. 1999. *Au coeur de l'Europe* (Entretiens avec Henri de Bresson). Paris: Le Pré aux Clercs.

Naïr, Sami. 1999. Intervention lors de la présentation de la liste *Construisons Notre Europe*. April. http://mdc-france.mrc-france.org/document/dis_nair.rtf.

Notat, Nicole. 2000. Je viens défendre l'Europe sociale. Interview in *Nice-Matin*. 5 December. *Confédération Française Démocratique du Travail* press archive. www.cfdt.fr/actu/presse/media/actumedia037.htm.

Pernot, Jean-Marie. 2001. Dedans, dehors, la dimension internationale dans le syndicalisme français. Unpublished doctoral thesis. University of Paris X (Nanterre). June.

Robert, Anne-Cécile. 1999. Les institutions européennes à l'épreuve. *Le Monde Diplomatique*. 16 March (dossier on the EU).

Rocard, Michel. 2002. La France et son nombril. *Le Monde*. 14 February.

Sarre, Georges. 2001. Communiqué on the Franco-German summit. 23 November.

Schmidt, Vivien. 2001. The Politics of Economic Adjustment in France and Britain: When does Discourse Matter? *Journal of European Public Policy* 8, no. 2: 247-264.

Sitter, Nick. 2001. The Politics of Opposition and European Integration in Scandinavia: Is Euro-Scepticism a Government-Opposition Dynamic? *West European Politics* 24, no. 4: 22-39.

SOFRES. 2001. Les Français et la mondialisation'. Poll for *Le Monde*. 18 July. www.sofres.fr/etudes/pol/180701_mondialisation_n.html).

Strauss-Kahn, Dominique. 2002. *La flamme et la cendre*. Paris: Flammarion.

Taggart, Paul. 1998. A Touchstone of Dissent: Euroscepticism in Contemporary West European Party Systems. *European Journal of Political Research* 33, no. 3: 363-388.

Taggart, Paul and Aleks Szczerbiak. 2002. The Party Politics of Euroscepticism in EU Member and Candidate States. Sussex European Institute Working Paper no. 46. Brighton: Sussex European Institute.

Usherwood, Simon. 2001. Opposition to the European Union in the UK and France. Paper presented to the European Consortium for Political Research. University of Kent at Canterbury. 6-8 September.

Van der Plaetsen, Jean-René. 2002. La Marseillaise de Chevènement. Special issue of *Le Figaro*, 'La présidentielle qui a fait trembler la Ve République': 94-99.

Wurtz, Francis. 2002. Résultats du Conseil européen de Barcelone. 20 March. Available on the United Left website: www.bouge-leurope.org.

Ysmal, Colette. 2002. L'Europe en toile de fond. Special issue of *Le Figaro*, 'La présidentielle qui a fait trembler la Ve République': 100-103.

EUROPEAN STUDIES 20 (2004): 83-98

GERMAN EUROSCEPTICISM

Klaus Busch and Wilhelm Knelangen

Abstract

The German perception of European integration has changed. The traditional attitude of consent (which was often above the European average) has given way to a more sober sentiment. It would be incorrect, however, to talk of fundamental Euroscepticism. The political parties, for instance, have so far not exploited the change of mood. What public scepticism there is appears focused on two key EU projects and their consequences: the single currency and enlargement. Until the end of the 1980s integration was linked to overall gains in growth and employment. Since then the single market and monetary union have led to greater intra-European competition, which will be heightened by enlargement. Many Germans fear that this situation will adversely affect employment, wages and social standards. There is reason to believe that these fears might well come true, providing an extra impulse to German Euroscepticism. This trend may be stopped if the current European monetary policies are supplemented by social policies.

Euroscepticism has not traditionally been associated with the Federal Republic of Germany. Since the beginning of European unification, German public opinion, the social elites and political parties have harmoniously supported integration in a manner that was seen as exemplary (Knodt and Staeck 1999, 4). In the academic debate on Euroscepticism the German example has frequently served as 'the exception', which stood out clearly from, for instance, the situation in Britain or Denmark. For a long time the question has been 'where are the German Eurosceptics?'

Since the early 1990s, however, this situation has changed. Germany's seemingly unlimited support for integration has given way to a much more cautious attitude. Opinion polls show that German approval of European integration has now reached, and in some cases even fallen below, the EU average. The increase in scepticism is particularly marked in attitudes towards two key EU projects which were either co-initiated or politically encouraged by German governments: the introduction of the single currency and enlargement.

As regards the 'big issues' of European unification, the coordinates of German European policy have not shifted significantly. There is no single party in the spectrum of German politics that poses a serious threat to Germany's traditional pro-European stance. As such Germany still remains an insignificant candidate when it comes to party-based Euroscepticism (Taggart and Szczerbiak 2002, 9-12). Yet it cannot be denied that Germany has changed its role on the European stage. Not only does it more confidently pursue its national interest, but the issue of integration appears now to be approached in a more instrumental manner. Short-term domestic success sometimes matters more than the attainment of the longer-term targets of integration (Hyde-Price and Jeffery 2001).

This article first maps the shift in public attitudes towards integration and then evaluates the effects of this increase in Euroscepticism on German party politics. The subsequent section argues that the hardening of public opinion cannot simply be equated with anti-Europeanism or 'hard' Euroscepticism. Instead, German scepticism seems motivated by the economic problems whose emergence has coincided with the introduction of the euro and the latest moves towards enlargement. Finally, some suggestions are made as to how European policies could be amended to allay the growing Euro-pessimism in German public opinion. The premise of this article is that the changed German attitudes are an expression of the changed socio-economic consequences of European integration. Until the end of the 1980s, Germany indisputably benefited from integration in the form of growth and employment yields. EMU and enlargement, however, have exposed the German economy to increased competitive pressures which might endanger wage levels and social standards. Only a paradigm shift from a 'liberal Europe' to a 'social Europe' can check the growing sense of pessimism which threatens to damage the long-term goals of the integration project.

Public opinion

The levels of approval and rejection of European unification have not been constant in the Federal Republic of Germany (Niedermayer 1995). In the 1950s, for example, Germans displayed well above-average enthusiasm for the idea of a unified Europe (Teschner 2000, 62). At the beginning of 1953, when the ECSC had only just started and negotiations had just begun on a European Defence Community, 41% of Germans believed they would live to see a 'United States of Europe', whereas 29% believed they would not. The latter group, however, has been in the majority as of the early 1960s, when the first EEC crises emerged. Yet, in 1979, after a decade of 'Euro-sclerosis', 31% of Germans still believed they would live to see a USE (Noelle-Neumann and Petersen 2002, 620).

From the beginning of European integration German approval has been above the European average. Until the early 1990s a large number of Germans responded positively to the *Eurobarometer* trend question of whether membership is considered a 'good thing' or a 'bad thing'. Since then, however, this level of approval has not only dropped in absolute terms, but also relative to the EU average (table 1). At the moment of writing just over half of those interviewed considered German membership a good thing. Nearly one third thought it neither a good or a bad thing and 9% thought it was a bad thing.

Table 1: *Membership is ...*

	1975/2		1980/2		1985/2		1990/2		1995/2		2000/2		2002/1	
	D	EC	D	EC	D	EC	D	EC	D	EU	D	EU	D	EU
... a good thing	56	63	62	53	61	60	73	69	51	53	48	50	52	53
... neither good nor bad	28	21	22	23	24	22	17	18	32	26	30	27	31	28
... a bad thing	8	9	6	16	8	11	5	7	10	15	14	14	9	11

Source: *Eurobarometer* 4, 14 (EC-9), 24, 34 (EC-12), 44, 54, 57 (EU-15)

In this respect, German public opinion thus tends to fall slightly below the EU average. Nevertheless, a relatively high level of support has been maintained. Using the *Eurobarometer* data, it is clear that hard Euroscepticism, in the sense of 'principled opposition to the EU and European integration' (Taggart and Szczerbiak 2002, 7), remains confined to only a small segment of German public opinion.

The response to the question whether membership has been beneficial to one's country reveals a similar trend. Until the early 1990s, a large majority of Germans thought that this was so. Since then, however, this figure has diminished and opinion has even swung the other way. By the late 1990s, the majority of Germans believed that EU membership brought them no advantages. Recently, opinion has reverted to a more positive attitude (table 2), but it remains a fact that in 2002 far fewer Germans (43%) believed that their country profited from membership than the EU average (51%). Only Finland, Austria, Great Britain and Sweden score lower on this point (41%, 40%, 36% and 29% respectively).

Table 2: *Has your country benefited?*

	1985/2		1990/2		1995/2		1997/2		1999/2		2001/2		2002/1	
	D	EC	D	EC	D	EU	D	EU	D	EU	D	EU	D	EU
benefited	53	53	57	59	40	44	37	46	39	47	44	52	43	51
not benefited	31	30	24	30	36	35	39	31	39	32	34	27	33	26

Source: *Eurobarometer* 24, 34 (EC-12), 44, 48, 52, 56, 57 (EU-15)

The *Eurobarometer* statistics thus reveal 1990 as a turning point in German attitudes towards the European Union. In this exuberant year of reunification German approval of European integration was exceptionally high. In the ensuing years, however, things changed. It is now widely accepted that 'permissive consensus' (Lindberg and Scheingold 1970, 38) has given way to more critical attitudes.

There are various possible explanations for this negative shift in German public opinion. First, the discussion surrounding the internal single market has changed. The focus on free trade and growth potential has given way to concerns about jobs and social standards in the face of heightened competition (Busch 1992). Second, the failure of the first Maastricht referendum in Denmark and the narrow French approval introduced topics into the debate which had hitherto received little attention. Questions were raised about the legitimacy and democratic quality of the project. In 1993 these questions became more acute when the German Federal Constitutional Court in its 'Maastricht judgement' placed both conditions and limits on further integration (Weiler 1995). The introduction of the euro was to cause considerable unrest. Rejection of this project was greatest in Germany, not just in terms of public opinion (table 3), but also amongst many prominent economists who expressed doubts about the stability of the new currency and the lack of fiscal discipline in the other member states (Ohr 1993). The debate took on an emotional aspect as the *Deutsche Mark* was not just perceived as a means of payment; it was seen above all as the national symbol of the German post-war economic success story.

Table 3: *Are you for or against a monetary union with one single currency (euro)?*

	1994/2 D EU	1996/2 D EU	1998/2 D EU	1999/2 D EU	2000/2 D EU	2001/2 D EU	2002/1 D EU
for	38 52	39 51	54 64	55 60	47 55	60 61	67 67
against	53 37	42 33	32 25	36 32	44 37	31 30	25 24

Source: *Eurobarometer* 42 (EU-12), 46, 50, 52, 54, 56, 57 (EU-15)

So far aversion to the euro has proved pretty tenacious. After a temporary upturn in public opinion, opponents regained the upper hand in the course of 2002. In September only 35% approved of the single currency (in January this was still 49%), while 40% were against (compared to 24% in January) (*Financial Times Deutschland*, 2 October 2002, 13).

Finally, the imminent enlargement of the Union has contributed to the downturn in German public support. It is feared that an influx of cheap labour migration will disrupt the labour market and negatively affect German wage levels and social standards. *Eurobarometer* surveys show that German support for enlargement is below the EU average, while there is more than average opposition (table 4). Only in France and Belgium is there more opposition to the accession of new members (24% and 23%). In Germany 10% stated that they expected their personal situation to improve following enlargement (EU-15: 11%); 54% expect no change (EU-15: 64%) and 20% expect their personal situation to deteriorate (EU-15: 12%). This means that in the EU, the Germans are the most pessimistic, followed by the Netherlands (19%) and Austria (17%).

Table 4: *The European Union should ...*

	Germany	EU
... not be enlarged to include any additional countries	18	14
... be enlarged to include only some of the countries wishing to join	47	44
... be enlarged to include all the countries wishing to join	12	21
... no opinion/ none of these	23	21

Source: European Commission 2002

The Maastricht Treaty marked the end of an era when the EC/EU appeared only of direct relevance to farmers. Before the 1990s, during the phase of 'permissive consensus', Europe was but 'a mirage on the horizon; visible but not within actual grasp' (Teschner 2000, 68). The EU has become politicised as it has become visible to the general public through the single market, the euro and preparations for enlargement (Agenda 2000). In other words, attitudes towards the EU are no longer based primarily on affective support, but rather now reflect a utilitarian motive. Depending on the extent to which Germans feel affected by 'Europe', they tend to express their opposition. This scepticism, however, appears not to be directed against the EU as such, but is focused on projects which are perceived as threatening.

Euroscepticism in German party politics

One might expect the German political parties to have exploited the critical stance of the public. This, however, has been the case only in a very limited sense. First of all, there are no major disagreements in the federal parliament (*Bundestag*) as regards the fundamental issues of integration. The major treaty reforms from the 1990s onwards were approved by overwhelming majorities, composed of the Christian Democratic parties (the CDU and the CSU), the Social Democratic Party (SPD), the Liberal Party (FDP) and the Greens (*Bündnis90/Die Grünen*) (table 5).[1] In the second chamber, the *Bundesrat,* in which the govern-

---

[1] Only the ex-Communist PDS, the successor to the East German state party, the SED, voted against the ratification of all the major treaties in the *Bundestag*. This is the only party in the *Bundestag* 'that has developed a sustained critique of the European consensus' (Lees 2002, 255). The Greens abstained in the vote on the ratification of the Amsterdam Treaty. In their view, the reforms introduced by the treaty were not far reaching enough.

ments of the German *Länder* are represented, no votes against the ratifi-
cations were recorded.

Table 5: Results of European policy votes in the *Bundestag* and *Bundesrat*

		Yes	No	Abst.
Ratification of the Maastricht Treaty	Bundestag (2.12.1992)	543 (95.6 %)	17	8
	Bundesrat (18.12.1992)	16	0	0
Ratification of the Amsterdam Treaty	Bundestag (5.3.1998)	561 (87.0 %)	34	50
	Bundesrat (27.3.1998)	16	0	0
Participation in the 3rd stage of monetary union	Bundestag (23.4.1998)	575 (93.5 %)	35	5
	Bundesrat (24.4.1998)	15	0	1
Ratification of the Nice Treaty	Bundestag (18.10.2001)	570 (94.4 %)	32	2
	Bundesrat (9.11.2001)	16	0	0

Source: Bundestag, Bundesrat (official records)

This does not mean, however, that the German parties blindly accept
integration or the various European projects. On the contrary, since the
1990s, German ambitions and their prospects of being realised have been
discussed very openly (Hyde-Price and Jeffery 2001). But criticism and
scepticism are usually expressed by individual politicians and are not
translated into party policies. This 'black sheep' strategy (Teschner 2000,
74) is not only employed by fringe politicians. In the mid 1990s, when
they were respectively minister-president of Lower Saxony and of Bavaria, the protagonists of the latest *Bundestag* elections, the Federal Chancellor Gerhard Schröder and his challenger Edmund Stoiber, strongly
highlighted the problems of the single currency. Nevertheless, both politicians approved the introduction of the third stage of monetary union in
the *Bundesrat* in 1998.[2]

---

[2] Only Saxony abstained, which was partly due to scepticism about the stability of
the euro, but it was also a protest against the European Commission blocking subsidies to the VW group (Lees 2002, 258).

The German federal system, with its sixteen regional electoral arenas, in fact facilitates exploitation of electoral 'mood swings'. Attempts to capitalise on the growing public concerns over Europe have, however, been unsuccessful (Lees 2002). The Social Democrats, for example, attempted to gain support by allowing individual politicians systematically to criticise the euro during the 1996 election in Baden-Württemberg. When the votes were counted, however, the SPD had suffered a 4% loss.

Rhetoric that wholly rejects European integration has scored even less well in German national elections. The hard Eurosceptic parties on the far right – the *Republikaner*, the *Deutsche Volksunion* (DVU) and the *Nationaldemokratische Partei Deutschlands* (NPD) – were not able to increase their national election results in the 1990s when opinion polls measured a particularly high level of resistance against the euro. They were all a long way away from the 5% threshold that German parties must meet to gain entrance to parliament. Indeed, it may be thought that the association of these far right parties with a Eurosceptic agenda has served to discredit this agenda (Lees 2002, 254), while at the same time contributing to a sense of an unacceptable 'radicalism' or untrustworthiness as regards the parties themselves.

Single issue conservative and liberal parties have also tried to gain votes on the subject of monetary union. Although the majority of the population rejected the euro, these parties only managed to gain modest results. In 1994, the *Bund Freier Bürger* was founded. Its leading figure, Manfred Brunner, is a former Bavarian FDP chairman and head of the 'Single Market Division' at the EC Commission. The core of the party programme was strict opposition to the introduction of monetary union. Hence the party campaigned under the name of the 'D-Mark Party'. It only gained 1.1% at the European Parliament elections in 1994 (Decker 2000, 177-180). The same lot befell the *Pro DM* party, which tried to turn the electorate's fears into votes by means of major advertising campaigns. Fewer than 1% of the electorate voted for the party at the 1998 *Bundestag* elections.

In Germany, as elsewhere, there is a high correlation between support for the European Union and the level of education or knowledge about European integration. Hence, one could hypothesise that the above-average levels of German scepticism towards enlargement and the euro might be attributable to particular educational deficiencies or to a lack of understanding of EU issues. It would seem more likely, however, that German scepticism is inspired mainly by economic issues. Enlargement has given rise to fears about increased competition and negative pressure on income levels and social standards. The euro project is perceived as a threat to the price and budget discipline on which the Germans have prided themselves for many decades. In the following paragraphs these root causes of German Euroscepticism are further examined and evaluated.

The euro and price stability

Ever since the creation of the EEC Germany has boasted a lower rate of inflation than most other member states. The anxieties of the majority of Germans that the euro will bring a higher rate of inflation are, therefore, understandable. So far, however, these negative expectations have proved unfounded, owing to the deflationary policies the EU states imposed upon themselves in the run-up to the single currency, and the restrictive monetary policy of the European Central Bank (Ohr and Schmidt 2001).

Since the introduction of euro notes and coins, however, the majority of Germans have again focused on the issue of inflation. The introduction of the new money led to widespread price hikes in the retail, catering and service industries. This seemed to confirm people's fears, and as a result the euro was soon dubbed 'Teuro' (Teuer meaning 'expensive'). As was stated above, in Germany the percentage of euro supporters fell from 49% in January 2002 to 35% in September. Conversely, opposition increased from 24% to 40%. Consumers reacted swiftly by buying less and switching to the discount market sector, thus forcing traders to change their practices. In spite of the release of figures which suggest that the introduction of the euro has not led to an increase in inflation, this negative attitude has not yet been reversed. The situation was obviously not helped by the fact that the European Stability Pact began to waver at the same time the debate on the 'Teuro' emerged.

Budgetary crises and the Stability Pact

During the EMU debate Germans feared that the excessive budgetary policies of some member states could endanger the monetary policy of the ECB and lead to higher inflation and interest rates. For this reason, the German government supported strict fiscal convergence criteria, as well as a procedure to avoid excessive deficits in the negotiations leading up to the Maastricht Treaty. Afterwards, in response to continual pressure from sceptics, the German government managed to make the heads of state and government agree upon a Stability and Growth Pact in June 1997. Despite this additional safety feature, the German public remained fearful that the pact would not be applied if it came to the crunch.

The Stability Pact was subject to its first endurance test in 2001/2002 when, as a consequence of the global economic crisis, the budgets of numerous Euroland states (Portugal, Germany, France and Italy) incurred growing deficits. Despite these circumstances the Commission is still officially adhering to the Stability Pact, though in September 2002 it suggested postponing the targets set for 2004 to 2006, amidst a debate (stimulated by Italy, France and Germany) whether the Stability Pact should be reformulated in view of its pro-cyclic effects. These events have been grist to the mill of German Eurosceptics, who claim that their fears about EMU have been confirmed (Hankel et al. 1998), and have undoubtedly encouraged the backlash in public opinion, which increasingly turned against the euro in the course of 2002.

Germany's competitive position

In the debate on the introduction of EMU the hypothesis that the strongest EU economy would also profit most from EMU was opposed by the sceptic opinion that the cheaper labour costs in many other Euroland states would endanger growth and employment in Germany. The period since the introduction of the euro has been too short to subject these hypotheses to serious empirical investigation. First indications are that the German economy has grown at a slightly under-average rate while labour costs have risen at a slightly above-average rate. It would appear that those Euroland states that quote under-average growth in labour and social costs (compared to a rise in productivity) will achieve above-average GDP growth and benefit most from EMU. Many experts believe that Germany will not fall into this category, due to its relatively strong trade unions, the high costs of its welfare state and its more comprehensive labour market regulations. If these predictions turn out to be true, German acceptance of the EU and the euro will probably continue to decline.

Migration

Sectors of the population feel deep anxiety at the prospect of migration from Eastern Europe following enlargement. In fact, cross-border integration of EU-labour markets has not been very pronounced: between

1973 and 1990, employees from other member states of the EU-12 made up only approximately 2-3% of all employees on the respective labour markets of the individual EU member states. The proportion of employees from non-EU member states (approximately 3% of gainfully employed persons) also remained largely stable during this period (Deutsches Institut für Wirtschaftsforschung 2000, 1; Molle 1994, 119 and 201). Nevertheless the significant differences in income between East and West give rise to fears that eastern enlargement could lead to much greater migration than was the case after southern enlargement. According to Eurobarometer results, 53% of Germans expect a considerable number of migrants after enlargement (EU-15: 48%) whereas only 25% do not expect this (EU-15: 30%). Of the 53% anticipating increased migration, 76% regard this as a negative development (European Commission 2002).

Whether or not enlargement will increase migration into Germany is a moot point. The *Deutsches Institut für Wirtschaftsforschung* expects that the number Eastern European residents in Germany will increase from the current number of 550,000 to 1.9 million by 2010, 2.4 million by 2020 and 2.5 million by 2030, by which time the long-term balance will have been attained. According to these figures, 3.5% of the overall population of Germany will originate from these states by 2030 (the current figure is around 0.6%). This survey shows that fears about Eastern European waves of immigrants are exaggerated. In the context of expected demographic changes in Germany and Europe, such developments would not only be manageable, they would even be desirable. According to predicted demographics, Germany requires a net influx of approximately 300,000 gainfully employed persons per year (Deutsches Institut für Wirtschaftsforschung 2000).

However, these figures are highly speculative as they are based primarily on experiences of migration between Germany and eighteen other countries between 1967 and 1998. It is not surprising, therefore, that another research institute, the *Ifo Institut für Wirtschaftsforschung*, predicts a considerably higher influx in its study on EU enlargement. It estimates the number of migrants living in Germany fifteen years after the accession of ten Central and Eastern European states at approximately 4 million people, while the DIW predicts approximately 2 million after thirty years (*Ifo Institut für Wirtschaftsforschung* 2001, 15ff; *Deutsches Institut für Wirtschaftsforschung* 2000, 1). Microeconomic studies on migratory potential in the would-be EU states introduce yet other figures into the debate.

They estimate a migratory potential of between 2% and 10% (Alecke and Untiedt 2001, 136ff).

Although the predictions differ, German anxieties about enlargement and its effect on the job market cannot simply be dismissed as the result of a low level of education or lack of information on the EU. Given that the above-mentioned economic studies show uncertainty about migratory flows from Central and Eastern Europe, it is by no means impossible that they will increase job competition in Germany. Hence, it was probably prudent of the German federal government to insist on a transition regulation regarding the freedom of movement of workers following enlargement.[3]

Wage policy and eastern enlargement

As was noted above, German Euroscepticism is concerned mainly with economic issues, for instance the possible effects on wages after enlargement. The substantial differences in income between East and West might indeed put pressure on Western wage levels in various ways. First, migration could lead to heightened competition, primarily in the low-wage sector. In border regions this effect will be multiplied by commuters and short-term migrants. Following freedom of movement, displacement effects rather than wage effects are to be expected in the low-wage sector, after which prices will be adjusted; in other words, wages will be reduced. This sector, therefore, might not stand to gain from eastern enlargement.

More than migration, EU wage levels will be affected by trade with the accession countries and their wage policies. A crucial factor is the development of unit labour costs and exchange rates. After the single currency has been introduced in the new countries – which will probably take place just a few years after 2004 – the essential question will be whether a neutral cost-level wage policy in the East and West can be implemented. If this is the case, competitive relations between the regions will not shift. However, the unit labour costs in the Central and Eastern European countries fell dramatically between 1997 and 2002. In

---

[3] In May 2001, the EU member states agreed that freedom of movement may be postponed for up to seven years after accession of the new countries. The regulation stipulates a transition period of five years, but after the first two years this may be re-examined. Throughout the transition period, the EU member states may regulate freedom of movement on a national basis, enabling them to take their specific labour market conditions into consideration.

fact, they fell to such an extent that the nominal upward revaluation of their currencies was massively overcompensated (The Vienna Institute for International Economic Studies 2002).

It is likely that this trend will continue, owing to the high levels of unemployment in the applicant countries and their weak trade unions. As a result foreign trade-induced pressure will be exerted on wage levels in the present EU member states, confirming German Eurosceptic concerns about enlargement. The EU will then be facing a repetition of the Ireland syndrome. In recent decades Ireland also reduced its unit labour costs below the European average, thus creating for itself competitive advantages which have led to double digit growth rates in GDP.

If the applicant countries were to introduce the single currency shortly after accession, which is not unlikely, this wage-dumping competition will increase considerably, for the strong capital flows to the East will then no longer lead to a nominal upward revaluation of the currencies (such revaluations at least alleviate competitive pressure to some degree). Given these perspectives, it is not surprising that the Euroscepticism of German workers has focused on the plans for enlargement.

Conclusion

German attitudes towards the EU have changed twice since 1990. On the one hand, general acceptance of European integration has fallen in comparison to the 1970s and 1980s. In Germany acceptance of European integration was above average until the 1990s, when the level of support fell to the EU average and sometimes even below.

It would be an exaggeration, however, to take this as a sign of widespread or 'hard' Euroscepticism. A large majority of the German population still approves of European integration and German membership of the EU. This majority, however, is more fragile than was previously the case, as surveys indicate that core projects, notably the single currency and enlargement, meet with greater rejection in Germany than elsewhere. Stephen Wood is justified in stating: 'Over the past decade Germany reveals a marked divergence between the aims and methods of elites and the desires of the public on major issues of European integration' (Wood 2002, 23).

This development cannot simply be explained with reference to abstract factors such as 'a greater national consciousness after German unification'. As argued above, Germany's changed socio-economic position within Europe is the major cause of the German change in attitude. Integration can no longer automatically be linked to gains in growth and employment. The single market and Economic and Monetary Union, which have been implemented with the blessing of all the main parties, have led to greater intra-European competition, which will be further heightened by Eastern enlargement. Many Germans clearly consider this a threat to employment and wage levels, as well as to social standards.

For this reason, it is inadequate to call this development a process of normalisation 'whereby attitudes towards European integration are formed on a more objective (utilitarian) than subjective (dutiful) basis' (Teschner 2000, 80). Instead, utilitarian motives have always been present, not just since the 1990s, but also during the preceding phase of phase of 'permissive consensus'. It is inevitable, therefore, that the economic consequences of today's European projects will have a significant impact on German Euroscepticism. Improving public education and introducing more transparency in EU decision-making – desirable as these reforms are – will not stem the tide of this dissatisfaction. In order to gain sustained acceptance of European integration it is essential not only to debate the merits of a European constitution, the competencies of the institutions or other structural reforms. Attention should also be refocused on the social traditions of Europe, or the 'European Social Model'. In the midst of the debate on the European constitution, the former French Prime Minister Lionel Jospin rightly pointed out that it is not the formal rules of politics that gain the trust of citizens, but the contents of policies (Jospin 2002).

In keeping with the idea of a European Social Model, two policies should be implemented so as to create a more stable union (Busch 2000; 2001). First, a European economic government should be introduced to supplement the monetary control of the ECB. Its brief should be to prevent European employment crises by means of growth-oriented macropolicies. To this end the static and pro-cyclic Stability and Growth Pact must be revised. Second, competition between the European member states should be checked by coordinating and regulating the national wage, social, tax and environmental policies at European level. Economic and social advancement in Europe will then go hand in hand. Under such a regime the process of the weaker developed states catching up will not lead to a relative drop in standards in the stronger developed countries, but to a gradual closing of the gap between East and West.

The single market, the euro and enlargement have been billed as projects that will bring general economic growth and employment. Only when the German public is not disappointed in these promises and does not experience a fall in employment, wage levels and social standards will growing Euroscepticism be halted. Only then will the project of European Union be assured of long-term security.

References

Alecke, Björn and Gerhard Untiedt. 2001. Das Migrationspotential nach der EU-Osterweiterung: Ein Überblick. *Osteuropa-Wirtschaft* 46: 125-150.

Busch, Klaus. 1992. *Umbruch in Europa : die ökonomischen, ökologischen und sozialen Perspektiven des einheitlichen Binnenmarktes.* 2nd ed. Cologne: Bund-Verlag.

Busch, Klaus. 2000. Economic Integration and the Welfare State: The Corridor Model as a Strategy for a European Social Policy. In *The Role of the Social Sciences in the Making of the European Union,* ed. Max Haller, 25-42. Berlin, Heidelberg, New York: Springer Verlag.

Busch, Klaus. 2001. Leitbilder des europäischen Integrationsprozesses und mögliche Schritte zur Vertiefung der Integration. In *Soziales und Gerechtes Europa. Von der Wirtschafts- zur Sozialunion,* eds. Barbara Krause, Rainer Krockauer and Andreas Reiners, 186-200. Freiburg im Breisgau: Lambertus Verlag.

Decker, Frank. 2000. *Parteien unter Druck. Der neue Rechtspopulismus in den westlichen Demokratien.* Opladen: Leske + Budrich.

Deutsches Institut für Wirtschaftsforschung. 2000. *Wochenbericht* 21. Berlin: DIW.

European Commission. 1974ff. *Eurobarometer: Public Opinion in the European Union.* Brussels: European Commission.

European Commission. 2002. *Eurobarometer Special Bureaux 2002: Getting Information on Europe, the Enlargement of the EU, Support for European Integration* 56.3. Brussels: European Commision.

Hankel, Wilhelm, Wilhelm Nölling, Karl Albert Schachtschneider and Joachim Starbatty. 1998. *Die Euro-Klage. Warum die Währungsunion scheitern muss.* Reinbek bei Hamburg: Verlag Rowohlt.

Hyde-Price, Adrian and Charlie Jeffery. 2001. Germany in the European Union. *Journal of Common Market Studies* 39: 689-717.

Ifo Institut für Wirtschaftsforschung. 2001. *EU-Erweiterung und Arbeitskräftemigration. Wege zu einer schrittweisen Annäherung der Arbeitsmärkte.* Munich: Ifo Institut für Wirtschaftsforschung.

Jospin, Lionel. 2002. Rede des französischen Premierministers zur 'Zukunft des erweiterten Europas' am 28. Mai 2001. In *Entwürfe einer europäischen Verfassung. Eine historische Bilanz,* ed. Wilfried Loth, 285-299. Bonn: Europa Union Verlag.

Knodt, Michele and Nicola Staeck. 1999. Shifting paradigms: Reflecting Germany´s European policy. *European Integration online Papers* 3. http://eiop.or.at/eiop/texte/1999-003.htm.

Lees, Charles. 2001. 'Dark Matter': Institutional Constraints and the Failure of Party-Based Euroscepticism in Germany. *Political Studies* 50: 244-267.

Lindberg, Leon N., and Stuart A. 1970. *Europe´s Would-be Polity: Patterns of Change in The European Community.* Englewood Cliffs, NJ : Prentice-Hall.

Molle, Willem. 1994. *The Economics of European Integration.* 2nd ed. Aldershot: Dartmouth.

Niedermayer, Oskar. 1995. Trends and Contrasts. In *Public Opinion and Internationalized Governance*, eds. Oskar Niedermayer and Richard Sinnott, 53-72. Oxford: Oxford University Press.

Noelle-Neumann, Elisabeth, and Thomas Petersen. 2002. Die Bürger in Deutschland. In *Europa-Handbuch*, ed. Werner Weidenfeld, 618-636. Gütersloh: Verlag Bertelsmann-Stiftung.

Ohr, Renate. 1993. Die ökonomische Kritik am Maastrichter Vertrag. *Wirtschaftspolitische Blätter.* 40: 27-37.

Ohr, Renate and André Schmidt. 2001. Europäische Geld- und Währungspolitik. In *Kompendium Europäische Wirtschaftspolitik*, eds. Renate Ohr and Theresia Theurl, 417-466. Munich: Verlag Vahlen.

Taggart, Paul and Aleks Szczerbiak. 2002. *The Party Politics of Euroscepticism in EU Member and Candidate States.* Opposing Europe Research Network Working Paper 6. Brighton: Sussex European Institute. sussex.ac.uk/Units/SEI/pdfs/wp51.pdf.

Teschner, Julia. 2000. No longer Europe´s Europhiles? Euroscepticism in Germany in the 1990s. *Journal of European Integration* 22: 55-86.

The Vienna Institute for International Economic Studies. 2002. *Transition Countries in 2002: Loosing Steam.* Research Reports 285. Vienna: The Vienna Institute for International Economic Studies.

Weiler, J.H.H. 1995. The state 'über alles': Demos, Telos and the German Maastricht Decision. In *Festschrift für Ulrich Everling.* Bd. 2. eds. Ole Due et. al., 1651-1688. Baden-Baden: Nomos.

Wood, Stephen. 2002. Germany and the Eastern Enlargement of the EU: Political Elites, Public Opinion and Democratic Processes. *Journal of European Integration* 24: 23-38.

EUROPEAN STUDIES 20 (2004): 99-126

EUROSCEPTICISM IN THE NETHERLANDS:
STIRRINGS OF DISSENT[*]

Robert Harmsen

Abstract

Recent years have seen the emergence of a markedly more critical discourse in the Netherlands as regards European integration. Concerns over both the size of the net national contribution to the European Union budget and the implications for the country of EU enlargement have given rise to high-profile public debates. An explicitly articulated discourse of national interest, centred on but not limited to the Liberal VVD, has become a staple of political debate. At the same time, movements with clearly Eurosceptic agendas (the Pim Fortuyn List and the Socialist Party) have enjoyed unparalleled levels of electoral success. Although not of significant electoral salience, 'Europe' has nevertheless emerged as an issue in Dutch politics. The present article examines these stirrings of dissent in an EU member state which had long been regarded as one of the most enthusiastic supporters of further integration.

The Netherlands has long been regarded as one of the most enthusiastic supporters of further integration amongst the European Union's member states. At least since the 1960s, Dutch governments have been strong supporters of the 'Community model' and the commensurate development of supranational institutional structures. Dutch public opinion has similarly tended to be amongst the most favourable towards European

[*] The author wishes to acknowledge the hospitality of Gerrit Voerman and his colleagues at the Documentatiecentrum Nederlandse Politieke Partijen (DNPP) at the Rijksuniversiteit Groningen. The resources of the DNPP were invaluable in the preparation of the present article. I would also like to thank Paul Lucardie of the DNPP and Gerrit Voerman, for comments on earlier versions of this paper.

integration. In *Eurobarometer* polls, the Dutch have routinely come near the top of the table of those who regard European integration as a 'good thing' (usually above the 70% mark in recent years). Yet, particularly from the mid-1990s onwards, a growing number of critical voices have also been heard. Recent surveys of Dutch European policy clearly reflect this critical turn, highlighting, for example, 'the growing doubts of a loyal member' (Soetendorp and Hanf 1997) or the new challenges facing a 'former founding father in search of control' (Hoetjes 2003).

The growth of a more critical Dutch European discourse was initially fuelled in large part by budgetary issues. Long a net recipient of Community funds, from the early 1990s onwards the Netherlands became a net (and progressively heavier) contributor to the Community budget. This led to increasing expressions of concern on the part of the Dutch government as to the load which it was expected to bear. The government, most notably, tabled a paper in the Dutch parliament in February 1995 setting out the existing budgetary situation and the case for reforms which would have the effect of reducing the net Dutch contribution (see Laffan 1997, 56-59). More generally, Liberal (VVD) Finance Minister Gerrit Zalm conducted an increasingly vocal campaign for budgetary reform. Zalm was careful to distance himself from a hard-line Thatcherite position, stressing rhetorically that he did not carry a handbag and substantively that he was seeking an overall solution to the Community's budgetary problems rather than a specific national rebate (*Trouw*, 21 February 1995). It remains, however, that the budget issue served to crystallise a reaffirmed sense of a distinctive Dutch national interest which would have to be more vigorously defended within Community institutions. To this end, the coalition agreement reached by the Labour Party (PvdA), the Liberals, and Democrats '66 (D'66) as the basis for the second 'purple coalition' in 1998 specified that the government was to seek a reduction in the annual net Dutch contribution of 1.3 billion guilders. The government was able to achieve this goal at the 1999 Berlin summit, winning a reduction in future contributions equivalent to 1.5 billion guilders per annum. This result, 'bringing home the silver fleet', was secured by an exceptionally high degree of interministerial co-ordination in aid of a clearly defined national policy goal (Werts 1999). More recently, the Dutch government again emerged as one of the strongest proponents of budgetary reform. One of the 'gang of four' arguing the case for pre-enlargement budgetary reform (together with Germany, Sweden and the United Kingdom), the

Netherlands eventually found itself in a 'gang of one' as the negotiations with the first wave of accession countries drew to a close.

Beyond the budget issues, recent years have further seen a more general change in the frame of reference of Dutch European policy. Both governmental position papers and academic commentators have highlighted the emergence of a 'new bilateralism' as a cornerstone of Dutch foreign policy (Pijpers 1999). While maintaining a strong commitment to multilateral institutions, both in the European arena and more generally, the Dutch government has increasingly sought to enhance its negotiating position within these multilateral fora by the strengthening of bilateral contacts with key national capitals. In this vein, Dick Benschop, at the time state secretary for European affairs, spoke of the emergence of a 'network Europe' (Benschop 2000). In Benschop's view, the traditional method of European integration, predicated on a top down approach and driven by strong supranational institutions, had largely run its course. In its place, a new dynamic of integration was emerging which placed greater reliance on both traditional bilateral contacts between capitals and a more general process of transnational learning, whereby the spread of 'best practice' and the use of 'benchmarking' techniques would increasingly replace the more rigid legal instruments of integration which had been necessary for the completion of the internal market. In taking this position, Benschop was, of course, significantly departing from the long-standing Dutch position of viewing a strong Commission role as the likely best guarantor of smaller state interests.[1]

One must, however, be careful not to overstate the change of direction in Dutch European policy. On the one hand, the perception that a federalist idealism drove Dutch European policy was never sustainable on the record (Koch 2001). Rather, Dutch policy is historically better characterised in terms of a pragmatic support for supranational institutional structures in areas where this corresponded to identifiable national interests. On the other hand, the recent development of a more critical approach must be understood as nuancing, rather than in any sense reversing a continuing, basic commitment to the integration process. As has often been said, European integration for the Netherlands remains

---

[1] This gave rise to a lively exchange between Benschop and the Brussels correspondent of the *NRC Handelsblad*, the latter arguing that the network model had significant disadvantages for a mid-sized state like the Netherlands. *NRC Handelsblad*, 31 March and 4 April 2000.

like the weather – one may complain about it, but it must be accepted as an inevitable part of life.

Against this background, the present article examines this limited, but significant critical turn in Dutch European debate. The first two sections survey the increasingly critical tenor of mainstream Dutch political debate on European issues. This shift is first highlighted with reference to the critical stances on European issues assumed by VVD leader Frits Bolke-stein in the 1990s and the reactions which this produced. This, in turn, provides the framework for understanding more recent, high-profile debates on enlargement. The following two sections of the paper then turn to a more detailed consideration of specific Dutch political move-ments which have assumed Eurosceptic positions. A number of parties fall under this rubric. Notably, both the 'small Christian parties'[2] and Green-Left[3] have, to varying degrees, identified themselves with Euro-sceptic positions. For reasons of space, however, the present discussion is confined to the movement founded by Pim Fortuyn and to the Socialist Party (SP). Both of these movements may readily be described as 'popu-list' or 'protest' parties, which have recently assumed a degree of promi-nence within the Dutch political arena. Both have also displayed signifi-cant elements of 'hard Euroscepticism', in the sense of advocating 'poli-cies towards the EU [which] are tantamount to being opposed to the whole project of European integration as it is currently conceived'

---

[2] The 2002 electoral programme of the Political Reformed Party (SGP) clearly spelled out its opposition to the creation of a 'European Political Union'. For the SGP, 'the autonomy and the distinctive character of the member states must be respected, so that citizens do not become further estranged from political authorities' (Staatkundig Gereformeerde Partij 2002, 53). To this end, the party opposes the institution of a directly elected European Commission president, a European senate, and a European constitution. It further views European citizenship as 'superfluous' (54). A similar message may also be found in the 2002 manifesto of the Christian Union. For the Christian Union, 'The Netherlands should remain a recognisable, unified political entity within the European Union' (ChristenUnie 2002, 61). In con-trast to the SGP, however, its more detailed proposals concerning the EU appear more willing to seek reform of the Union on its own terms – stressing the need for a more stringent application of the principle of subsidiarity and the need for a clearer division of powers between the national and the European level.

[3] The 2002 electoral programme of Green-Left is highly critical of a 'Europe of market and money, in which people and the environment are of secondary impor-tance' (GroenLinks 2002, 56). Nevertheless, the party's proposed remedy is that of 'more Europe', with, among other measures, the adoption of a 'European constitu-tion' (to be ratified in an EU-wide referendum) and the strengthening of social policy co-ordination.

(Taggart and Szczerbiak 2002, 7). The paper concludes by attempting to situate the Dutch case relative to the broader literatures on Euroscepticism and the (non-)impact of European issues on national party systems.

First stirrings: Frits Bolkestein

VVD parliamentary leader Frits Bolkestein was the most prominent figure associated with the growth of a more critical discourse surrounding European integration in Dutch political circles during the 1990s. Memorably reproached by former Christian Democrat (CDA) leader Enneüs Heerma for being an 'un-Dutch politician' (Cited in van Weezel and Ornstein 1999, 9), Bolkestein consciously sought to place himself outside of the strongly accommodationist traditions usually taken to characterise Dutch politics. Most prominently, this took the form of a sharp criticism of the much heralded 'polder model' (Bolkestein 1999), seen by its proponents as having allowed the Netherlands to square the circle of maintaining a high level of social welfare provision with a competitive, flexible economy through a culture of consensual decision-making. For Bolkestein, actual practice fell well short of this idealised model, with the Dutch economy in need of a further dose of liberalisation in order to maintain a competitive edge. The VVD leader also appeared to take a more general delight in breaking political taboos, placing sensitive and often side-stepped questions such as immigration squarely at the centre of political debate (Maas, Marlet and Zwart 1997). Bolkestein's critical stance on European issues must thus, in good part, be seen in the light of this more general bid to shake up what he viewed as the overly cosy consensus of Dutch politics.

Bolkestein consistently rejected any form of European federalist blueprint. In his view, one could not meaningfully speak of a 'European identity'. Indeed, as he never tired of repeating, many European countries continued to have stronger affinities with countries outside of the European Union than with their fellow member states. In the case of the Netherlands, for example, its 'individualistic and open, democratised culture shares greater similarities with Canada than with Italy' (*Elsevier*, 20 April 1996).[4] This absence of a strongly shared identity, in turn, precludes the formation of a meaningful political community at the European level. As he put it in an interview published on 13 December 1996 by the newsweekly *HP/De Tijd*:

---

[4] All translations from the Dutch, unless otherwise noted, are those of the author.

The EU shall never become a federation in the sense of the United States or of Germany. This is because there is no European people, no European language, no European legal system, and no European public opinion. And I also think that it is not desirable for the Netherlands, in a future European Union, to accept a position like that of the state of Bavaria in Germany.

Bolkestein was equally disparaging as regards the idea of a European citizenship. The 'Union citizen'- an *'Unieburger'* in Dutch – he derided as something that one could not even find at McDonald's. More seriously, Bolkestein argued that the continued acceleration of the integration process, in the absence of a deeper sense of shared community, risked opening a particular serious breach between citizens and the political process. In this, he sought directly to turn the usual pro-integrationist arguments on their head. For Bolkestein, the danger lay not in a loss of forward momentum, but rather in the creation of an artificial momentum by elites disconnected from national realities. Future developments should be governed by a strict adherence to a principle of subsidiarity (if not parsimony), whereby delegations of power to the European level should be kept to the strict minimum necessary for the accomplishment of particular tasks. In sum (Bolkestein 1992, 89):

> Nowhere is the danger of an unbridgeable distance between the citizen and politics so great as in the European Community. This means that national politicians must operate very cautiously as regards the transfer of sovereignty to the European level. If the elites get too far ahead of the national music, then they may well find things ringing hollow.

The European integration project, in Bolkestein's view, thus had to remain a relatively limited one. Essentially, it should not extend much beyond a narrowly defined economic dimension, creating and maintaining a large, unhindered internal market. This vision of European integration was critically characterised by Green-Left leader Paul Rosenmöller as that of a 'customs union plus' (*De Volkskrant*, 18 June 1999). Yet, though intended as a criticism, it is uncertain whether Bolkestein himself would greatly dissent from this description. When asked in a 1996 interview what the EU meant for him (*HP/De Tijd*, 13 December 1996), Bolkestein candidly replied 'The heart is the internal market, with hopefully European Monetary Union. For the rest you must work pragmatically'. He followed this by emphasising that 'The focal point of the European Union is and shall remain economic'.

More specifically, in an earlier piece, Bolkestein (1992, 88-89) had clearly spelled out three 'core tasks' against which all existing and future delegations of power to the European Union should be judged. These core tasks were: 1). The removal of economic barriers between the member states; 2). The handling of trans-border problems which cannot adequately be dealt with at the national level; and 3). Areas where clear advantages of scale may be enjoyed at the European level. Applying a strict subsidiarity test, competence would be vested in the Union only insofar as it was demonstrably necessary to discharge these specified tasks.

In practical terms, this meant that Bolkestein was a strong proponent of European-level market liberalisation measures. Essentially, he could be seen to have backed a fairly classic 'negative integration' agenda – concerned with the removal of trade barriers, but largely adverse to the creation of new, 'positive' supranational-level obligations (Rozemond 1996, 27-34). Yet, in notable contrast to UK Eurosceptics, Bolkestein was a consistent supporter of European Monetary Union – at least for a small group of lead countries. Beyond EMU, however, Bolkestein was a fierce critic of both the social chapter and of the structural funds. He opposed these attempts at (re-)regulation and redistribution on economic grounds as market distorting measures, as well as on political grounds as unacceptable intrusions into areas which should remain within national jurisdiction (Bolkestein 1992, 92-95). Interestingly, however, he had a rather more nuanced view of the Common Foreign and Security Policy. Bolkestein saw the CFSP as a potentially positive development, providing certain 'economies of scale' (Bolkestein 1992, 95-97). Nevertheless, he was also insistent that developments in this area be maintained under a strictly intergovernmental rubric, with national veto rights fully intact.

Bolkestein's European *prises de position*, as with his interventions on other policy areas, disturbed a comfortable elite consensus. His pronouncements clearly fell outside of a well-established, if largely tacit pro-integrationist consensus. In part, the fault lines created can be understood in fairly classic left/right terms, pitting advocates of a 'social Europe' against those, like Bolkestein, who saw market liberalisation largely as an end in itself. Indeed, in this regard, one can see signs of an interesting Europeanisation of national political debate, with proponents of competing 'Rhineland' and 'Anglo-American' versions of capitalism carrying on a debate which simultaneously encompassed both domestic and European policy choices. Bolkestein's dissent from the established consensus also rekindled long dormant questions concerning the position of the

Netherlands within the broader geopolitics of European integration, as well as the manner in which the country's national interest should be defined and defended.

Bolkestein was adamant that the Netherlands should not attach itself too closely to the Franco-German axis. As he provocatively phrased it, 'I do not belong to those Dutch politicians who believe that the Netherlands should seek shelter in the armpit of the Franco-German axis' (Bolkestein 1998b, 105). In his view, the axis itself was apt to be of decreasing importance over time, as a reunited Germany, legitimately, pursued its own national interests without seeking prior accommodations with Paris (Bolkestein 1998a, 168-170). In such a scenario, it was clear that the Netherlands would be part of a Northern 'free trade' camp, in opposition to a more 'protectionist' Southern grouping. This further implied the need to maintain or to enhance the Netherlands' close relationship with the United Kingdom, ensuring that London was not marginalised within the EU. In essence, Bolkestein can thus be seen as re-opening, within the contemporary framework of European integration, a long-standing historical discussion concerned with the balancing of 'Continental' and 'Atlantic' orientations in Dutch foreign policy. The Continentalist rebuttal was not long in coming.

Bolkestein's critics argued that his vision risked marginalising the Netherlands within the European integration project. As Green-Left leader Paul Rosenmöller put it (*De Volkskrant*, 18 June 1999), the adoption of a policy along the lines suggested would undesirably lead to a gradual 'sliding away' of the Netherlands from the European 'core countries' as it grew towards the 'minimalist' position held by Great Britain, Denmark, and Sweden. This risk of marginalisation had also been given voice earlier on by Ad Melkert (interview with *De Volkskrant*, 27 March 1996), at the time social affairs minister and a prominent PvdA strategist. For Melkert, Bolkestein's outlook ran the risk of closely associating the Netherlands with the UK at a time when 'England had entered the last phase of its European splendid isolation' and would soon have to change tack. Melkert went on, more strongly, to underline the undesirability of this misplaced Anglophilia in European affairs:

> One thing remains unchanged. If you stand on the beach at Scheveningen and look longingly across the North Sea, this does imply that you are standing with your back to Europe. What must not be allowed to happen is that the emergency brake is pulled at every moment.

Beyond the specific Atlantic/Continental divide, Bolkestein's interventions also served to place more general questions concerning the Dutch 'national interest' explicitly back on the political agenda. Most particularly, in a controversial speech delivered to a VVD foreign policy seminar at Noordwijk on 25 February 1996 (reprinted in Bolkestein 1998a, 163-171), Bolkestein forcefully set out the case for what he regarded to be the neglect of the national interest in the formulation and execution of Dutch foreign policy. In his view, the Dutch 'internationalist' tradition had led to a situation in which the country gave in too easily in international negotiations, rather than 'fighting its corner' as it should. As regards the EU, Bolkestein argued that it is the states which most stubbornly hold out, notably the Southern member states, which are the biggest net beneficiaries in budgetary terms (*'wie dwarsligt, wordt beloond'*; Bolkestein 1998a, 166). The time had thus come, in his view, for the Dutch government to play the same game. Specifically, this entailed the adoption of a strong line demanding a fundamental reform of both the Common Agricultural Policy and the structural funds. More generally, there had to be a 'cultural break' (*cultuuromslag*) in the conception of Dutch foreign policy, allowing the national interest to occupy its rightful, central place.

Bolkestein's remarks produced a predictable storm of criticism. Unsurprisingly, Dutch foreign ministry officials let their consternation be known to the press (*De Volkskrant*, 3 March 1995; *Het Parool*, 4 March 1995). Apart from mounting a strong defence of the vigour with which the Dutch diplomatic corps promotes the national interest, the leaks suggested that Bolkestein was opportunistically creating a 'negative sphere' around the EU in national public opinion, which risked compromising the Netherlands' position in Europe. This critical response also found an echo in some political circles. For example, Democrats '66 MEP Laurens Jan Brinkhorst portrayed Bolkestein's vision of Dutch foreign policy as a 'return behind the waterline' (*NRC Handelsblad*, 1 March 1995), implying a retreat behind the defensive fortifications of an insular nationalism. More positive reactions were, however, also forthcoming. Notably, two prominent national political commentators, J.L. Heldring writing in the *NRC Handelsblad* (2 March 1995) and Bart Tromp writing in *Het Parool* (8 March 1995), welcomed Bolkestein's frank evocation of the idea of the national interest. Both saw this as usefully breaking the unhelpful silence which had come to surround the underlying objectives of national foreign policy. Yet, in doing so, they also both clearly spelled out their disagreement with certain aspects of Bolkestein's own definition of this interest. In the perpetual contest between the *koopman* (the merchant) and the *dominee* (the clergyman) which has long been taken to define Dutch foreign policy, it is not difficult to paint Bolkestein as having gone entirely – and perhaps counterproductively – over to the mercantile side (see also the commentary by former CDA leader Piet Bukman in *Trouw*, 8 March 1995).

The more immediate question is, however, that of whether Bolkestein's views on European integration may be described as 'Eurosceptical'. In the first instance, it might be noted that the term Eurosceptic has been regularly used in connection with Bolkestein by Dutch commentators, as is perhaps most readily exemplified by Sam Rozemond's 1996 study *Bolkestein en de Euroscepsis*. Bolkestein's Euroscepticism was also a source of particularly acute controversy at the time of his nomination in 1999 to be the Dutch member of the College of Commissioners. Dutch Euro-parliamentarians, in particular, expressed their reservations at the thought of the Netherlands being represented in Brussels by a 'Eurosceptic' (*NRC Handelsblad*, 7 and 16 June 1999). This opposition found its most concrete expression in a pamphlet published by the Dutch Green MEP Joost Lagendijk, together with Richard Wouters, which brought together a collection of Bolkestein's major 'Eurosceptic' pronouncements (Lagendijk and Wouters 1999). The pamphlet, issued in four languages, was intended to provide MEPs with ammunition which could be used in the course of Bolkestein's confirmation hearing before the parliament.

Bolkestein himself has wavered over time as to the applicability of the term. Asked directly in a 1996 interview, 'Are you a Eurosceptic?', he replied 'In some regards, yes' (*HP/De Tijd*, 13 December 1996). There was, however, a marked change of tone as the possibility of a move to Brussels came into the picture. In a well-publicised speech to the European Liberal Democrat and Reform Party (ELDR) congress in Berlin on 30 April 1999, Bolkestein struck an uncharacteristically 'pro-European' note, heralding European integration as 'one of the three most important events of the century' (*NRC Handelsblad*, 30 April 1999). He also took great pains, during his confirmation hearing before the European Parliament, to eschew any connection with a hard-line Euroscepticism. Replying to a question from the British ELDR MEP Diana Wallis, Bolkestein emphasized the distance between himself and political figures readily identified elsewhere as Eurosceptics:

[W]hen I think of the word Eurosceptic, [I] think of politicians like Mr. Michael Portillo or Mr. John Redwood, or in France Mr. Charles Pasqua. Now I have no desire to polemicize with politicians who are not present in the room and therefore cannot defend themselves. I only want to say that I have nothing in common with the European ideas that these three gentlemen have and people like them[,] so if that is what you mean by Euroscepticism, and certainly that is the definition that I would follow, then suffice it for me to say that I have nothing in common with them.[5]

This protestation of European faith was somewhat disingenuous, but not fundamentally inaccurate. It is undeniable that, on the road to Brussels, there had been a change of tone. Yet, it also true that there had been no real change of substance. Bolkestein had consistently championed the cause of a limited, but significant European project centred on a core of economic activities. Moreover, his European pronouncements were also unquestionably both a reflection and a catalyst of a wider sea-change in Dutch attitudes towards European integration. It is telling that the positions defended by Bolkestein in the 1990s from the relative margins of Dutch European debate have, to a significant degree, now become accepted as part of a new mainstream consensus. As previously detailed, evocations of the national interest and the need for a major reform of the EU budget have become staples of Dutch European discourse. These, moreover, also formed the parameters for later debates concerning the Dutch position *on* and, by implication, *in* an enlarged Union.

Recent debates: the enlargement issue

European Union enlargement assumed a comparatively high-profile place in Dutch political debate in 2002. During the course of an exceptionally tumultuous year in Dutch politics, the question of EU enlargement figured during both the May 2002 and the January 2003 parliamentary election campaigns (see further Harmsen 2002; 2003). In neither campaign, it should be stressed, did European issues have a significant impact on the outcome of the poll. In the Netherlands, as elsewhere, 'Europe' has not shown any signs of emerging as a realigning issue which may reshape the terms of party competition. Yet, it is equally clear that European issues

---

[5] European Parliament, Judicial Affairs Committee, Hearing of Mr. Bolkestein, 8 September 1999, column 1-014. See also Bolkestein's letter to the *NRC Handelsblad* of 19 August 1999, in which he took exception to the 'insinuation' in the paper's reporting that he had 'in the past been an opponent of European integration'. Bolkestein, amongst other points, noted his support for both the Maastricht and the Amsterdam treaties.

have become significantly politicised, in the sense of occupying an increasingly prominent place on party and media agendas. In 2002, differences between the main parties over the handling of the enlargement issue were, literally and figuratively, 'front-page news' in the Netherlands. This was, moreover, a debate which also had substantial echoes elsewhere. Indeed, at one stage, it briefly seemed that Dutch doubts about enlargement might delay the entire process (*Financial Times*, 16 October 2002).

Enlargement first flared up as a potentially significant political issue during the last phase of the campaign for the 15 May 2002 parliamentary election. In an interview with *De Telegraaf* on 4 May 2002, VVD leader Hans Dijkstal expressed serious reservations as regards the enlargement process. Dijkstal was highly critical of the possible consequences of enlargement for existing member states, stressing the threats which might be posed to the value of the euro and the maintenance of the stability pact. He also clearly affirmed his view that the Netherlands should be prepared to veto enlargement if adequate reforms to the operation of the Common Agricultural Policy (CAP) and the Structural Funds could not be secured prior to the accession of the new member states.

Dijkstal's remarks drew a sharp and immediate response from leading figures in the other established parties. State Secretary Benschop of the PvdA referred to Dijkstal's remarks as 'irresponsible' and as, in his view, blocking any possibility of Labour and the Liberals working together again in government if this position were to be maintained (*Algemeen Dagblad*, 6 May 2002). In a similar vein, both Christian Democrat leader Jan Peter Balkenende and Democrats '66 leader Thom De Graaf expressed surprise at Dijkstal's remarks, stressing that they appeared to stand at odds with previous VVD support for the enlargement process (*De Telegraaf*, 6 May 2002).

This flurry of criticism was, however, somewhat disingenuous relative to the previous evolution of party positions on the enlargement issue. First, it should be emphasised that Dijkstal's statement, though somewhat more strongly worded than his previous pronouncements on this issue, nevertheless did not represent a major, substantive change of policy. Dijkstal (2002, 48) had previously made clear his view that 'Reform of the EU should take place before 2004, before the accession of new countries. This is true even if it delays the enlargement process.' While admittedly the word 'veto' was not used, it is difficult to see how this earlier statement differs fundamentally from the VVD leader's later comments to *De Telegraaf.*

The VVD leader's remarks must, moreover, be placed in the context of a growing number of calls being made in Dutch governmental circles for a fundamental, pre-enlargement reform of the EU budget. Not the least, in January 2002, State Secretary Benschop himself, speaking on behalf of the government, gave voice to a Dutch demand for a fundamental reform of the CAP prior to enlargement. Although carefully avoiding the term 'veto', such reform was cited as a key factor conditioning Dutch support for the accession of new member states (*De Volkskrant,* 29 January 2002).

Beyond governmental circles, Dijkstal's suggestion of the need for a hard-line Dutch position in the final stages of the enlargement negotiations also corresponded to the position being staked out by CDA leader (and future prime minister) Balkenende. While Balkenende reaffirmed the Christian Democrats' traditional attachment to a 'strong and federal Europe' (*NRC Handelsblad,* 14 December 2001), he further stressed the need for the European Union to engage in a process of radical reform so as to maintain its otherwise threatened credibility (Balkenende 2002a, 129-145). This credibility, amongst other issues, would hinge upon a strict insistence that all new member states met the accession criteria in full. Balkenende put on the record his doubts concerning the readiness of some of the candidate countries and counselled against a softening of the accession criteria which would lead to a more general weakening of the Union. In his words, 'the EU member states must dare to say No to those countries which have not yet put their houses in order as regards essential areas of EU legislation' (*NRC Handelsblad,* 14 December 2001). Balkenende took a similarly assertive position on the budget issue. The CDA leader directly criticised what he regarded to be the Commission's view that enlargement and budgetary reform could be treated as separate issues. To his mind, the two questions had to be handled together, with a review of the CAP and the Structural Funds preceding enlargement. Were this not to be done, the Union would be confronted with financial problems which 'cannot be trivialised' (Balkenende 2002b, 34).

Whatever debate might have been triggered by Dijkstal's remarks was, nevertheless, cut short by the premature halt to campaigning agreed in the climate of shock and anger which followed Pim Fortuyn's assassination on 6 May 2002 (see below). Yet, as negotiations started in earnest for the formation of a new government after the May election, the European issue again came to the fore. It was clear, from a relatively early stage in the negotiations between the Christian Democrats, the Liberals and the Pim Fortuyn List (LPF), that the new government would adopt a fairly hard-line stance as regards the last stages of the enlargement process (*NRC Handelsblad*, 3 June 2002). While most prominently driven by the VVD, it should be stressed that this position was echoed in the LPF and, as discussed above, found sympathy within the CDA.

In keeping with the tenor of the negotiations, strongly worded passages concerning the future handling of the enlargement issue figured in the July 2002 'Strategic Accord' concluded by the three parties as the basis for the governmental coalition. The Strategic Accord specified that the 'accession of new member states should be subject to the strict application by country of the Copenhagen criteria' (CDA-LPF-VVD 2002, 27). It further committed the government to seeking agreement on the reform of the Common Agricultural Policy (CAP) prior to enlargement. This was to be achieved either through the non-application of the existing system of direct income subsidies to the new member states or, as a fall back position, through the gradual phasing out of such subsidies for existing member states. It remained, however, to determine precisely how these parameters were to be incorporated into the government's negotiating brief. Particularly, the question arose as to whether the Dutch government would exercise a 'veto' as regards either individual countries deemed not to meet the accession criteria or the process as a whole in the event that a satisfactory result could not be achieved on CAP reform.

It was precisely this question which led to considerable (and widely reported) frictions within the cabinet in the run-up to the October 2002 EU summit in Brussels (*NRC Handelsblad*, 11 and 12 October 2002; *De Volkskrant*, 11 October 2002). It became clear that the CDA Foreign Minister, Jaap de Hoop Scheffer, essentially wished to endorse the position of the European Commission with minimal qualification. While recognising that problems remained in the candidate countries, this represented a strong endorsement for a 'big bang' enlargement, maintaining the first wave of entrants on an equal footing and poised for entry in 2004. The VVD ministers in the government, conversely, expressed (somewhat late in the day) reservations concerning the 'big bang' approach. In particular, they sought to obtain the adoption of a range of safeguard clauses to ensure that candidate countries would continue to be held to account for a strict respect of the *acquis* both during the run-up to accession and in a transitional period afterwards. A compromise was eventually achieved between de Hoop Scheffer and the state secretary for European affairs Atzo Nicolaï of the VVD, setting out a series of demands for strict safeguard clauses but removing the threat of a Dutch veto on individual countries. The compromise was, however, immediately rejected by VVD parliamentary leader Gerrit Zalm. This set the stage for a marathon thirteen hour pre-summit debate in the Dutch parliament on the government's position statement.[6]

In the debate, Zalm underscored the position of the VVD parliamentary group that a number of candidate countries were not yet ready for accession (naming Poland, Slovakia, Lithuania, and Latvia). In the VVD view, these countries variously failed to meet minimum standards in such areas as the fight against corruption, the development of appropriate administrative structures to deal with EU legislation, food safety, taxation regimes, privatisation, and industrial restructuring. To this end, it was argued that the countries concerned should be required to undergo periodic re-examinations to determine whether they met the accession criteria, thus potentially being excluded from the first wave of new members. The Dutch government was called upon to insist on the adoption of this strict 'country-by-country' approach at Brussels. The government was further called upon to demand the reform of the CAP, in the terms set out in the Strategic Accord, as a pre-condition for enlargement. In Zalm's words, the government would have to show itself a staunch ('*bikkelhard*') defender of the national interest at this critical juncture and had, in effect, undermined its own position by relinquishing the threat of a veto.

The government, in turn, argued the case for a more flexible position. It stressed the historic and economic opportunities represented by EU enlargement, as well as, more particularly, the undesirability of the Netherlands becoming isolated in the EU by an insistence on a politically untenable set of demands. In the end, the government position carried the day, but only by relying on the support of the opposition. The PvdA joined with the CDA and other smaller groups to back the government, while both the VVD and the LPF groups voted against the government position. The Netherlands was thus represented at the Brussels summit by a caretaker government (it had resigned prior to the EU debate over

---

[6] Tweede Kamer, Handelingen 2002-2003, nr. 12, 575-660 (23 October 2002). The full text of parliamentary debates, together with attendant documentation, may be accessed on-line via parlando.sdu.nl/cgi/login/anonymous.

an unrelated matter) whose position, though supported by the (left) opposition in the chamber, had been rejected by two of the three parties in
the outgoing coalition. The vote stands, if nothing else, as a strong
(though by no means unproblematic) example of Dutch parliamen-
tary/executive dualism.

If sharp, the divide on the government's negotiating strategy nevertheless proved to be short lived. On returning from Brussels, Prime Minister
Balkenende was able to point to a number of minor victories.[7] The Dutch
government was able to play a significant role in shaping the mechanics
of the safeguard clauses put in place as regards the new member states.
Dutch influence may be seen in a lengthening of the time period after
accession when such clauses may be invoked (from 2 to 3 years), a specification of the areas in which they may be imposed, and the consultative
involvement of the Council of Ministers in their removal. While unable to
do much about a (in Dutch eyes) very unfavourable Franco-German
budget compromise reached before the summit, the prime minister was
nevertheless able to secure a reduction in the inflation correction mecha-
nism in the CAP from 1.5% to 1%. This, overall, was enough to prompt
Zalm to compliment Balkenende for his handling of the negotiations in
Brussels, given the parameters within which the prime minister had to
operate. Perhaps rather more to the point, the VVD had, by this stage, no
interest in deepening a rift on an effectively closed issue with a party with
whom they hoped to continue in government after the January 2003
election. Although the Liberals had earlier signalled an intention to make
enlargement a campaign issue (NRC Handelsblad, 17 and 21 October
2002), they had rapidly backed off from this position, concluding that the
question was unlikely to be a successful mobilising theme.

The post-summit debate largely closed off the debate on the European issue. There was, however, one addendum worthy of note. The
Dutch parliament, on 5 November 2002, backed two motions concerned
with the holding of referenda on European issues. A majority backed a
motion, put down by Democrats '66 leader de Graaf and others, which
called on the government to consider the possibility of holding a referendum on EU enlargement and to report back to parliament on its feasibility by the end of November 2002.[8] The parliament also turned its attention to the European Convention, charged, under the chairmanship of

---

[7] Tweede Kamer, Handelingen 2002-2003, nr. 14, 733-760 (30 October 2002).
[8] Tweede Kamer, Vergaderjaar 2002-2003, 23 987, nr. 23.

former French president Giscard d'Estaing, with putting forward proposals for the reform and consolidation of the EU treaties. A majority backed a PvdA sponsored motion calling for a Europe-wide referendum on the results of the Convention or, failing that, a national referendum in the Netherlands prior to the ratification of any resulting treaty reform.[9] In each case, the referendum motion was backed by the (left) opposition together with the LPF parliamentary group, over the combined opposition of the CDA and the VVD. The government, on 29 November 2002, reported back to the chamber on the feasibility of an enlargement referendum, unsurprisingly making the case for insuperable problems of logistics and timing.[10] Yet, though an enlargement referendum has been taken off the table, the proposal for a referendum on treaty reform remains very much a live issue. Members of parliament from the Labour Party, Green-Left and the Democrats '66 put down a new motion in May 2003 setting out a framework for a national consultative referendum on such treaty reforms as may emerge from the Intergovernmental Conference convened to follow up the work of the Convention.[11] For the sponsors of the motion, the holding of such a referendum would serve both to legitimate the adoption of a 'European constitution' and to enhance citizen participation in the integration process more generally.[12] At the time of writing, it is unclear if this referendum proposal enjoys the support of a parliamentary majority, with the Christian Democrats remaining resolutely opposed and the Liberal Party divided (*NRC Handelsblad*, 17 June 2003). Nevertheless, whether or not the referendum takes place, the serious and repeated discussion of the possibility must in itself be seen as a striking gauge of the evolution of Dutch European debate in recent years.

Euroscepticism of the right: Pim Fortuyn

The meteoric rise to prominence of the maverick populist Pim Fortuyn in late 2001 and early 2002 appeared, momentarily, to shake Dutch politics to its core. A sometime academic and journalist (notably, a columnist for the newsweekly *Elsevier*), Fortuyn unexpectedly captured a strong under-

---

[9] Tweede Kamer, Vergaderjaar 2002-2003, 21 502-20, nr. 197.
[10] Tweede Kamer, Vergaderjaar 2002-2003, 23 987, nr. 28.
[11] Tweede Kamer, Vergaderjaar 2002-2003, 28 885, nr. 2.
[12] Tweede Kamer, Vergaderjaar 2002-2003, 28 885, nr. 3.

current of discontent with the Dutch political establishment. Perhaps even more, Fortuyn's assassination shortly before the May 2002 election threw the nation into a state of shock, eliciting waves of sympathy well beyond those who shared his political agenda. In manifold ways, the comfortable certainty that 'it couldn't happen here' had been unsettled.

The Pim Fortuyn List, in the May 2002 election, secured 26 seats in the 150 seat Dutch parliament on 17% of the vote. This result, the single most important breakthrough ever made by a new party in a Dutch parliamentary election, secured a place in government for the LPF. However, bereft of its leader and lacking a clearly defined organisational structure, the movement rapidly succumbed to highly public internecine squabbling. By October 2002, the bickering between two senior LPF ministers, Eduard Bomhoff and Herman Heinsbroek, triggered the break-up of the governmental coalition. In the ensuing January 2003 parliamentary election, the party was reduced to only 8 seats on 5.7% of the vote. The LPF will, perhaps, be able to carve out a longer-term role for itself as a niche player in the Dutch party system, staking out a position to the right of the VVD. Any thoughts of a broader realignment of Dutch party politics would, however, seem to have disappeared as rapidly as they first emerged on the horizon. Yet, the underlying discontent which took shape in the 'Fortuyn phenomenon' cannot be ignored. Beyond a specific concern with the issues of asylum and immigration, the LPF electorate was marked out by a deep feeling of cynicism as regards the political process in general (van Holsteyn and Irwin 2003; van Praag 2003). In this regard, though Dutch politics has 'normalised' in party political terms, it remains for the mainstream parties to find the means to reconnect with an electorate that has displayed both an increasing volatility and a troubling estrangement.

It is against this more general background that the nature and influence of Fortuyn's Euroscepticism must be understood. Europe, it should be stressed, did not emerge as a significant mobilising theme for the LPF electorate (van Holsteyn and Irwin 2003, 62). Nevertheless, a strongly articulated Eurosceptic discourse formed a clear and consistent part of Fortuyn's political message. Though advocating neither Dutch withdrawal from the EU nor the abolition of the EU itself, Fortuyn was a radical critic of the European integration project. He envisaged a major retrenchment of EU competence and a reshaping of EU institutional structures which would, in effect, redefine the nature of the integration process. As such, Fortuyn's thought continues to merit examination as the most pronounced example to date of a populist Eurosceptic discourse in the Netherlands – incorporating a radical critique of the EU into a broader and initially very successful anti-establishment movement.

In keeping with the more general development of his thought, Fortuyn's views on Europe did not at first depart much from mainstream Dutch opinion. While still involved with the PvdA, Fortuyn, indeed, described European integration as 'indispensable' (Cited in Lucardie and Voerman 2002, 39). His views on Europe, however, later shifted in keeping with the more general radicalisation and rightwards shift of his thought. Most notably, in 1997 Fortuyn published a book with the telling title (in translation) of *Soulless Europe: Against a Europe of Technocrats, Bureaucrats, Subsidies and Inevitable Fraud.* As suggested by the title, he attacked European integration as a project created by political and bureaucratic elites to serve their own interests, to the detriment of those of the population at large. Fortuyn characterised the EU as the 'private affair' (*onderonsje*) of those elites (Fortuyn 1997, 95), allowing them to escape accountability for their actions behind the mask of policies presented to national electorates as '*faits accomplis*' (Fortuyn 1997, 102). As a result, wasteful expenditure and outright fraud were endemic. In contrast to this corrupt system, he argued that power must be exercised more closely to individual citizens, necessitating a reaffirmation of national sovereignty.

Fortuyn's criticism of the EU was, in good part, grounded in a nationalist discourse. While Fortuyn's writing is not very evocative of the values or the characteristics of the Dutch nation in particular, it puts forward a very strong affirmation of the continued importance of the nation-state in general. For Fortuyn, it is the nation which remains the basic unit of effective political organisation; it is with the nation that the individual is able to establish a meaningful, transcendent political bond. As he puts it, 'It is the nation-state which allows us to feel that we are a people and which gives us an awareness that standing above our individual interest there is something else of great worth, the general interest' (Fortuyn 1997, 100). It is the nation-state which is, moreover, 'the bounded bit of territory where people feel secure, in which they are looked after, and within which they can feel themselves to be united as a people through the existence of a shared language, culture, and mentality' (Fortuyn 1997, 101). It is thus the nation which must remain the primordial unit of political organisation and social solidarity.

Although Fortuyn muted his Eurosceptic views during his short lived tenure as leader of the Liveable Netherlands (LN) movement in late 2001

and early 2002, this proved to be only a brief and unrepresentative inter-
lude. After his removal from the LN leadership in February 2002, Fortuyn returned to advocating a more thoroughgoing reform – effectively a
substantial dismantling – of the EU *acquis*. His thoughts on the European
question were detailed in the authored book, *The Ruins of Eight Years of the
Purple Coalition*, published in lieu of a traditional party manifesto for the
May 2002 election. In connection with a generally hard-line stance on
immigration issues, Fortuyn advocated the renunciation by the Netherlands of the Schengen Accord as a necessary precondition for the integral
re-establishment of border controls (Fortuyn 2002, 166). Beyond this, he
put forward a nine-point plan for the radical reform of the European
Union. These points are as below (Fortuyn 2002, 180-181):

1. Renegotiation of the size of the Dutch budget contribution, with
   the population size and prosperity of the country relative to other
   member states used as the base point.

2. Abolition of agricultural subsidies and renationalisation of agricultural policy.

3. Abolition of all structural funds.

4. A new, time-limited structural fund created for the new member
   states, allowing them to bring their economies up to the EU-level.

5. The new member states will, for the time being, be excluded from
   Economic and Monetary Union.

6. The Netherlands will hold politically binding referenda on the
   admission of new members, by groups of states.

7. The Netherlands would support the holding of an EU 'subsidiarity
   conference', to review those powers which may be returned to the
   national level and those which should remain in Brussels.

8. The European Parliament will be the subject of a critical review.
   Fortuyn, who had earlier written that the EP 'would be missed as
   one misses a toothache' (Fortuyn 1997, 24), expressed the personal
   view that the EP could be abolished and replaced by a senate
   made up of national members of parliament.

9. The Netherlands Parliament will take a more concentrated interest
   in EU affairs, holding ministers to binding, limited mandates in
   EU negotiations.

In *The Ruins* as elsewhere, a strong anti-establishment discourse figures prominently in Fortuyn's critique of European integration. The EU in general is seen as above all a little game of political elites and civil servants. Dutch leaders in particular are criticised for having used the EU as a means to escape 'the swampy morass of the low countries' (Fortuyn 2002, 178). The Dutch political class is accused of having sought to enhance their personal standing on the wider European stage at the cost of routinely agreeing compromises which poorly reflected national interests. Europe thus continues to be portrayed as an elite instrument used to escape genuine accountability – with decisions from Brussels assuming the character of a 'natural law' (Fortuyn 2002, 178) which cannot be questioned through normal democratic channels.

Fortuyn is, however, also careful to underline what he regards as the positive achievements of European integration. The European Union is referred to as a 'phenomenal experiment' (Fortuyn 2002, 177) which has brought both peace and prosperity to its member states. The EU, to his mind, is 'a project which has delivered considerable economic advantage to us, has allowed us to get to know one another better, and has created a situation in which matters which are best handled at the Community level may be handled at the Community level' (Fortuyn 2002, 178). In other words, Fortuyn is careful to stress that he is not opposed to European co-operation *per se* – insofar as, respecting the principle of subsidiarity, there is a clear value-added to undertaking action at the European level. Rather, he casts his argument in terms of an objection to 'unnecessary' transfers of sovereignty to the European institutions, in ways taken to reflect elite or institutional interests, but not the public interest.

This qualification is of considerable importance in situating Fortuyn's ascendancy relative to wider European trends. Fortuyn himself adamantly objected to being classed with such extreme right politicians as Jean-Marie Le Pen or Jörg Haider (*Financial Times*, 10 April 2002). There is much to justify this objection. Fortuyn's agenda, at least as regards Europe, bears little resemblance to the overtly xenophobic and strongly protectionist stances typically adopted by parties of the far right. Rather, it might be suggested that Fortuyn's views on European integration, in keeping with his more general political philosophy, are better understood in terms of a somewhat contradictory mixture of populist, nationalist, and liberal strands (Lucardie and Voerman 2002).

In Dutch terms, the most obvious point of reference is Frits Bolkestein. It bears emphasis that Bolkestein prefaced Fortuyn's 1997 *Soulless*

Europe. In his preface, the VVD leader revealingly commended the work
for raising issues that had too long lain dormant in the Netherlands, while
at the same time criticising the book for its tendency towards exaggeration (In Fortuyn 1997, 8).[13] At base, the two men share certain core conceptions concerning the nature and extent of European integration. They
both display a deep scepticism of 'European federalism'. Both equally can
be seen as proponents of a 'common market' in the narrow sense, supporting economic integration divorced from a broader range of political
commitments. Fortuyn's expression of these ideas is, however, clearly of
a more extreme variety, to the point of opening up obvious inconsisten-
cies. Unlike Bolkestein's position, it is difficult to see how even the limited 'Europe' which Fortuyn desired could be maintained without at least
some of the institutional structures which he simultaneously sought to
dismantle. The parallel with Bolkestein's thought, insofar as it may be
sustained, is nevertheless a telling one. Fortuyn's views on European
questions can, in many respects, be read as a radical prolongation of
mainstream Dutch right-wing liberalism.

The final word in this regard might, however, be left to Fortuyn himself. His reference point in European matters was already clearly indicated in *Soulless Europe*, where he expressed an unbounded admiration for
Mrs. Thatcher's stance on Europe (Fortuyn 1997, 91-93). The former UK
Prime Minister was lauded for having broken up the all too cosy 'boy's
club' in Brussels, as well as for having publicly railed against the excessive, wasteful bureaucratisation which the EU had foisted upon its members. Fortuyn, in fact, went so far as to propose that Mrs. Thatcher
should be the chair of a newly created European audit committee charged
with paring back the Union's expenditures to more reasonable levels
(Fortuyn 1997, 96-97).

Euroscepticism of the left: the Socialist Party

The Socialist Party represents the most prominent instance to date of a
left-wing Euroscepticism in the Netherlands. Originally founded in the
1970s as a Maoist movement, the SP has, from the 1980s onwards, rein-
vented itself as something of a 'tribune' party, with a strong grassroots
implantation. Entirely absent from parliament prior to the 1994 election,
the party has seen its level of support gradually rise to the point where in

---

[13] Bolkestein later emerged as a strong critic of Fortuyn during the 2002 election
campaign. See, for example, *Trouw*, 2 May 2002.

both the 2002 and the 2003 elections it was able to win around 6% of the vote and 9 seats in the 150 seat parliament. The SP is active in the anti-globalisation movement and advocates Dutch withdrawal from NATO, as well as adopting a comparatively 'hard' Eurosceptic stance. The Party has consistently campaigned against the further transfer of powers to what its leader, Jan Marijnissen, has termed 'untransparent, fraudulent, bureaucratic Brussels' (Marijnissen 2003, 131). For Marijnissen, European integration is producing a situation in which the member states are pro-gressively coming to resemble 'the powerless provinces of a supreme and uncontrollable superstate' (Marijnissen 2003, 89).

The core of the Socialist Party critique of the European integration project is two-fold. First, the EU, in its present form, is viewed as a neo-liberal project, serving business interests to the detriment of ordinary citizens. The scope created by the EU for tax competition, placing gov-ernments under pressure to lower taxation with a corresponding decline of public services, is highlighted as an example of the realisation of this corporate agenda (Socialistische Partij 2002, 58). Second, the EU is sharply criticised for its lack of democratic accountability. To this end, the 2002 SP electoral programme called for the holding of national refer-enda in the Netherlands on both the enlargement of the Union and the ratification of such new or consolidated treaty texts as may come out of the deliberations of the European Convention (Socialistische Partij 2002, 57). The SP further sought directly to limit the remit of European law, proposing that European regulations should not have effect in the Neth-erlands without the prior and explicit approval of the Dutch parliament. The role of the national parliament in the EU legislative process was also more generally to be enhanced, most notably acquiring a right of free access to the minutes of deliberations of the Council of Ministers.

The economic and democratic elements of the SP critique are most clearly brought together in the Party's strong opposition to Economic and Monetary Union. For Marijnissen, the establishment of a monetary union in the absence of a political union is the sign of a process which is 'advancing entirely the wrong way around' (Marijnissen 2003, 92). The single currency is seen as having been driven forward by the interests of big business, most prominently the 'captains of industry' represented in the European Round Table. This, in Marijnissen's view, is storing up more general problems. He foresees an escalation of political tensions, as national governments are forced to make increasingly unpalatable policy choices in order to remain within an artificially imposed monetary straightjacket. The 2002 SP electoral programme, in keeping with this analysis, called for the adoption of an 'emergency plan' for the restoration of the guilder, in the event that the 'greatest monetary experiment in history' proved not to work (Socialistische Partij 2002, 57). On a more day-to-day level, the party has also made considerable mileage out of the generalised concern over a rounding up of prices after the transition to the euro.

The SP's European agenda is thus very much consonant with a more general 'alternative Europe' discourse shared by much of the West European far left. The current EU appears largely as a subset of a more general neo-liberal international economic order and is rejected as such. This is, in the case of the SP, further complemented by a strong focus on issues of democratic accountability and, relatedly, an insistence on the preservation of national sovereignty. The European issue, it should be noted, does not figure with particular prominence on the SP agenda. The 'anti-elite' tenor of its message on the issue does, however, serve to enhance its overall profile as a 'people's party of the left', in contrast to a Labour Party which may be cast as a 'party of officials and advisors' (*NRC Handelsblad*, 8 November 2002).

Conclusion

The past decade has seen a 'critical turn' in Dutch European debate. The 'automatic' pro-integrationist reflex which had marked Dutch European discourse at least since the early 1960s has been replaced by a more explicit discourse of national interest, stressing the need for a careful assessment of the costs and benefits of further integration. Initially fuelled by budgetary issues, this new attitude found its most prominent expression to date in the comparatively hard-line position assumed by the Dutch government during 2002 over EU enlargement. While this 'Eurocritical' discourse has been centred on the VVD, it has resonated more broadly amongst mainstream parties. Recent years have also seen unparalleled success for parties adopting comparatively strong Eurosceptical stances, with the emergence of the Pim Fortuyn List and the growth of the Socialist Party. In neither case was the European issue a major mobilising theme for these movements of 'populist discontent'. Nevertheless, breaking with conventional wisdom, a Eurosceptic stance proved at the very least not to be an impediment to electoral success.

The Dutch case largely corresponds to the findings of the more general literature on Euroscepticism and the (non-)impact of European issues on national party systems. Clearly, in keeping with the strong general trend (Mair 2000), Europe has not been a realigning issue in Dutch politics, nor does it show any likelihood of becoming so. Divisions on European integration, moreover, follow the pre-existing cleavage structure underpinning the Dutch party system. In particular, the VVD stands as an archetype of the 'liberal-conservative' position identified by Marks and Wilson (2000). Consistent with this position, the VVD favours economic integration 'as a means to lower trade barriers and institutionalize free markets', while opposing 'the social democratic project for regulated capitalism at the European level' (Marks and Wilson 2000, 449) and broader forms of political integration. The Dutch case also provides confirmation for Taggart's (1998) 'touchstone of dissent' thesis, insofar as the stronger forms of Dutch Euroscepticism all form part of more general anti-establishment programmes directed by protest movements against the mainstream ('cartel') parties. The evidence as regards Sitter's (2001) argument that the development of party-based Euroscepticism must be understood relative to a government/opposition dynamic is mixed. The Dutch case offers support for the argument that 'the strategies of the core parties set the parameters for new politics and new populist party-based Euroscepticism' (Sitter 2001, 36). In particular, the growth of a more critical European discourse amongst the mainstream parties appears to have created a more permissive climate in which parties holding overtly Eurosceptic positions could find broader audiences than might otherwise have been the case. Conversely, the Dutch case offers no evidence of the mainstream parties themselves adjusting their positions on European issues in relation to distinctive governmental or opposition strategies. The European issue does, however, appear to have given rise to a particularly robust reading of the Dutch doctrine of parliamentary/executive dualism. The VVD parliamentary party, first under Frits Bolkestein and more recently under Gerrit Zalm, has been a frequent critic of governmental European policy, thus publicly assuming a distance from the positions accepted by the VVD ministers in those governments. While not unproblematic in terms of maintaining the cohesion of the governmental majority, this dualist practice nevertheless provides an interesting example of a particular institutional opportunity structure facilitating the expression of dissent on European issues (see further Lees 2002).

The overall pattern is thus one of a discernible discursive shift which has not, however, been accompanied by significant changes in the terms of party competition. Dutch European discourse as a whole has become more critical, but the issue (of still comparatively low salience) has not been used as a mobilising theme by individual parties. This critical turn is, moreover, likely to be sustained over the coming years. Budgetary issues will continue to preoccupy Dutch governments on the European stage, as the country seeks to reduce the level of its net contribution. The Dutch will also continue to exhibit what Milner (2000) has termed a 'healthy scepticism', questioning the levels of democratic accountability provided by EU institutions relative to pre-existing national standards. More generally, the Netherlands will continue to search for its place in a post-enlargement Union where there will, inevitably, be a much lower level of 'natural congruence' with its national interests than had been the case in the past. Historically caught between 'Atlanticist' and 'Continentalist' impulses, the Netherlands will now have to adjust to life near the western edges of a much enlarged Union. The relatively recent stirrings of dissent from the polder thus look set to become an enduring feature of the European political landscape.

References

Balkenende, Jan Peter. 2002a. *Anders en beter: Pleidooi voor een andere aanpak in de politiek vanuit een Christen-democratische visie over de samenleving, overheid en politiek.* Soesterberg: Aspekt.

Balkenende, Jan Peter. 2002b. Europe is asleep, it's time to awaken her!. In *Europa in de Nederlandse Politiek*, ed. J.Q.Th. Rood, 27-37. The Hague: Nederlands Instituut voor Internationale Betrekkingen ('Clingendael'). On-line version available at www.clingendael.nl/cli/publ/essays/rood_2002_april.pdf.

Benschop, Dick. 2000. De dynamiek van Netwerk Europa: Nederlands oude en nieuwe partnerschappen. *Internationale Spectator* 54, no. 4 (April): 186-190.

Bolkestein, Frits. 1992. *Woorden hebben hun betekenis*. Amsterdam: Prometheus.

Bolkestein, Frits. 1998a. *Boren in harden houd*. Amsterdam: Prometheus.

Bolkestein, Frits. 1998b. *Liberalism in a Changing World*. The Hague: VVD/Liberal International.

Bolkestein, Frits. 1999. The Dutch Model: The High Road that Leads out of the Low Countries. *The Economist*, 22 May 1999: 115-116.

CDA-LPF-VVD. 2002. *Werken aan vertrouwen, een kwestie van aanpakken. Strategisch akkoord voor kabinet CDA, LPF, VVD*. 3 July. www.minaz.nl/kabinets formatie/20020703akkoord.pdf .

ChristenUnie. 2002. *Durf te kiezen voor normen: Verkiezingsprogramma 2002-2006.* www.verkiezingen.christenunie.nl/.

Dijkstal, Hans. 2002. Staten in verandering, staatkundige verandering. In *Europa in de Nederlandse Politiek*, ed. J.Q.Th. Rood, 39-49. The Hague: Nederlands Instituut voor Internationale Betrekkingen ('Clingendael'). On-line version available at www.clingendael.nl/cli/publ/essays/rood_2002_april.pdf.

Fortuyn, Pim. 1997. *Zielloos Europa: Tegen een Europa van technocraten, bureaucratie, subsidies en overmijdelijke fraude.* Utrecht: A.W. Bruna.

Fortuyn, Pim. 2002. *De puinhopen van acht jaar Paars: Een genadeloze analyse van de collectieve sector en aanbevelingen voor een krachtig herstelprogramma.* Rotterdam: Karakter.

GroenLinks. 2002. *Overvloed en Onbehagen: Verkiezingsprogramma 2002-2006.* www.groenlinks.nl/visie/GroenLinksVerkiezingsprogramma2002-2006.pdf.

Harmsen, Robert. 2002. Europe and the Dutch Parliamentary Election of May 2002. Opposing Europe Research Network/Royal Institute of International Affairs Election Briefing No. 3. www.sussex.ac.uk/Units/SEI/pdfs/oern/no3.pdf.

Harmsen, Robert. 2003. Europe and the Dutch Parliamentary Election of January 2003. Opposing Europe Research Network/Royal Institute of International Affairs Election Briefing No. 9. www.sussex.ac.uk/Units/SEI/oern/ElectionBriefings/no9.pdf.

Hoetjes, Ben J.S. 2003. The Netherlands: A Former Founding Father in Search of Control. In *Fifteen into One? The European Union and its Member States*, eds. Wolfgang Wessels, Andreas Maurer and Jürgen Mittag, 315-336. Manchester: Manchester University Press.

Van Holsteyn, Joop J.M. and Galen A. Irwin. Never a Dull Moment: Pim Fortuyn and the Dutch Parliamentary Election of 2002. *West European Politics* 26, no. 2: 41-66.

Koch, Koen. De valse tweedeling van federalisme en intergouvernementalisme: Terughoudendheid als traditie in Nederlands Europees beleid. *Internationale Spectator* 55, no. 9 (September): 429-434.

Laffan, Brigid. 1997. *The Finances of the European Union.* Basingstoke: MacMillan.

Lagendijk, Joost and Richard Wouters. 1999. *Een Euroscepticus in Brussel?: Frits Bolkestein over de Europese Unie, een bloemlezing.* Utrecht: Stichting GroenLinks in de Europese Unie.

Lees, Charles. 2002. 'Dark Matter': Institutional Constraints and the Failure of Party-based Euro-scepticism in Germany. *Political Studies* 50, no. 2: 244-267.

Lucardie, Paul and Gerrit Voerman. 2002. Liberaal patriot of nationaal populist? Het gedachtegoed van Pim Fortuyn. *Socialisme en Democratie* 59, no. 4: 32-42.

Maas, Ad, Gerard Marlet, and Rutger Zwart. 1997. *Het brein van Bolkestein.* Nijmegen: SUN.

Mair, Peter. 2000. The Limited Impact of Europe on National Party Systems. *West European Politics* 23, no. 4: 27-51.

Marijnissen, Jan. 2003. *Nieuw optimisme.* Soesterberg: Aspekt.

Marks, Gary and Carole J. Wilson. 2000. The Past in the Present: A Cleavage Theory of Party Response to European Integration. *British Journal of Political Science* 30: 433-459.

Milner, Susan. 2000. Introduction: A Healthy Scepticism? *Journal of European Integration* 22, no. 1: 1-14.

Pijpers, Alfred, ed. 1999. *Nederland zoekt het tweegesprek: Neobilaterale accenten in de Europese politiek.* The Hague: Nederlands Instituut voor Internationale Betrekkingen ('Clingendael').

van Praag, Philip. 2003. De LPF-kiezer: Rechts, cynisch of modaal?. In *Documentatiecentrum Nederlandse Politieke Partijen Jaarboek 2001*, 96-116. Groningen: Rijksuniversiteit Groningen. On-line version available at. www.rug.nl /dnpp/jaarboeken/jaarboek2001/lpf.pdf.

Rozemond, Sam. 1996. *Bolkestein en de Euroscepsis.* The Hague: Nederlands Instituut voor Internationale Betrekkingen ('Clingendael').

Sitter, Nick. 2001. The Politics of Opposition and European Integration in Scandinavia: Is Euro-scepticism a Government-Opposition Dynamic? *West European Politics* 24, no. 4: 22-35.

Socialistische Partij. 2002. *Eerste weg links: Actieprogramma SP 2003-2007.* www.sp.nl/partij/theorie/program/eerste_weg_links.pdf.

Soetendorp, Ben and Kenneth Hanf. 1997. The Netherlands: Growing Doubts of a Loyal Member. In *Adapting to European Integration: Small States and the European Union*, eds. Kenneth Hanf and Ben Soetendorp, 36-51. London: Longman.

Staatkundig Gereformeerde Partij. 2002. *Tot uw dienst: SGP-Verkiezingsprogramma 2002-2006.* www.sgp.nl/1.1.6.2.1.pdf.

Taggart, Paul. 1998. A Touchstone of Dissent: Euroscepticism in Contemporary West European Party Systems. *European Journal of Political Research* 33, no. 3: 363-388.

Taggart, Paul and Aleks Szczerbiak. 2002. The Party Politics of Euroscepticism in EU Member and Candidate States. Sussex European Institute Working Paper no. 51. Brighton: Sussex European Institute. www.sussex.ac.uk/ Units/SEI/pdfs/wp51.pdf.

van Weezel, Max and Leonard Ornstein. 1999. *Frits Bolkestein: Portret van een liberale vrijbuiter.* Amsterdam: Prometheus.

Werts, Jan. 1999. Agenda 2000: Hoe Paars stilletjes in Berlijn de 'Zilvervloot' haalde. *Internationale Spectator* 53, no. 9 (September): 463-470.

EUROPEAN STUDIES 20 (2004): 127-149

BRITISH EUROSCEPTICISM

Menno Spiering

Abstract

Britain is the home of the term Euroscepticism. Coined in this country in the mid-1980s, the word has since been widely used in the media and has been adopted by many individuals and organisations, in as
well as outside Britain. This article first deals with the 'when', 'what',
'where' and 'why' of British Euroscepticism. After locating the phenomenon in time and place, its characteristics are examined in greater
depth. It is argued that British Euroscepticism is in part the product
of British 'differentness' as manifested in the electoral and party political system, the condition of the press and a tradition of regarding the
country and people as distinct from Europe and the Europeans.

Almost all studies on 'Britain and Europe' which have appeared since the
early 1990s mention the term Euroscepticism, and tend to do so in relation to the entire postwar period. In his monumental *This Blessed Plot:
Britain and Europe from Churchill to Blair* Hugo Young labels the former
Labour leader Hugh Gaitskell (1906-1963) 'the first Eurosceptic' (Young
1999, 161). Stephen George grants the honour to another Labourite of
the 1960s, James Callaghan (George 2000, 16). As the word first appeared
only in the 1980s, one could argue that using it in such a wide, temporal
context is anachronistic.[1] Having said that, the reason for this practice is
obvious. Anglo-European relations did not start, nor did they start to be
troublesome, in the 1980s. Although the term Euroscepticism might be
relatively young, in Britain what it appears to denote goes back a long
time. This article, therefore, will follow the trend and apply the term *avant
la lettre*.

---

[1] The earliest citation in the Oxford English Dictionary is from *The Times* of 30 June 1986.
In fact the same newspaper used the word some months earlier, on 11 November 1985.

What is British Euroscepticism?

In origin the word is evidently journalese and in the years to come it might well be superseded by yet another catchy Euro-word. However, at the start of the 21st century, almost twenty years after its inception, the term seems only to gain in currency in Britain and elsewhere, and is increasingly attracting academic attention, as witness this volume of *European Studies* and various other publications. An attempt at definition, therefore, is in place.

There is clear consensus that the 'Euro' in Euroscepticism refers to the European Union and its precursors, while 'sceptic' means 'doubtful'. The majority of scholars and commentators leave it at that, and consequently regard every British doubt, past and present, about the European institutions as a sign of Euroscepticism. Anthony Forster's (2002) *Euroscepticism in Contemporary British Politics* is a case in point. Its subtitle reads 'Opposition to Europe in the British Conservative and Labour Parties since 1945'. Forster, together with many others, employs the term in a non-specific way, as a portmanteau for every British reservation ever expressed about postwar European cooperation and integration. Winston Churchill, Harold Wilson, Margaret Thatcher, they were all Eurosceptics, albeit in their own ways. In a similar vein the two editions of Martin Holmes' *Eurosceptic Reader* bundle together a wide variety of articles and speeches on Britain and Europe, ranging from calculated analyses to frenzied tirades against 'Brussels' (Holmes 1996; 2002).[2]

Evidently, such a broad interpretation of British Euroscepticism is possible and popular, but it renders the concept almost meaningless. Very occasionally more specific definitions have been suggested. Stephen George, for instance, writes: 'it has to be said that in Britain the term has come to refer to a rather stronger position which is hostile to British participation in the European Union' (George 2000, 15). It is a valid observation. Coined at a time of great tensions between Margaret Thatcher and the European Commission (and within her own administration) Euroscepticism immediately acquired connotations of extremism. In *The Times*, in the first articles that mention the term, 'Euro-sceptic' (then still hyphenated) is freely mixed with 'anti-Marketeer', the word reserved for those who had altogether rejected continued EEC member-

---

[2] To date there is one other Eurosceptic 'Reader' on the market, edited by Ronald Tiersky (2001). This book, however, also deals with Euroscepticisms outside Britain.

ship during the 1975 referendum.[3] In the following years the word became solidly associated with Mrs. Thatcher's famous 'No, No, No' (pronounced in 1990 in respect of moves towards more European integration) and with John Major's epic struggles with his own, increasingly EU-hostile MPs and ministers. One of these sceptics, Norman Lamont, suggested at the 1994 Conservative Party conference that the time had come for the UK seriously to consider complete withdrawal from the EU.

There are further indications that British Euroscepticism is at heart about rejecting UK membership. First, the term is sported as a badge of honour by those who actively seek to withdraw Britain from the EU. The Internet bristles with British organisations calling themselves Eurosceptic and demanding that the UK 'get out'. Most can be found under the umbrella of the 'Eurosceptic Web Resource' (www.euro-sceptic.org)[4]. One of the oldest is the Campaign for an Independent Britain, which was formed in 1976 as the Safeguard Britain Campaign. It changed its name to the British Anti-Common Market Campaign in 1983 and changed again in 1989 to form the CIB. It explicitly calls itself Eurosceptic, designates its opponents as 'Europhiles' and seeks the unconditional repeal of the 1972 European Communities Act under which EU directives take precedence over UK law. 'Once self-government has been recovered, the United Kingdom would be free, as an independent state, to co-operate and trade with its neighbours in Europe and with countries elsewhere in the world without the restrictions imposed by EU membership' (www.cibhq.co.uk). One of the CIB's stickers says it all: 'Free Britain from Euro Union' (figure 1).

Figure 1: Sticker produced by the Campaign for an Independent Britain

---

[3] 'Tomatoes Throw Europe's Summit Progress', *The Times*, 11 November 1985, 19. 'Thatcher Still the Sceptic in Europe', *The Times*, 30 June 1986, 9. 'Testing Time for European Unity', *The Times*, 2 July 1986, 10.

[4] An excellent site listing Eurosceptic parties and groups throughout Europe, is maintained by Simon Usherwood at www.susherwood.fsnet.co.uk/weblinks.htm.

Second, 'Eurosceptic' is eschewed as an inappropriate sobriquet by British persons and groups that are critical of the EU, but do not advocate withdrawal. The New Europe group, chaired by the former Foreign Secretary David Owen, is against British participation in EMU, but explicitly states they are not 'sceptics' because they aim for the UK to remain 'a dedicated member'. Under the heading 'We Are Good Europeans' the group declares: 'We wish to make clear at the outset that the United Kingdom should continue to be a fully committed member of the European Union, displaying an innovative and constructive attitude to policy issues as they arise. We are not sceptics about the EU' (www.new-europe.co.uk). Similarly, the 'Europe Yes, Euro No Campaign' says it is 'anxious not to be seen as sceptic' (www.no-euro.com). Instead of the word Eurosceptic, these and similar-minded activists prefer other compounds, such as 'Eurorealist' or 'Europragmatist', to mark their position, while claiming that those who call themselves Eurosceptic are in fact 'Europhobes'.

In conclusion, though Euroscepticism can and is used in a general sense, as a label for all views more-or-less critical of the EU, in Britain the term has always had radical connotations. Following Paul Taggart's and Aleks Szczerbiak's suggestion, British Euroscepticism must be classified as 'hard' (Taggart and Szcerbiak 2002, 7). A British Eurosceptic aims to withdraw the UK from the EU, or perhaps one should say 'promotes the idea that Britain withdraw'. Without this qualification one of the great role models of all Eurosceptics, Margaret Thatcher, would not quite qualify for the tag. Her arguments against the EU have been such that anyone can be forgiven for thinking that termination of membership is the only British option left. Strictly speaking, however, she has, to date, not advocated this course of action.

Where is British Euroscepticism?

As elsewhere in this volume, this article focuses on Euroscepticism in national politics, the press and public opinion. Wherever possible, it will, however, also provide a regional context. Always valuable, such specification is a prerequisite now that devolution in the UK is a fact. The European Commission has separate offices in Cardiff and Edinburgh, and Brussels is host to both Scottish and Welsh representatives. Hence, where data are available, the paragraphs below also examine manifestations of Euroscepticism in Scotland and Wales.[5]

Though the word Euroscepticism began to be used (and acquire its radical connotations) as of the 1980s, its creed has long been a real force in British politics. In the 1950s, this was highlighted by the refusal of the various British governments and parties to participate in the European cooperation schemes then being initiated by France and Germany. From the early 1960s to the 1980s, it is the rejectionist attitude of much of the Labour Party and leadership which stands out, ranging from Hugh Gaitskell's passionate dismissal of 'Europe' in his 1962 Labour Conference speech, to Harold Wilson's contortions over EEC membership in the early 1970s, to James Callaghan's outcry of 'non, merci beaucoup!' in 1971, and finally to the 1983 pledge in the Labour manifesto 'to extricate ourselves from the Treaty of Rome and other Community treaties.' Not long after this the Conservative Party began to express serious unease about EU membership, first under Margaret Thatcher and then under John Major. This culminated in the episodic revolts of an ever growing and ever more vocal group of Eurosceptic Conservative MPs. Finally, the 1990s were marked by the rise of Eurosceptic single issue parties (the Referendum Party and the UK Independence Party), dedicated to terminating UK membership of the European Union.

The political agenda in Scotland and Wales is to an important degree set by the nationalist parties, the Scottish National Party (SNP) and, in Wales, Plaid Cymru. Though relatively small, both parties are potential vote catchers, forcing the major parties to take account of the nationalist programmes. There are significant differences between the SNP's and Plaid Cymru's objectives and tactics, but as regards their stance on Europe a similar pattern has emerged (Cabrol 2002; Keating 1997; Mitchell 1998). In the 1940s and 1950s both parties appeared positive about European integration, though the issue was by no means central to their message. The 1960s and 1970s, by contrast, was a period of Euroscepticism for the Scottish and Welsh nationalists. Partly driven by a wish to protect Welsh farmers and Scottish fishermen, but also by a strong desire to distinguish themselves from the major UK parties, the SNP and Plaid Cymru campaigned against British EEC membership during the 1975

[5] Northern Ireland is also host to a European Commission Representation. However, due to the special situation there, this article does not investigate Euroscepticism in this part of the United Kingdom.

referendum, brandishing slogans such as 'NO, ON ANYONE ELSE'S TERMS!' and 'EUROPE YES, EEC NO!' (Mitchell 1998, 114). In time, however, both parties were to reverse their positions. First Plaid Cymru and then the SNP began to embrace the EU as a means of gaining independence. If small countries like Luxembourg could be independent EU members, then so could Scotland and Wales.

This non-Eurosceptic agenda has forced the main parties to play up their European credentials when campaigning in Scotland and Wales. Perversely, however, some figures (albeit dated) show that in Scotland withdrawal from the EU was supported most by SNP voters (24% in 1992). The Scottish Conservative and Labour voters, on the other hand, were considerably less Eurosceptic, also compared to their English counterparts. In 1992 12% of the Scottish Conservative electors favoured withdrawal from the EU (in England this was 22%). For the Labour Party these figures were, respectively, 17 and 27% (Mitchell 1998, 125). One reason for the relatively high instance of Euroscepticism amongst SNP voters might lie in the fact that the nationalist strongholds are in the Northeast of Scotland, where the EU remains unpopular because of its fishery policies (Keating 1997, 13).

Moving from politics to manifestations of Euroscepticism in the British press, what can readily be established is that a good many British newspapers have traditionally been outspoken in their criticism of the EEC. During the first negotiations for entry the *Express*, for instance, took a firm Eurosceptic stance by declaring that the UK should not get involved on any count. It greeted de Gaulle's veto with the headline 'GLORY GLORY HALLELUJAH!' (30 January 1963). However, broadly speaking, the British press were long supportive of the EEC. At the time of the 1975 referendum anti-Marketeers complained with some justification about the pro-Community bias of much of the news coverage (Wilkes 1998, 195). But from the mid-1980s the tone began to change. The British print media not only invented the word Euroscepticism, but helped give it the connotations of extreme censure. Spectacular tabloid campaigns attracted (and still attract) international attention, with the *Sun* setting a benchmark on 1 November 1990 when, under the heading 'UP YOURS DELORS', it invited its readers to kick the French (and by extension the Europeans) in 'the gauls'.

Concentrating on the 1990s Anderson and Weymouth claim that 'although the discourse of Euroscepticism was to be found in every title [they] examined, it was most consistently in evidence in the *Mail*, the *Sun*, the *Express*, *The Times* and the *Daily Telegraph*, as well as in their Sunday stablemates' (Anderson and Weymouth 1999, 63). This conclusion needs some qualification if we do not just label any criticism of the EU as Euroscepticism, but only apply the term to demands that the UK terminate its membership. Though all of the above titles at times allow individual Eurosceptics to plug their views, none have made total withdrawal a consistent point of editorial policy. In reality, however, this qualification is somewhat academic. Much of the reporting is such that to 'get out' offers itself as the only possible option.

In the light of the more positive appraisal of the EU outside English Britain, it is unlikely that the Scottish and Welsh national press have plumbed the same depth of Euroscepticism. No detailed studies, however, of the Euro-reporting of these segments of the media are available. The major Scottish newspapers, in any case, do not appear to see themselves as sceptics. Speaking in 2001, at a conference on Scotland and Europe organised by the Scottish Parliament, Murray Ritchie, political editor of the *Herald*, declared that his paper and the *Scotsman* have 'tried to be fair about Europe. We [are] not like some of the English Eurosceptic newspapers' (Murray 2001, 36). Elsewhere in this volume (p. 152), however, Peter Anderson suggests that things might be changing as he perceives that 'there is now a strong Eurosceptic presence within the Scottish press'.

Next to politics and the press, Euroscepticism can be located in British public opinion, understood as the view on a defined issue of a defined population as expressed by representative samples interviewed in various opinion polls. It should be noted that these choices preclude using newspaper readerships as indicative of public opinion. It is not reasonable to conclude (as some have done) that the British are Eurosceptic because many of them read Eurosceptic newspapers (the circulation of *The Sun* alone is around four million). Large it may be, but this group does not constitute a representative sample of the population as a whole, and in any case there are strong indications that readers do not necessarily agree with the views pushed by their papers (Mortimore et al. 2000, 10).

One of the first, and also the biggest poll testing the Euroscepticism of the British public was the '1975 Referendum on the United Kingdom's continued membership of the Common Market'. Only two years after having acceded to the European Communities the electorate was given the opportunity to take the UK out again. With 67% in favour of staying in and 33% voting to get out, that year a third of the British public appeared Eurosceptic. However, this seemed to change in the following years. In 1977, in answer to the MORI-poll question 'if there were a referendum now on whether Britain should stay in or get out of the EEC, how would you vote?', 53% expressed a wish to stay in, with 47% opting for withdrawal. In 1980 the latter category rose to an overwhelming 71%. In the following years, the potential Eurosceptic vote oscillated markedly, before settling down to a relatively steady figure of around 44% in most of the 1990s. In the entire period covered by the MORI poll (1977-1999) an average of 45.8% of the British public revealed itself Eurosceptic by claiming they would vote to withdraw their country from the EC or the EU (Worcester 1999, 7).

Other polls, asking slightly different questions, suggest a lower percentage of public Euroscepticism, but even so, the figures appear high, in absolute terms, but also relatively in the EU context, judging by what data is available on public opinion in the other member states (see the other chapters in this volume).[6] This trend is confirmed by the findings of the EU sponsored public opinion survey, *Eurobarometer*. Responses to its question on whether one considers membership a 'good thing' or 'a bad thing' consistently show that in the UK public regard for EU membership is significantly lower than the EU average (European Commission 2002, 37). Over the last years only Swedish public opinion has displayed a deeper dislike of the EU. Not thinking highly of EU membership is in itself not an explicit expression of Euroscepticism (which we defined as a tendency to reject British EU membership altogether), but these findings nevertheless suggest that to 'get out' is not anathema to a large section of the British public. This impression is underscored by the result of one other *Eurobarometer* trend question, which invariably shows that the UK public would feel 'least sorry' if the EU was scrapped (European Commission 2002, 36).

The conclusion that in the context of the UK itself, and the EU as a whole, Euroscepticism is clearly manifest in British public opinion needs one important qualification: all the signs are that this scepticism is of a passive kind. So far the intentions measured by the polls have not been translated into actions. As was shown above, in Britain there are many Eurosceptic organisations, movements and campaigns, but in the day and

---

[6] According to a report on 'British and European Social Attitudes', in response to the question 'Do you think Britain should continue to be a member of the European Union or should it withdraw?', an average of 30% opted for withdrawal between 1983 and 1997 (Evans 1998, 174).

age of the Internet 'many' is a relative concept. A good number of these Eurosceptic groups appear only to exist as web pages of single individuals. The established organisations, such as the CIB, refuse to disclose their membership numbers, a likely sign that the British public are not exactly queuing on their doorsteps.

Election results are another indicator that British public opinion is Eurosceptic mainly in theory. At the Uxbridge by-election of 1997, the Monster Raving Loony Party scored ten times the vote of Dr Alan Sked's UK Independence Party, and in spite of a lavish campaign, the Referendum Party only pulled 1.5% of the vote at the 2001 general elections. Obviously, in the minds of the British public 'getting out of Europe' is not an unattractive notion, but it has no priority. Polls indicate that when people are asked 'what are the important issues facing Britain today?' Europe is never even near the top of the list (Worcester 1999, 6). It might even be so that the British public is prepared to abandon its Eurosceptic stance if it thinks this might lead to gains in other fields. In the early 1990s, when the Margaret Thatcher was pushing through the extremely unpopular poll tax measures, the public appeared to punish her by not following her Eurosceptic lead. According to the MORI figures, in those years public support for 'staying in' temporarily shot up to a figure exceeding that of the 1975 referendum (Worcester 1999, 7).

In the light of this passive, even fickle public behaviour, it is not surprising that British Eurosceptics at times seem to despair of ever mobilising public support. Many, therefore, take the line that the British should be 'woken up'. A *leitmotif* in Eurosceptic discourse is that the people have been misled and duped into accepting EU membership by an elite determined to conceal the loss of national sovereignty this has entailed. Once this 'treason' has been sufficiently exposed, the public, so it is hoped, will finally take action. But, of course, to date they haven't. To make it happen anyway, an increasing number of sceptics have taken refuge in the controlled world of fiction. In the Eurosceptic novels *The Aachen Memorandum*, by Andrew Roberts (1995), and *Division*, by Graham Ison (1997), the British public do what they are supposed to do and finally demand instant withdrawal. Provoked by endless Brussels directives, the loss of their culture and by a deceitful incorporation of the UK into Economic and Monetary Union, the British people at last rise in violent protest against their oppressors. At the end of *The Aachen Memorandum* the public cries out in a 'profound fury' after having listened to an emotional address by King William IV: 'This great country was tricked, conned, cheated into joining a Union which has been disastrous for her economy, her world standing, her true interests and her God-given independence' (Roberts 1995, 275, 269).[7]

The level of Euroscepticism in Scottish and Welsh public opinion is difficult to establish as little data is available. The 1975 referendum suggested that at that time the people of both these countries were significantly more in favour of withdrawal than the English. In England 31.3% voted against continued membership, but in Wales this figure was 35.2%, and in Scotland 41.6% (Butler and Kitzinger 1996). As was shown above, in the 1990s the Scottish electorate was less Eurosceptic than their English companions, but *Eurobarometer* data suggests that in public opinion the Scots have remained relatively more Eurosceptic. In 2001, 26.7% of those polled north of the border thought membership of the European Union 'a bad thing' (in contrast to the UK average which evened out at 25.2%). In that year, the Welsh, on the other hand, scored below the UK average with 14.8% (European Commission 2001, 129).

It is perhaps tempting to assume that devolution, or 'the break up of Britain', has also led to subnational splits over Europe in public opinion, with the resentful English turning more and more Eurosceptic as the emancipated Scots and Welsh look to Brussels rather than London. Yet another dystopian novel, *England, England*, by Julian Barnes, describes how Scotland, as an independent member of the European Union, 'reconquers' parts of England with the blessing of the Europeans (Barnes 1998, 253). The few figures that are available, however, suggest that even the most moderate version of such a scenario is unlikely to unfold. There are no clear indications that the Scots are champing at the bit to trade the United Kingdom for a united Europe, nor that 'Euroscepticism has become an essentially English phenomenon' (Cabrol 2002, 1). At most one could speculate that in England Euroscepticism is less passive than elsewhere in the UK. In the 1997 elections the Referendum Party and the United Kingdom Independence Party attracted many more votes in England than in Scotland or Wales. In 2001 this pattern persisted with

---

[7] Britain's first Eurosceptic novel is *The Old Men at the Zoo* by Angus Wilson (1961). Published at the time of the UK's first application to join the EEC, the novel describes how 'Uni-European' troops invade Britain after the country has refused to join the Union. To date about a dozen Eurosceptic novels have appeared in Britain. A recent example is Edwina Currie's *The Ambassador* (1999).

the United Kingdom Independence Party drawing 1.7% in England, as compared to 0.9% in Wales and 0.1% in Scotland. That the English are somewhat more active in their Euroscepticism is further suggested by the fact that, judging by their addresses, the many Eurosceptic organisations that grace the Internet tend to be based in England (only the CIB boasts a Scottish Branch). Finally, some polls imply that in Scotland and Wales, Europe is seen as even less of a priority issue than in England. Compared to the English, fewer Scots and Welsh identify with Britain, but they do not feel more European (MORI 2002).

The why of British Euroscepticism

The following paragraphs do not seek to list in detail the reasons advanced by the Eurosceptics. Studies and collections of their arguments against EU membership are widely available. The *Eurosceptic Readers* mentioned earlier, and Anthony Forster's *Euroscepticism in Contemporary British Politics*, are but a few recent examples. The aim, rather, is to explore the possible reasons for the British Eurosceptic phenomenon as such. What reasons can (and have been) supplied to explain the British rejectionist impulse? As shown above, Euroscepticism has been present in Britain longer, and is stronger than in the other member states. Not surprisingly, therefore, the analyses tend to focus on British 'differentness'.

First, it is widely recognised that after the Second World War British governments perceived the international position of their country to be dissimilar to that of the Continental countries. For the latter, cooperation and even integration was a dire necessity, but the UK was different. It could pursue other options, notably, to continue its association with the Commonwealth, or to cultivate the 'special relationship' with the USA. Thus Britain could afford to be Eurosceptic because the European choice was but one of many. Or 'thought' it could afford to do so. It is now fashionable to argue that for too long the UK put too much faith in what it saw as alternatives, ignoring at its cost the developments on the Continent. How Britain 'missed the bus' in Europe is a central argument of many post-war histories.

'Differentness' is also central to the argument that links British Euroscepticism to the country's political structures. Britain's first-past-the-post electoral system creates a particular dynamic of party competition, marked by a strong 'winner takes all' logic. This situation, which does not prevail in the other member states, invites polarisation (Papamikail 1998; Wilks 1996; Forster 2001, 4). In 1962, in his famous Eurosceptic speech, Labour leader Hugh Gaitskell was chiefly concerned to carve a clear divide between his party and the Tory government of the day, which was in the process of piloting the UK into the EEC. 'It may be the view of the government that this is the only way Britain can put its house in order', he exclaimed, 'but it is not something we in the Labour Party can accept' (Holmes1996, 15). Later the roles reversed. While the Tories grew more sceptic, Labour revised its stance and laid itself open to Eurosceptic attack. As John Major declared to the House of Commons on 22 March 1994:

> We shall not do what the Labour Party do, which is to say yes to everything that comes out of Europe, with no critical examination whatever. The Opposition would sign away our votes, our competitiveness and our money. The right honourable and learned Member for Monklands East [the then Labour Leader John Smith] is the man who likes to say yes in Europe. Monsieur Oui, the poodle of Brussels.[8]

The British adversarial political system can be charged with generating Euroscepticism in other ways. Unlike their Continental counterparts, the one-party British governments are evidently not used to sharing power. This fact alone makes it natural for the UK to reject supranational partnerships (Papamikail 1998, 218). Simon Usherwood (2002) advances that in Britain radicalisation does not only occur between, but also in the main parties. Building on a model proposed by Mark Aspinwall (2000), Usherwood shows that, under proportional representation electoral systems, radical parties, which tend to be small, stand a good chance of entering parliament, but not of forming a government. If they do, this must be in coalition with a bigger middle of the road party, which means they must considerably tone down their objectives. In the British first-past-the-post system, on the other hand, political activists will be more inclined to join one of the main parties. These, however, do not normally allow radical opinion to determine policy. Large parties, after all, stay large by following public opinion, and the European option of total withdrawal, while not altogether rejected, is not top-of-list for the majority of the electorate. As a result, Eurosceptics are pushed to the party fringes where they feel justified in forging alliances with the various, zealous Eurosceptic pressure groups. These groups thus have access to main party politics through their MP associates, especially when the party concerned only

---

[8] All quotations from Parliamentary debates are taken from Hansard as published on the United Kingdom Parliament webpage: www.parliament.uk/hansard/hansard.cfm.

commands a small majority. In the mid-1990s, John Major, for instance, was in no position to ignore his party's Eurosceptics as he needed every vote he could get. Hence the 'bastards' (as he once called his most persistently Eurosceptic fellow MPs), and with them their comrades in the pressure groups, found themselves in a strong position of leverage.

The adversarial character of British politics is further reflected in the British press, which provides one reason for the fact, observed earlier in this article, that Euroscepticism flourishes in sections of the British print media. Many titles identify closely with one of the main parties and are therefore prone to amplify their statements and allegations. Commercial considerations, however, are far more important than political affiliations. Here, again, British Euroscepticism is linked to British 'differentness'. The situation of the British press, claims Jeremy Tunstall, 'differs from the rest of Western Europe' (Tunstall 1996, 7). In the UK, due to socio-economic circumstances and early technical innovations, intense rivalry between mass-produced dailies has been a long established phenomenon. At the end of the twentieth century, with the rise of the electronic media and the concentration of newspaper ownership in a few mega concerns, this rivalry quickly developed into 'super competition' (Tunstall 1996, 31; Wilkes and Wring 1998, 205; see also Peter Anderson's article in this issue of *European Studies* on the London-based Eurosceptic press). The British public, which comprises 'significant numbers of adults at the lowest level of literacy', is lured by means of special travel offers and money prizes, but above all by sensational stories, and 'world exclusives'(Anderson and Weymouth 1999, 173). The pressure to sell is only intensified because in Britain few papers are sold by subscription. Every day the reader has to be captured again. The tabloids in particular cannot afford to lose sales as they are primarily dependent on circulation, rather than advertising revenue (Tunstall 1996, 12). As stated above, none of the British newspapers have made withdrawal from Europe a principle of editorial policy, but ever hungry for sensational copy, Euroscepticism is nevertheless grist to their mill. After all, the proposal that Britain might be better off outside the EU can easily be reduced to stories about foreigners trying to lord it over 'us', or about absurd rulings imposed on the UK by alien institutions. Selling such stories is all the easier as in Britain knowledge of the EU is the lowest of all member states.[9] In the 1990s

---

[9] That is, 'self-perceived knowledge of the EU'. In the *Eurobarometer* surveys the British score lowest when asked how much they feel they know about the European Union.

shock reports about crazy directives which would ruin the British way of life reached such a pitch that the London office of the European Commission was spurred into publishing a booklet rectifying what they dubbed 'Euromyths' (European Commission in the United Kingdom 1994). It makes interesting reading. The story that rocked the tabloids in 1992 (that fishing boats would be forced to carry condoms), turns out to be based on a liberal interpretation of Council Directive 91/493 which aims at ensuring that 'strict hygiene conditions are met in fish processing plants.'

Next to international relations, political and press traditions, psychological reasons have been mustered to explain British Euroscepticism. Again, the British situation is regarded as different. Its leaders, for instance, are said to have undergone different formative experiences to their Continental counterparts. Whereas the Europeanism of Schuman, de Gasperi and Adenauer is traditionally linked to their growing up in disputed border territories (Milward 1992, 327), Margaret Thatcher's Euroscepticism is supposed to have originated in Grantham, the Lincolnshire town where, as a fourteen-year-old, she listened to Churchill's warnings on the wireless that Europe was turning Fascist and that Britain should rearm. (Edward Heath's enthusiasm for the EEC, by contrast, has been linked to his being born in Broadstairs, Kent, where 'on very clear days it was possible to see the coast of France.' Campbell 1993, 119).

Mostly, however, the psychological reasons behind Euroscepticism are located at the national level. Explaining Britain's wavering over membership, Hugo Young, for instance, regularly refers to the peculiar workings of the 'national psyche' or 'the British mind' (Young 1998, 67). A common way to account for early, postwar Euroscepticism is to diagnose this psyche as having been in a state of arrant aloofness. Having won the war and with some of their Empire still intact the British suffered from delusions of grandeur and regarded the Continental countries from 'de haut en bas' (e.g. Porter 1983). By way of illustration it is often recalled that Britain deigned to send a 'mere' undersecretary of the Board of Trade to the discussions following the 1955 Messina Conference where plans for a European Economic Community were first launched. Leaving these discussions prematurely, the civil servant is alleged to have declared: 'I have to tell you that the future Treaty which you are discussing has no chance of being agreed, if it were agreed, it would have no chance of being ratified, if it were ratified, it would have no chance of being applied. Monsieur le Président, messieurs, au revoir et bonne chance.'[10]

But the EEC was a success and Britain was left out. British Euroscepticism of later years has been linked not so much to aloofness, as to national feelings of resentment. How could it be that the countries which had only recently been liberated by Britain and its allies were now so prosperous? And was it right that Germany, the aggressor, was now rapidly gaining a position of leadership? It is, indeed, not difficult to illustrate that feelings of resentment, but also of downright Germanophobia, form an important aspect of British Eurosceptic discourse. The CIB suggests that Edward Heath appeased the Germans even more than Neville Chamberlain, and the Eurosceptic press regularity insinuates that the EU is but the Third Reich in disguise. Under the headline 'THE BATTLE FOR BRITAIN' the *Daily Mail* of 15 April 1997 exclaimed 'How long will it be before our mortgage rates are set in Frankfurt? A unified European VAT and income tax system is imposed on Britain? Our gold reserves shipped to Germany to ensure the dubious stability of the single currency?' In a book called *Europe's Full Circle* Rodney Atkinson (a brother of 'Mr Bean') unfolds the theory that the European Union is in fact a plot of former Nazis to restore Germany to its rightful place at the heart of Europe:

> What the Nazis said and planned before, during and after the war, is now to be seen in the present activities of the German state, in the words of its leaders, in the philosophy of its collaborators in Belgium and France and in the power of the European Union, which Nazis designed and which 'democratic' Germans have forced on the once free peoples of Western Europe (Atkinson 1997, 125).

And then, of course, there was the secret seminar at Chequers in 1990 where Margaret Thatcher is alleged to have claimed that the Germans were trying to achieve through economic imperialism what they could not attain through world wars. They could not do otherwise, it was in their 'unreliable character' (Urban 1996, 124). Shortly afterwards her thoughts were echoed in public by her Secretary of State for Industry, Nicolas Ridley, who in *The Spectator* of 14 July 1990 suggested that the European Community was just 'a German racket'. 'I'm not against giving up some

---

[10] There are many variants of this valediction, which makes Hugo Young decide the story is probably apocryphal (Young 1998, 93). French sources in particular are fond of quoting this example of British recalcitrance. This version was taken from Paul Everio and Pierre Servent 1993, 67.

sovereignty in principle, but not to this lot. You might as well give it to Adolf Hitler.' That the EU is the Reich reborn, finally, is a stock theme of British Eurosceptic novels. In Graham Ison's *Division,* the British traitor who devastates his country during a chaotic time of Euro-riots was trained in Germany. Similarly, in *The Aachen Memorandum,* Andrew Roberts portrays Britain in the year 2044 as an insignificant province of a European Union ruled no longer by Brussels but by Berlin; even the English language is on its way out as the British Europhile elite starts to imitate the tongue of its masters.

From the national psyche it is a small step to national identity. Frequently British Euroscepticism is regarded as a product not just of postwar delusions or resentment, but of deep-rooted national attitudes. Eurosceptics who seek to vindicate their cause, as well as academics who try to explain it, often do so with reference to a British identity which is (again) 'different'. Hugh Gaitskell's exclamation 'we are not Europeans' (in his previously cited 1962 Party Conference speech) was widely echoed during his own time and has been ever since. Responding to a poll organised by *Encounter* in 1962-1963, Sir Herbert Read pronounced the Common Market first and foremost a threat to national identity, while David Marquand wrote: 'Like Orwell, I rejoice in the differentness of England and detest the inverted Blimps who believe that continental ways must be smarter, more up to date, or more dynamic than English ways' (Marquand 1963, 70). It is not hard to trace similar statements in later Eurosceptic discourse, predominantly of the right. In a bid to explain why the UK does not belong in the EU, the former Conservative Party chairman Norman Tebbit declared in 1990: 'different as our Continental neighbours are from each other, we are even more different from each of them' (Tebbit 1990, 77).

Scholars, too, have linked British Euroscepticism with the question of national identity. Many mention a national 'identity crisis', brought about by a too sudden loss of empire. The demotion from world power to middle ranking European state left the British baffled and bewildered about who they really are. Their Euroscepticism, their rejection of active participation in the 'New Europe', is thus diagnosed as the product of a traumatised national sense of being. Dean Acheson, the US Secretary of State between 1949 and 1953, is usually quoted to illustrate the point. 'Great Britain', he famously claimed, 'has lost an empire and not yet found a role' (Young 1998, 171).

Britain's identity crisis is sometimes considered the consequence not of the demise of Empire, but of the break-up of the country itself, culminating in the various devolution Acts of the late 1990s which, especially amongst the English, created uncertainty about the essence of their nationality. Now that Britishness no longer equals Englishness, the English need to redefine their identity, and they are doing so in the time-honoured manner of contrasting their ownness against the otherness of a significant out-group: the Europeans. The Euroscepticism of the 'English Tribe', argues Stephen Haseler, is provoked by the perception that the EU has assisted in the 'breaking asunder of the unitary character of the United Kingdom' (Haseler 1996, 7). The argument is temptingly logical. However, as shown above, there is no factual evidence that in British public opinion Euroscepticism is more rife in England. Concerns about their place in post-devolution Britain the English might have, but as yet there are few indications that this 'identity crisis' has been a particular source of Euroscepticism.

It is not just the postwar crisis in British (or English) national identity that scholars have marked as a root cause of Euroscepticism. There is also a broad acceptance of the Eurosceptic thesis that the British identity *per se* is different. They are (or at least perceive themselves to be) so unlike 'the Europeans' that non-membership appears the only option. The fact that 'British politicians and voters of all partisan persuasions find it difficult to accept the dictates of the EEC', says Linda Colley, 'indicates how rooted the perception of Europe as the Other still is' (Colley 1992, 328). In his study of 'Britain and the Continent' Jeremy Black concludes that Britain's reluctance to embrace the Union is in part due to the determination of its politicians to 'defend the configuration and continuity of British practices (...) of their own society and identity' (Black 1994, 270). Anthony Forster argues in his *Euroscepticism in Contemporary British Politics* that the matter of identity – 'hating Europeans and championing British' – has persistently dogged postwar Anglo-European relations (Forster 2002,136). Finally, in *Patriots: National Identity in Britain 1940-2000*, Richard Weight also constructs a direct link between British Euroscepticism and national feelings of differentness.

These are sweeping claims, but having said that, some figures suggest that, at least in British public opinion, Euroscepticism and questions of national identity are, indeed, linked. Just as the British score high on the wish to withdraw, so too do they stand out for both their attachment to their own national identity and their dearth of 'European feelings'. This is confirmed by data presented in the fifteenth report on *British and European Social Attitudes*. Writing about 'national identity and national pride', McCrone and Surridge (1998, 4) highlight that the British score lowest in 'feelings of attachment to Europe', at only 22%. Even the Swedes score higher with 39%, while the Spanish top the list with 63%. These conclusions are confirmed by *Eurobarometer*. The proportion of people who identify solely with their own nation and not with Europe is by far the highest in the UK (71%), as compared to the runners up, the Finns, who score 59% (European Commission 2001, 14). The MORI report on 'Reluctant Europeans' agrees that the 'cultural identity of the British is antipathetic to Europe, with only a quarter of the British "feeling" European' (MORI 1999, 6). Finally, a European Commission report on *Perceptions de l'Union européenne* also finds that it is primarily the British who regard the Union as a threat to their national identity. A high percentage see 'Europe' as something exterior and, when asked, refuse point-blank to consider themselves as Europeans. 'Au delà de leurs résistances à l'Union européenne, les Britanniques manifestent plus généralement la faiblesse de leur sentiment européen, voire affirment avec force leur non-européanité' (European Commission 2001, 44).

These figures notwithstanding, some commentators are understandably hesitant to analyse British Euroscepticism in terms of national culture and identity. These issues, after all, are complex and difficult to measure. Simon Usherwood starts his analysis of Euroscepticism by noting that in the British case perhaps too many have fallen for 'the temptation (...) to concentrate on cultural and historical explanations of "Otherness"' (Usherwood 2002, 211). Others might disagree, seeing cultural issues and feelings of identity as the true forces, *les forces profondes*, in history and politics (Renouvin 1968, xiii). William Bloom goes as far as to claim that there is now an 'academic basis (...) to the popular notion that distinctive types of national character lead to distinctive types of foreign policy behaviour; that nations states have particular aggravated psychological tendencies which directly influence and motivate their foreign policy decisions' (Bloom 1990, 18).

The importance of national identity in politics and international relations can be overstated, as Bloom probably does, but should not be ignored in the case of British Euroscepticism. In Britain the tendency to see Europe as an undifferentiated 'abroad' is deeply ingrained. As of the sixteenth century in the English language the terms 'Europe' and 'European' began to be used also to denote an outside, even alien entity, reflecting a growing national trend to contrast the English (or British) with 'the Europeans' (Spiering 1997). There is nothing special about defining one's identity vis-à-vis an outgroup. To be French means not to be German, and so forth. What is special about the British case is that one of these out-groups is, and has been for a long time, the Europeans *en masse*. In other European countries such a differentiation makes no sense.

The identity contrast between 'the British' and 'the Europeans' lends British Euroscepticism two special qualities. First, it infuses the debate with an emotiveness only matched perhaps in some of the Scandinavian countries, where perceived differences between a 'Nordic' and more southern European identity have also led to impassioned arguments (see Milena Sunnus' article on Sweden elsewhere in this volume). There is little doubt that Hugh Gaitskell's words about the British not being Europeans were genuinely felt. Equally, Margaret Thatcher's face showed conviction when in the 1993 BBC series *The Downing Street Years*, she declared: 'There is a great strand of equity and fairness in the British people. This is our characteristic. There is no strand of equity and fairness in Europe. They are out to get as much as they can. This is one of those enormous differences.'

Second, and perhaps more importantly, because Anglo-European relations can so easily stir emotions about 'enormous differences', Euroscepticism is a resource to be exploited by politicians and the press alike. Many of the tabloids routinely carry reports about nation-threatening directives which are dreamt up not just by 'Brussels', but by 'the Europeans'. Politicians, too, have embraced Euroscepticism not so much as a matter of principle, but because of its rich seams of rhetoric. All member states at times seek to deflect criticism of their policies onto the EU, but in Britain this practice carries an extra premium. On 12 May 1996, at the height of the BSE crisis, all the media reported the tragic story of an English farmer who, unable to export his beef, took his own life. He allegedly left a note saying: 'My cows are all I have and now the Europeans won't let me sell them anywhere' (*Daily Telegraph* 14 May 1996). In Parliament many were happy to follow this reasoning: it is 'the Europeans' what done it. 'Does she [the Parliamentary Secretary to the Ministry of Agriculture, Fisheries and Food] agree that British minced beef is a prime product and that the Europeans are mugs to miss out?', was one of the more dispassionate questions cast at the government in the House of Commons on 18 July 1996.

Conclusion

This article has examined the what, when, where and why of British Euroscepticism. 'Hard' in nature, it first resisted UK participation in the EEC and then demanded withdrawal from the EU. These sentiments have been manifest (in various degrees and with regional differences) in politics, the media and public opinion. As to 'why', the reasons suggested centre on British differentness. The tradition of adversarial politics and intense media competition, the demise of Empire, as well as aspects of the national psyche and identity have fuelled British Euroscepticism. This inventory of possible causes raises two final points. First, how valid is this idea of British exceptionalism? It is impossible reach a definite conclusion. The articles in this volume show that national contexts matter. Different circumstances and different histories precipitate different kinds and levels of Euroscepticism. On the other hand, within these contexts many similarities may be discerned, as is borne out by the work of the European Parties, Elections and Referendums Network (EPERN) at the Sussex European Institute, and is further demonstrated in first chapter of this issue of *European Studies*. In the end, what matters is that the idea of British differentness is widely accepted. It forms part of received opinion, and as such it is real just as nations are real. 'Imagined communities' they may be, but people live and die by them.

The second point that can be made is that the suggested reasons for British Euroscepticism are not of the same order. They can, in fact, be divided into two categories. On the one hand, some of the reasons point to *forces profondes*: a tradition of literal *Euro*-scepticism, a long-established wariness not just of European integration, but of all things European. Other reasons consider Euroscepticism a product of national practices which in themselves have little to do with either 'Europe' or even the European Union: the rituals of an adversarial political system and the commercial needs of the written press. The first category of reasons, those that invoke the profound forces of sentiment and national identity, suggest that British Euroscepticism is built on deep cultural foundations. The second category is more concerned with how this scepticism is expressed and shaped by the much more fickle forces of party politics and media interests. For a proper understanding of British Euroscepticism both aspects have to be taken into account. It is important to realise that one is dealing with a political and media show brimming with caricature and distortions. The failure, so far, of the UK Independence Party and other explicitly Eurosceptic parties might well be an indication that the public is aware of this fact. However, nothing comes from nothing. Euroscepticism provides good copy for politicians and journalists alike because it resonates with long established British perceptions of Europe and the Europeans.

References

Anderson, Peter J., and Anthony Weymouth. 1999. *Insulting the Public: The British Press and the European Union.* New York: Addison Wesley Longman.

Aspinwall, Mark. 2000. Structuring Europe: Powersharing Institutions and British Preferences on European Integration. *Political Studies* 48, no. 3: 415-442.

Atkinson, Rodney. 1997. *Europe's Full Circle: Corporate Elites and the New Fascism.* Newcastle: Compuprint Publishing.

Barnes, Julian. 1998. *England, England.* London: Jonathan Cape.

Black, Jeremy. 1994. *Convergence or Divergence: Britain and the Continent.* London: Macmillan.

Bloom, William. 1990. *Personal Identity, National Identity, and International Relations.* Cambridge: Cambridge University Press.

Butler, David and Uwe Kitzinger. 1996. *The 1975 Referendum.* London: Macmillan.

Cabrol, Karine. The European Challenge of Devolution in Scotland. Paper presented at *Diversity, Difference and Democracy: Political Responses to the Challenge of Identity.* Jean Monnet Center for European Studies, University of Wales, 22-25 April 2001. solcidsp.upmf-grenoble.fr/publications/articles/cabrol_devolution_scotland.htm.

Campbell, John. 1993. *Edward Heath: A Biography.* London: Random House.

Colley, Linda. 1992. *Britons: Forging the Nation 1707-1837.* New Haven: Yale University Press.

Currie, Edwina. 1999. *The Ambassador.* London: Little, Brown.

European Commission. 2001. *Perceptions de l'Union européenne: Attitudes et attentes à son égard. Etude qualitative auprès du public des 15 Etats membres et de 9 pays candidats à l'adhésion Rapport Général.* Brussels: European Commission.

European Commission. 2001. *Eurobarometer: Public Opinion in the European Union: Report Number 56.2.* Brussels: European Commission.

European Commission 2002. *Eurobarometer: Public Opinion in the European Union: Report Number 56.* Brussels: European Commission.

European Commission in the United Kingdom. 1994. *Do You Believe All You Read in the Newspapers? The Euromyths.* London: The European Commission in the United Kingdom.

Evans, Geoffrey. 1998. How Britain Views the EU. In *British and European Social Attitudes. The 15th Report: How Britain Differs,* eds. Roger Jowell, J. Curtice, A. Park, L. Brook, K. Thomson and C. Bryson, 173-189. Aldershot and Brookfield (USA): Ashgate, 1998.

Everio, Paul and Pierra Servent. 1993. *L'Europe de Yalta à Maastricht 1945-1973*. Paris: Le Monde.

Forster, Anthony. 2002. *Euroscepticism in Contemporary British Politics: Opposition to Europe in the British Conservative and Labour Parties since 1945*. London: Routledge.

George, Stephen. 2000. Britain: Anatomy of a Eurosceptic State. *Journal of European Integration* 22, no. 1. 15-33.

Haseler, Stephen. 1996. *The English Tribe: Identity, Nation and Europe*. London: Macmillan.

Holmes, Martin. 1996. *The Eurosceptical Reader*. Houndmills and New York: Palgrave.

Holmes, Martin. 2002. *The Eurosceptical Reader 2*. Houndmills and New York: Palgrave.

Ison, Graham. 1997. *Division*. Sutton: Severn House Publishers.

Keating, Michael. 1997. Scotland and the Union. *Revue Française de Civilisation Britannique* 9, no. 2: 10-17.

Marquand, David. 1963. Going into Europe. *Encounter* 114 (March): 70.

McCrone, David, and Paula Surridge. 1998. National Identity and National Pride. In *British and European Social Attitudes. The 15th Report: How Britain Differs*, eds. Roger Jowell et al., 1-13. Aldershot and Brookfield (USA): Ashgate.

Mortimore, Roger, Simon Atkinson and Gideon Skinner. 2000. *What the Papers Say: Do Readers Believe What the Editors Want Them To?* London: MORI.

Milward, Alan. 1992. *The European Rescue of the Nation State*. London: Routledge.

Mitchell, James. 1998. Member State or Euro-Region. In *Britain for and Against Europe: British Politics and the Question of European Integration*, ed. David Baker and David Seawright, 108-129. Oxford: Clarendon Press.

MORI. 2002. *Britain One Nation?* mori.com/digest/2002/c020125.shtml.

Pappamikail, Peter Brown. 1998. Britain Viewed from Europe. In *Britain for and Against Europe: British Politics and the Question of European Integration*, ed. David Baker and David Seawright, 206-221. Oxford: Clarendon Press.

Porter, Bernard. 1983. *Britain, Europe and the World 1850-1986: Delusions of Grandeur*. London: George Allen and Unwin.

Read, Herbert. 1963. Going into Europe. *Encounter* 112 (January): 56.

Renouvin, Pierre. 1968. *Histoire des Relations Internationales*. Paris: Librairie Hachette.

Ritchie, Murray. 2001. *Scotland and Europe: A European Seminar*. Edinburgh: Scottish Parliament, 35-37.

Roberts, Andrew. 1995. *The Aachen Memorandum*. London: Weidenfeld and Nicolson.

Spiering, Menno. 1997. Why the British are not Europeans. *Europa* 1, no. 2. intellectbooks.com/europa/number5/spiering.htm

Taggart, Paul and Aleks Szczerbiak. 2002. *The Party Politics of Euroscepticism in EU Member and Candidate States*. Opposing Europe Research Network Working

Paper 6. Brighton: Sussex European Institute. sussex.ac.uk/Units/SEI/pdfs wp51.pdf.

Tiersky, Ronald. 2001. *Euro-Skepticism: A Reader.* Lanham, MD: Rowman and Littlefield.

Tunstall, Jermey. 1996. *Newspaper Power: The New National Press in Britain.* Oxford: Clarendon Press.

Urban, George R. 1996. *Diplomacy and Disillusion at the Court of Margaret Thatcher: An Insider's View.* London: I.B. Tauris.

Usherwood, Simon. 2002. Opposition to the European Union in the UK: The Dilemma of Public Opinion and Party Management. *Government and Opposition* 37, no. 2: 211-230.

Weight, Richard. 2002. *Patriots: National Identity in Britain 1940-2000.* London: Macmillan.

Wilkes, George, and Dominic Wring. 1998. The British Press and European Integration: 1948 to 1996. In *Britain for and Against Europe: British Politics and the Question of European Integration,* eds. David Baker and David Seawright, 183-205. Oxford: Clarendon Press.

Wilks, Stuart. 1998. Britain and Europe: An Awkward Partner or an Awkward State? *Politics* 16, no. 3: 159-167.

Wilson, Angus. 1961. *The Old Men at the Zoo.* London: Secker and Warburg.

Worcester, Robert. 1999. *The British: Reluctant Europeans: Britain and the Euro. Forecasting the Result.* London: MORI.

Young, Hugo. 1998. *This Blessed Plot: Britain and Europe from Churchill to Blair.* London: Macmillan.

EUROPEAN STUDIES 20 (2004): 151-170

A FLAG OF CONVENIENCE?
DISCOURSE AND MOTIVATIONS OF THE LONDON-BASED EUROSCEPTIC PRESS

Peter J. Anderson

Abstract

After an initial investigation of the motives underlying the Euroscepticism of three tabloid newspapers (the *Sun*, the *Mail* and the recently
schizophrenic *Express*), this article focuses in detail on the sceptic
broadsheets, the *Times* and the *Daily Telegraph*. It examines the discourses of nationalism present in these papers' reporting on the European Union, prior to suggesting that in most cases this nationalism
appears, to varying degrees, to be a facade masking the commercial
interests of the papers' proprietors. The article concludes by looking
at the implications for British democracy of the manner in which the
UK Eurosceptic press reports on the EU.

It is important to understand from the outset that Euroscepticism is not
the privileged reserve of the recognised EU-hostile press within the UK.
Elements of Eurosceptic discourse can be found in Europhile papers
such as the *Guardian* (Anderson and Weymouth 1999, 102) and on the
BBC (McLeod 2003). Rather than being the sole owners of such discourse, therefore, the recognised Eurosceptic press is simply the forum in
which it is found in its most vigorous and concentrated form.

On the other side of the proverbial coin, Europhile journalism can be
found even within the traditionally 'EU-unfriendly' Murdoch stable in the
form of Peter Riddell, a highly respected commentator within the *Times*.
Indeed, the new *Times* editor, Robert Thomson, while hardly an enthusi-
ast for unqualified and rapid British entry into EMU, is EU-friendly

enough to have been a serious candidate for the editorship of the *Financial Times*. From time to time, even Conrad Black's *Daily Telegraph* will allow prominent pro-Europeans to have their say within its pages. To be as precise as possible, therefore, the Eurosceptic press consists of those papers in which Euroscepticism is the dominant, but not necessarily the exclusive discourse on the EU.

Eurosceptic papers can be found locally and regionally as well as nationally within the UK. There is now a strong Eurosceptic presence within the Scottish press, for example. There is not the space within a journal article to look at all of the papers involved. Those papers with the largest circulation, therefore, would seem to be the most logical to select for examination on the simple basis that their size and reach gives them the greatest potential influence over the UK electorate. The London-based sceptic tabloids have been examined already in some detail in a recent paper by the author (Anderson 2003) and in a 1999 book jointly written with Anthony Weymouth (Anderson and Weymouth 1999). A summary of those findings will be presented here for comparative purposes. The main focus, however, will be on the London-based Eurosceptic broadsheet dailies, the *Times* and the *Daily Telegraph*.

The core concern in the analysis that follows will be with the nature and underlying motives of Euroscepticism within the UK sceptic press. In this regard it will ask what does the discourse of the Eurosceptic press suggest actually drives the Euroscepticism within it, and to what extent does the appearance match the reality? To be more specific with regard to the second question, what evidence is there to suggest that the Eurosceptic press is being driven primarily by nationalist or other considerations, given that it has been in the habit of portraying itself as speaking in the national interest when it addresses issues relating to the EU?

The findings from the above mentioned work on the tabloids will be presented first in summary form in answer to these questions (after the kinds of nationalism that are relevant to the discourse of the Eurosceptic press in the UK have been explained). These will be followed by case study analyses of the sceptic broadsheets. This exercise will provide an overall portrait of the essence of the London-based daily Eurosceptic press. In its conclusions, the article will consider briefly the implications of the manner in which the sceptic press reports the EU, most particularly in terms of its impact on the UK electorate and traditional notions of the 'Fourth Estate'.

Wrapped in the flag or hiding behind it?

As mentioned above, the UK Eurosceptic press is in the habit of using the language and sentiments of nationalism and patriotism in its EU-related discourse. In a previous paper (Anderson 2003), the author defined nationalism in a manner designed specifically to be relevant to an analysis of the sceptic press. It was described as a feeling of belonging to, and 'active' pride in, a particular group of people who describe themselves as a nation, whether or not the group concerned is in control of a state. (By 'active' pride is meant simply the preparedness either to promote the objectives of a nation as a result of one's pride in it, or to defend them, and indeed the nation itself, against the perceived attacks of others.) The paper then set out six different types of nationalism that can be identified within the Eurosceptic dimensions of British politics. Of those the following three were found to be relevant to the study of the UK Eurosceptic press as it is constituted presently:

Co-exclusive nationalism. This is a form of nationalism which will accept one or just a very few other forms of nationalism as equal or superior, but which regards all other nationalisms as inferior, subsidiary or servile (this does not mean that in many cases co-exclusive nationalists will not be keen to do business with other societies in order, for example, to keep the wheels of trade and profit moving). The strongly pro-American right of the dominant Eurosceptic wing of the British Conservative party could be argued to fit within this category.

Cooperative nationalism. This is a form of nationalism which, while proudly promoting its own values as far as they are attainable, holds that some of its key goals are best achieved in a level of cooperation with other nationalisms that is so close that it involves a degree of the sharing of sovereignty. Its relevance to this analysis will be seen when the *Express* is discussed below.

Qualified co-exclusive nationalism. This characterises the people who, while holding to the central tenets of co-exclusive nationalism and believing that British integration with the EU should make no or, at most, very little further progress, nevertheless are prepared to live with the limited sharing of sovereignty that the Thatcher government signed up to with the Single European Act. Their preparedness to make this sacrifice is driven by economic ideology and their belief that the EU's single market is a sensible way of boosting and maintaining the economic growth of Britain. Those who have accepted this situation, therefore, constitute an additional category. However, because their inclinations remain predominantly co-exclusionist, it is necessary to reflect this fact in the category title chosen. It would seem appropriate to refer to them as 'qualified co-exclusionists' (Anderson 2003).[1]

As mentioned above, the previous paper focused almost exclusively on the Eurosceptic tabloids and the reader is referred to it for detailed analysis of those papers and the full list of different types of nationalism that was set out there. The present analysis will focus primarily on the extent that nationalism, both apparently and genuinely, underlies the discourse of the two Eurosceptic quality broadsheets. Where nationalism is not found to be the prime mover, an attempt will be made to establish what is. However, before doing this, what can be noted here are the conclusions of the previous paper as to how the two virulently Eurosceptic tabloids, the *Sun* and the *Daily Mail*, and the third now schizophrenic, but previously staunchly sceptic tabloid, the *Daily Express*, can be categorised. These can then be compared with the results of the analysis of the Eurosceptic qualities that will follow shortly.

The tabloids

The application of a 'custom-built' simple critical analysis framework to case studies of the sceptic tabloids from the period 2000-2002, when combined with the findings of a previous much more comprehensive study of how the EU is covered across the British press (Anderson and Weymouth 1999), led to the conclusion that the *Sun*, on the surface, displays all of the characteristics of a paper that is driven by co-exclusive nationalism. Very clearly, the balance of its discourse shows a preference for the UK-USA relationship over Britain's membership of the EU. It is vigorously and virulently Eurosceptic, conjuring up an image of the EU as a corrupt and untrustworthy interventionist predator, driven by a Franco-German plot to damage British economic interests, British security and British sovereignty. The discourse style is highly dense and conversational and is characterised by such vivid headlines as, 'FRENCH BOOT US IN THE GAULS' and 'WILL THE LAST COUNTRY OUT OF THE EU PLEASE TURN OFF THE LIGHTS'. The USA, on the other hand, is presented as the trustworthy, traditional partner that is the best guarantor of Britain's security (Anderson 2003).

---

[1] Because this paper is in the process of being updated final page numbers are not yet available.

However, once the surface appearance was penetrated by more detailed analysis it was found that the *Sun* simply is not accurately classifi-
able as a paper that is driven primarily by nationalism. Among other
reasons for this, it was noted that all of the available most credible evidence demonstrates both that the *Sun*'s agenda on the EU is still driven
primarily by its proprietor, Rupert Murdoch and that he most certainly is
not driven by nationalism. While Murdoch recently – in the *Financial
Times* of 11 June 2002 – protested his concern for Britain's sovereignty
and the threat posed to it by the EU, it proved impossible to judge this
alleged motive to be anything other than a mask for much more fundamental commercial motives. The reasons underlying this judgement
included the fact that, while Murdoch was indeed part-educated within
the UK, he has not made the country his permanent abode and has not
chosen to take up British citizenship. Indeed, when commercial motives
dictated, he changed his nationality from Australian to American, not
British. This was hardly a move that suggested a man primarily driven by
a concern for Britain and British sovereignty.

Former key employees, such as one-time *Sunday Times* editor Andrew
Neil, also have provided testimony of Murdoch's preparedness at all
times to sacrifice his political fundamentalism when commercial motives
dictate (Neil 1996, 169). In line with this, it was noted how his stance on
the EU varied throughout his stable of newspapers in the British Isles,
from the London *Sun* to the *Times* to the Irish *Sun* (Anderson 2003).

While Murdoch undoubtedly dislikes the EU intensely, on the testimony of himself and others, and while Neil is accurate in his judgement
that the London *Sun* speaks with Murdoch's voice on the EU (Neil 1996,
174), his primary concern would seem to be a commercial one. There is
no evidence whatsoever to suggest that nationalism plays any role in his
motivations. Furthermore, the *Sun* speaks with his voice simply because
its readership profile allows him to decide that it should. The *Times*' profile means that his voice has to be moderated if it is to retain its circulation figures and remain financially viable, given its very different readership, and very clearly moderated it is. While, on 19 March 2002, the *Sun*
was effectively calling for Britain to consider leaving the EU (Anderson
2003), the *Times* was preparing for a new era under an editor whose apparent views on the EU would have made it difficult for him to have
taken the job should he have been required to promote the same line,
even if he does seem to be very much a 'wait and see' man as far as British membership of EMU is concerned. Should there be any lingering

doubts as to Murdoch's primary motivation and the irrelevance of nationalism as compared to commercial considerations, he himself provided the
evidence by which they can be removed by stating: 'I was more of an
Australian nationalist when I was younger. Today I would describe my-
self as being totally internationalist, free market' (Shawcross 1992, 550).
While these findings make it unnecessary to pursue any further the question of what it is that primarily drives the Euroscepticism of the *Times*
(the above quotation establishes beyond doubt that it is 'global capitalism'
and not nationalism), it will still be useful to identify the type of nationalism that its EU-related discourse uses as a surface device. This will enable
the concerns relating to the intended, actual impact of press Euroscepticism, which were outlined above, to be addressed more fully. For this
reason, the discourse of the *Times* will be subjected to detailed analysis
shortly.

Like the *Sun*, the *Daily Mail*'s discourse on the EU was found to be
characterised by a world full of Franco-German plots, threats to Britain's
sovereignty and security by an advancing European superstate, allegedly
untrustworthy European partners and a preference for the USA over the
EU. However, a key difference between the two papers was discovered.
The *Mail* was judged to be a paper that not only presented itself as a co-
exclusionist nationalist voice on the surface, but which also proved to be
exactly the same 'under the skin'. The success of Paul Dacre, its editor-in-
chief, in increasing and maintaining circulation, had given him the freedom under the previous and the present proprietor to write what he
wanted on the EU. What the readers got, therefore, was an undiluted
version of his own 'dry Tory' dislike of 'Brussels'. For example, in the
Daily Mail of 2 January 2002, a simple statement by Peter Hain, the UK's
Minister for Europe, that the pound might at some stage be replaced by
the euro, was described in *Sun*-like manner as 'apocalyptic'. Similarly, on
21 November 2000, an EU announcement concerning the establishment
of a Rapid Reaction Force for purely collective security purposes was
presented as if it was a device designed to both destroy NATO and undermine Britain's relationship with the USA. Like the *Sun*, in pursuing
this and other stories, the *Mail* freely engaged in omission and misrepre-
sentation in mediating the EU to its readers and left them poorly served,
no matter what their point of view on 'Brussels'.

The *Daily Express* was the proverbial joker in the pack. It was included
in the previously mentioned study (Anderson 2003) on the grounds that,
historically it was one of the most 'pungent' of the Eurosceptic papers in

the eyes of its critics. From 1998 onwards, under the editorship of Rosie Boycott, it attempted to reorientate itself in a more EU-friendly direction, partly in the hope of attracting a new and younger readership. However, due to the continuing importance of its more traditional readership within its overall profile, and the need to retain them for financial reasons, it found itself in the curious and rather confused position of oscillating between items that were strongly Eurosceptic and surprisingly (in the light of its traditions) EU-friendly. In this sense it was reduced to being a partial and slightly eccentric member of the Eurosceptic club. Boycott has long gone and there have been several editorial changes within the Express group since, the paper's circulation figures remain a problem and a new and somewhat unusual (even in UK-newspaper terms) proprietor has taken over, making it difficult to judge as to which side of the EU fence, if any, the *Daily Express* will choose to settle over the next two or three years. Because of this uncertainty, the comments that are made here refer only to its coverage of 'Europe' up until January 2002.

The split personality that it has ended up with has meant that while it has one foot in the qualified co-exclusive nationalist section of the Eurosceptic camp, it also displays many of the features of a cooperative nationalist approach within the Europhile half of its nature. In short, it is clearly not primarily driven by any coherent form of nationalism at the moment. The key driving force behind it would seem to be the simple economic need to secure a healthier balance sheet by continuing to try to acquire new readers without losing too many of the old ones.

Now that the conclusions regarding the tabloids have been summarised, it is possible to move on to look at the two Eurosceptic broadsheets. Before this is done, a brief note is necessary concerning the analytical approach that will be employed.

The framework

In a past book by the author and Anthony Weymouth, *Insulting the Public? The British Press and the European Union* (1999), a simple 'reader friendly' framework was employed to analyse the discourse of both the Eurosceptic and Europhile press. The framework, which derived from the work of Fairclough (1995), Fowler (1991) and others, was designed to achieve a workable compromise between what some preceding theorists had argued strongly should be ideal types of framework for analysing media discourse and the practical necessity of being able to produce useful research findings within strict word limits. The framework was well received and those aspects of it that were relevant specifically to the analysis of nationalism within press discourse were used within the previously mentioned Eurosceptic tabloid study (Anderson 2003). They will be used here as well. Primarily, they take the form of the two kinds of bias that are often simultaneously present within discourse. The tabloid-focused paper noted that:

> The first of these is overt political or commercial bias, that which sets out to be openly persuasive. The second type is covert by nature, and this might most easily be thought of as that which is implied or presumed to be part of the shared 'lifeworld' in the media discourse. For Fairclough, this type of bias is referred to as ideology and the implicit assumptions made within it are derived from previous discourses (Anderson 2003).

The purpose underlying their use, in conjunction with the three category types of nationalism outlined above, is to identify the types of nationalism that on the surface appear to underlie the discourse of the Eurosceptic broadsheets. Very simply the range of voices which are revealed by the analysis of bias within the sceptic broadsheets will be matched against the appropriate categories of nationalism.

The discussion which follows this exercise will look at bias from a different point of view, focusing on key parts of the evidence that might suggest motives for it, most particularly in relation to the proprietor of the *Daily Telegraph*. It will be concerned also with investigating the extent to which nationalism is genuinely (again, bearing in mind that nationalism can be a mask for other motives) behind the *Telegraph*'s Eurosceptic reporting on the EU and Britain's relationship with it. This task largely has already been undertaken in relation to the *Times* within the above discussion of Rupert Murdoch, and a summary of the relevant findings was presented at the beginning of this article. Only brief additional comments will therefore be made in this section. The purpose of still looking at the *Times*' discourse below, as stated previously, is to see how apparent nationalism is manipulated within its Eurosceptic reporting and commentary in order to serve Murdoch's economic ideology-driven dislike of the EU.

As in the case of the earlier tabloid case studies, the present study is facilitated greatly by the extensive survey and analysis of media texts, drawn from the two case study periods of 1997 and 1998, which were reported within *Insulting the Public*? First, as in the tabloid case studies, conclusions relating to the apparent presence of nationalism in the re-

porting on the EU of the Eurosceptic broadsheets will be extracted from
the detailed analysis of the relevant papers carried out within *Insulting the
Public?* Second, the extent to which these initial conclusions remain valid,
or need to be updated, will be shown via the analysis of a small but representative selection of texts taken from the period 2000-2002. These will
be taken almost exclusively from items within the Eurosceptic broadsheets which reacted directly to the announcement of the European
Rapid Reaction Force (RRF) in November 2000 (in addition, more recent
texts will be referred to where relevant). These will be analysed in the
manner outlined already. An examination of the genuineness of the nationalism on display (given that nationalism can simply be used as a mask
for other motives) will be left to the second section, using traditional
evidence-based academic 'detective work'. However, an attempt will be
made in this section to try and identify some of the apparent forms of
that nationalism using the categories identified earlier.

The Eurosceptic broadsheets' hostile reaction to the EU proposals
relating to the Rapid Reaction Force is chosen as the main focus of study
because it provides the most revelatory 'nationalist' coverage of any recent event. This is because defence and security issues lie at the heart of
national sovereignty and therefore automatically touch the rawest of all
nerves where nationalists are concerned. When those nerves are seriously
jarred, nationalist feelings tend to come out in their most detailed and
strongest forms.

The easiest way in which the findings from the first two of the above
tasks can be presented in a readily comparable format is simply to take
the two London-based Eurosceptic broadsheets one after the other,
summarising the relevant findings from the 1999 book and then comparing these immediately with the results from the period 2000-2002.

The Times

The *Times* is the one UK quality broadsheet in the Murdoch stable. Unlike its tabloid sister, the *Sun*, during the period in question it regularly
permitted a journalist who is a dissenter from its Eurosceptic 'gospel' to
express his opinions within its pages. Peter Riddell's views were available
to readers as an interesting counterpoint during 1997-98 when he chose
to write on EU related issues.

In the 1999 study the *Times'* discourse on the EU was found to be
substantial in a quantitative sense. As far as the representational function
was concerned, its informational dimension was found to be strong, and

to contain the principal underlying assumptions of Euroscepticism on both an overt and a covert level. The ideological dimension was well developed and can be summarised as follows:

> The single currency potentially is a source of political and social unrest; the single currency is a threat to sovereignty because it will lead to federalism; a common foreign and defence policy is a federalist ambition; the unified Germany still retains its historic dreams of expansionism; the EU is interventionist and should therefore be kept at arms length (Anderson and Weymouth 1999, 70).

While the overall discourse of the *Times* revealed that there were clearly things that it did not like about the economic and social policies and ambitions of the EU, what can be seen from the above is that there was a strong focus on British sovereignty in its European coverage and a clear suggestion that the EU was a major threat to this. The more recent examples of its discourse that follow below would seem not only to confirm that the original emphasis of its EU coverage has remained intact, but also to make it possible to pin down the type of nationalism that appears to underlie the discourse of the *Times*. The word 'appears' is particularly important in the case of this newspaper, of course, for the reasons that were explained in the earlier discussion of Murdoch and the *Sun*.

The *Times'* reaction to the RRF was of a mixed and detailed nature. As noted above, Peter Riddell's freedom to act as a counterpoint to the editorial view on the EU is an interesting feature of the newspaper, and it was on display again within its coverage of the RRF. The general tenor of his view is well reflected in the headline to his commentary piece of 23 November, 2000: 'Over-reaction Reveals Opponents Stuck in the Past'. But Riddell is something of a voice crying in the wilderness when the overall tone of the paper's response is considered. No less than two top-of-column leaders were devoted to the RRF announcement. The title of each piece conveys their general flavour. The first leader, in the *Times* of 21 November, bore the headline: 'PHANTOM ARMY: An Unwarranted Risk with European Security'. The second headline of Thursday, November 23, was: 'A CASE UNMADE: The Defence Tests that the EU's New Force Needs to Meet'. Both pieces are characterised by a failure to explain to readers the distinction between collective security and collective defence, an omission which casts an entirely different (and inaccurate) light on the proposals to the one that is shed if the actual agreements and declarations upon which the RRF is based are consulted.[2] The pieces concentrate instead on the alleged budgetary and functional impracticalities of the new force. The leader item of November 21 concludes by saying:

> Yesterday the EU spoke airily of relying on NATO defence planning mechanisms, almost as though NATO were a convenience store where it can 'buy in' US technical and logistical assets. Were the US to put this rhetoric to the test, the EU would fail miserably. Tony Blair has departed from Britain's constant position that nothing must undermine NATO. He has taken a leading role in creating this phantom army – not out of conviction, but for a mess of political potage.

The piece goes on to assert that as a result of the above, Blair has weakened Britain's credibility with the American government and may find that he has weakened NATO too. Underlying all of this is the implication that only the United States is a worthy full alliance partner and that the less reliable Europeans are not worth putting such a partnership at risk for. The failure to explain the distinction between collective defence and collective security, pointed to above, and the further failure to put this in the context of the NATO foundational treaty's section on collective defence, gives the reader the false impression that the core of the NATO treaty is under direct threat. Factually, this is simply incorrect. The leader of November 21 makes considerable efforts, via innuendo and the use of convenient but inappropriate quotation from the US NATO ambassador, to create the impression of such a threat.

The underlying agenda, of course, is the same as that identified in the paper's discourse during the 1997-1998 case studies, namely that the common foreign and defence policy, of which the RRF is a product, is driven by a federalist ambition and must therefore be resisted at all costs. The RRF is therefore seen, and indeed portrayed, not on the basis of what the underlying agreements and statements say it is, but on the basis of what the *Times* leader writer assumes that it will become. The familiar Eurosceptic agenda of Britons being deceived by mendacious Europeans is also present in the background here.

Elsewhere within the paper, however, far more strident views are expressed at considerable length. The following extract is taken from a

---

[2] See, for example, Council of the European Union. 1999. *Conclusions of the European Council meeting in Helsinki, held on 10 and 11 December 1999* (extracts only), 99/253, wwwarc1.iue.it/iue/efpball?nd=99%2t253.

long and vigorously nationalist piece by Michael Gove in the *Times* of November 21, 2000.

BEWARE THIS EURO ARMY'S LICENCE TO MEDDLE

Are you happy to have your children die for Javier Solana? Are you sanguine at the thought that the bodies of British servicemen will, in future, be laid to rest under an azure flag bearing a crown of golden stars with Senor Solana, high representative of the European common foreign and security policy, taking the salute? If you are, then you'll doubtless raise a cheer at the creation today of an EU army. The rest of us can only steel ourselves for tears. The decision by European leaders to create a new EU military structure (...) will (...) accelerate the drive towards a European super-state.

After a great many words in similar vein, the piece concludes by asserting that British servicemen are only prepared to make the ultimate sacrifice because they are, 'a national force'.

All that was merely covert within the leaders is fully overt here. In case any readers had missed the paper's dominant message, a cartoon is included within page 22 (the comment page) on November 23 which shows a somewhat neanthanderal soldier aiming a bazooka. The barrel, which is inscribed, 'Rapid Reaction Farce', stretches over his shoulder and curls round to align itself neatly with his backside.

Overall, the declaredly nationalist stance of Rupert Murdoch's *Times* is made clear here. It regards the EU as a federally minded meddler whose proposals for further integration should be treated with deep distrust and resisted. Its core aim is that British sovereignty should be preserved from further diminution within Europe and to persuade its readers that when security, the heart of sovereignty, is touched upon, then only the United States can be trusted. To this extent, the *Times* is therefore adopting a co-exclusive nationalist position. As it does not advocate withdrawal from the EU, however, (or at least did not during the original case study and subsequent sampling periods) then, in terms of the definitions outlined at the beginning, it should most accurately be classified as a qualified co-exclusionist. This conclusion would seem to be confirmed by Murdoch's appointment of Robert Thomson, a relatively EU-friendly (although not particularly euro-friendly) individual, to the editorship of the *Times* during 2002 and the previously-mentioned apparent freedom of Peter Riddell to say what he thinks on the EU within the paper. While, as was noted earlier, Murdoch was to insist in June 2002 that, come a referendum on the euro, Thomson and the *Times* must follow the *Sun* and 'say no', he could hardly expect his new editor to go several stages further and argue completely against what appears to be his core belief that Britain should at the very least remain within the EU.

Because this position is so clearly established here, and has not been contradicted by further random sampling (on 19 March, 2002, for example, the T2 supplement ran a piece by Margaret Thatcher titled, 'The euro will fail') it is not proposed to investigate further case studies at present. Time alone will tell how much Thomson is able or willing to persuade Murdoch to let him consolidate a more EU-friendly face for the *Times*. It was, at the time of writing, too early to make a judgement on this matter beyond the above-mentioned references to Murdoch's clearly stated opinion of June 2002.

The Daily Telegraph

The *Telegraph* was vigorously Eurosceptic in both the overt and covert bias that characterised the representational dimension during the 1997-1998 case study period. The ideological content of the *Telegraph* as identified during this period can be summarised as follows:

> The single currency is a threat to sovereignty and potentially a source of social unrest; the Social Chapter would be a burden for British manufacturing; on matters of foreign policy and security the EU is more disunited than united; Britain needs the EU less than the EU needs Britain; not only is Germany the driving force behind the single currency but this is linked to its continuing attachment to its dreams of expansion in Europe; Germany and France remain Britain's rivals in Europe; British pro-Europeans are to be associated with 'treason' and will abandon the veto, surrender the pound and sign away traditional British rights (Anderson and Weymouth 1999, 76).

The strong vein of nationalism that ran throughout the *Telegraph*'s discourse on the EU during the periods analysed can be seen clearly from the above. Britain's major EU partners simply were not to be trusted and the persistently interventionist policies of 'Brussels' were a serious threat to the traditional freedoms of the United Kingdom. It will be seen from the results of the more recent case studies below that the overall emphases of this perspective have been retained.

The *Telegraph*'s coverage across its issues of 21 and 23 November 2000 provides a voice for a cross-section of official views on the new RRF. Overall, the balance is tilted marginally, but noticeably, in favour of the Eurosceptic viewpoint across most of its various correspondents' reports. However, its underlying view is made fully explicit within its leaders on 21 November, 2000 and twelve months later, on 24 November, 2001.

The first of these is a generalised attack on the New Labour government, but which concludes on a twin-themed EU note which includes a swipe at the RRF:

LABOUR LOSES ITS WAY

(...) The Prime Minister thought he could help NATO by backing a European army: instead he is undermining it. First, he tried to dismiss fears about the Nice Treaty as 'froth': now, his Foreign Secretary is arguing for more majority voting. These matters are inextricably linked to Britain's future and freedom. There is a growing sense that the Government can't be trusted with either.

The core Eurosceptic tactic of describing the RRF as an 'European army' is designed, as in the case of the *Times*, to blur the crucial distinction between collective security and collective defence and therefore to create the false impression that the RRF proposal hits at the heart of the original NATO treaty. (To damage the core of the NATO Treaty, of course, is to damage Britain's key relationship with the United States.) This is a common tactic used across the Eurosceptic response to the RRF proposal at this time. A second core Eurosceptic agenda item lies behind the RRF's alleged threat to Britain's freedom, namely the assumption that the new force, like other proposals involving further European integration, is a thinly disguised device for the advancing of the goal of a European 'super-state'.

The RRF also gets a mention in a *Telegraph* editorial twelve months later (24 November 2001). The main theme of the piece is a speech on the euro made by Tony Blair on the previous day. The *Telegraph*'s feelings about the Prime Minister's alleged determination to move towards membership of the single currency are captured neatly in the title of the piece, 'Softening Us Up'. His stance on the RRF is almost ritually attacked half way through the item.

SOFTENING US UP

(...) he has sought compensation for exclusion from Europe's inner councils, at least on monetary matters, by launching with France the European Rapid Reaction Force. That half-baked construct has alienated America without noticeably strengthening the European pillar of NATO.

Where security matters are concerned, the prominent mention of France often is used as Eurosceptic code to indicate that a policy or proposal is anti-American or likely to antagonise America. It is mentioned here, presumably, to strengthen the force of the assertion that the RRF has alienated America, which traditionally has been advocated as Britain's primary and most trustworthy partner in security matters by the *Telegraph*.

Across the two leaders it can be seen that the *Telegraph*'s position would seem to be most suitably classified as co-exclusionist, given its continuing distrust of proposals involving Britain's security which appear to involve British reliance on its European partners instead of the United States, no matter how limited the range of military tasks that are involved. This impression is convincingly confirmed by a long article by columnist Daniel Johnson in the 21 November, 2000 issue. A relevant extract follows below.

WHY TONY BLAIR SHOULD BEWARE
OF HIS NEW BEST FRIEND

For the first time in modern history, a large military force is being formed without any clear strategic purpose. Nobody knows what threat the European army is intended to defend against. Its function appears to be one of political symbolism: the nascent European federation needs to give martial expression to its claim to full sovereignty over the nation states. Militarily, it will be more use on the parade ground than the battleground. Seen from Moscow, however, it looks like a godsend: a tool with which Russian diplomacy may engineer the demise of the Atlantic alliance.

In case the reader misses the central message, the paper has gone to the trouble of inserting into the centre of the article, in large print, the allegation that, 'Vladimir Putin – the butcher of Grozny – intends to use the new European army as a tool to engineer the demise of the Atlantic alliance'. The purpose of the article within the *Telegraph*'s overall discourse on the Rapid Reaction Force announcement is prominent and clear. Not only is the new 'army' a threat to the central plank of Britain's traditional defence policy, the relationship with the USA and NATO, as a result of the challenge that it is implied incorrectly to present to the heart of the Washington Treaty, but it also opens up a second front of attack by giving the Russians a golden opportunity to undermine the alliance.

Periodic sampling since has not revealed any significant changes in the nature of the *Telegraph*'s discourse on the EU. Indeed, amongst the items covered in the 24 November, 2001 issue, referred to previously, is another collection of 'old favourites', in addition to its coverage of the euro and the RRF. In a single report headlined as 'France and Germany Seek EU Constitution', for example, the *Telegraph* succeeds in merging the 'Franco-German plot', beloved of much Eurosceptic discourse, with the ultimate federalist threat, an EU constitution.

In short, the above evidence would seem to suggest clearly that the *Telegraph* fits within the co-exclusionist category of nationalism. British sovereignty is seen as something that must be preserved from further federalist advances towards an European 'superstate', and Britain's European allies are seen as very much second rank players as far as the core security dimension of sovereignty is concerned. The NATO alliance and the key UK-USA partnership are seen as the foundations upon which everything else must rest. However, as in the case of the *Times*, given that the *Telegraph* did not advocate complete withdrawal from the EU in any of the case study periods investigated, it would on the surface seem that it must most appropriately be classified as a qualified co-exclusionist paper.

The real motives behind the Eurosceptic discourse of the broadsheets

Most of what needs to be established about the motivations primarily underlying the Eurosceptic discourse of the *Times* has already been set out in the earlier discussion relating to the *Sun*. What can be seen clearly from the specific analysis of the *Times'* discourse on the EU, however, is that within it, and prior to the arrival of Thomson, Murdoch fostered a style of reporting and commentary that, while less strident than that of the *Sun*, nevertheless constructed a coherent nationalist framework to use as a vehicle for his ideologically and commercially-driven non-nationalist opposition to the European Union. The logical assumption must be that he hoped that the two papers' individual, 'market-tuned', pseudo-nationalist Eurosceptic discourse would both help persuade his readers of the need to resist moves towards the further European integration that he so obviously detests from a commercial/economic point of view, and at the very least make it more difficult for British governments to participate in such moves. As has been pointed out already, it remains to be seen to what extent he might allow this position to be moderated under Thomson. Certainly, his statement on the euro of 11 June 2002 would seem to suggest that, if there is any long-term change in the *Times'* position, it will not be radical.

While the precise nature of the motives underlying Rupert Murdoch's stance on the EU took a little unravelling, Conrad Black, the proprietor of the *Daily Telegraph*, provides a much clearer cut case. This is simply because he has laid down his personal views on the EU so publicly and so strongly. Perhaps the best guide to what Black thinks is provided by a lengthy lecture which he gave to the Thatcherite Centre for Policy Studies in 1998. The lecture title, 'Britain's Final Choice: Europe or America?'

does not leave much to the imagination. It is in the field of economics, perhaps, that he feels most strongly. At one point he claims that:

> (...) we could now probably assert a stronger and more positive influence from outside the European Union. We could export successfully into it, liberated from its costs and interferences and demonstrate the superior competitiveness and ultimately humanitarian value of the so-called Anglo-Saxon model (Black 1998, 3).

Should any of the audience have been left in any doubt still as to where precisely Black stands on the EU he dots the i's and crosses the t's in the next paragraph:

> There is no credible version of Eurointegration that does not involve a massive transfer of authority from Westminster, which has served this country reasonably satisfactorily for centuries, to the institutions of Brussels and Strasbourg, which are by Anglo-American standards rather undemocratic and unaccountable. Nor is there any definition of Eurointegration that does not run a large risk (...) of imposing European pre-Thatcher taxing and spending levels and industrial relations. And I fail to see how any aspect of a special relationship with the United States and Canada could survive monetary union and a common European defence and foreign policy (Black 1998, 3,4).

In short, Conrad Black's preference is that Britain should leave the EU and enter into what he believes would be a far more fruitful replacement relationship with North America. It is not unreasonable to assume that at least part of the *Telegraph*'s agenda in reporting and commenting on the EU is to convince its still large readership that this is the logical conclusion after all of the alleged ills of 'Brussels' have been taken into account. While it has been claimed that Black is playing a relatively back-room role with regard to his newspapers now that he has secured his peerage (Preston 2002), there are plenty of reasons for supposing that the *Telegraph* still reflects his overall preferences on the EU and other contentious subjects. Given that 'Europe' has been so much a core topic for him, it would be difficult to conclude otherwise. The fact that he has a reputation for correcting the *Telegraph* within the recent past when it has deviated too far from his line (McKie 2000), will remind its editorial team that, even if he is not a daily presence on the bridge, it still would be wise to keep within the broad parameters of his preferences.

However, like Murdoch, Black appears to be a man who moderates the views expressed in his papers in line with commercial reality. The fact that the *Telegraph* did not directly call for Britain to leave the EU during the case study and sampling periods would seem to be explicable most credibly in terms of a perception that such a position could lose it some of its readers. Most particularly, these would be the business people among its audience who, while probably not being in favour of further integration, nevertheless benefit economically from the EU single market and who have a vested interest in its continuance. By transferring the suggestion that Britain should consider leaving to a covert agenda, he could be argued to be having the best of both worlds, in so far as he is able to keep the paper in sync with his own preferences, albeit 'between the lines', while simultaneously not damaging its sales.

Now that he is both a UK citizen and a member of the House of Lords, as well as being someone who has argued vigorously that various aspects of the EU are against key British national interests, all of the formal criteria would seem to be in place for arguing that, in its coverage of the EU, the *Telegraph* is driven primarily by an agenda that is of a qualified co-exclusionist nationalist nature on a declaratory level, after moderation by the commercial interests of the proprietor, but most probably of an unqualified co-exclusionist nature on a covert level. This judgement is made specifically within the parameters set by the definition of nationalism outlined at the beginning of the article. However, given the strength of Black's dislike of the economic philosophy on which he feels the EU is based, and the extent to which he stresses this, there are grounds for suspecting that a significant part of his Euroscepticism is based on disapproval of an organisation that he regards as disadvantageous to his business interests, which, by strong implication in his lecture to the CPS, he clearly feels are best served within an Anglo-Saxon commercial framework rather than an EU one. However, it should be borne in mind that Black commonly refers to 'Anglo-Saxon' free trade economics in a way that appears to try and identify it with British national interests and the 'British way' and his business interests. He could therefore still try and argue that his interests were entirely driven by a nationalist agenda.

The conclusion here is that, at minimum, the *Telegraph* is driven primarily by a mixture of co-exclusive nationalism and the business interests of its proprietor. Whether personal business interests could be identified convincingly with British nationalism, thereby making a foolproof case for nationalism being the sole driving factor, is a matter of debate.

Conclusions

This study has shown that only two of the five London-based dailies in which a Eurosceptic discourse has been at its most vigorous in recent years – one broadsheet and one tabloid 'blacktop' – currently could be seen as being driven primarily by the nationalism that their stances at various times have suggested as their determining motive. Even then, and unsurprisingly, economic motives could be argued to be mixed in to one extent or another and in the case of the *Telegraph*, could legitimately be suspected to be at least as important as nationalism in driving its Euroscepticism. In the case of the remaining Eurosceptic papers, the tabloid *Sun* and *Express* together with the broadsheet *Times*, economic considerations alone are the primary driving force behind their discourse. The fact that many of the readers of the Eurosceptic press are being sold a nationalist line on the European Union by papers which are not most fundamentally driven by a belief in the nationalism that is being espoused is a cause for concern in the context of the UK democracy and the supposed role of the press within it. When this hypocrisy is considered in tandem with the extent to which the papers involved have chosen to omit or distort basic facts about the EU in their pursuit of an agenda that is at root driven primarily by proprietorial economic motives, it can only be concluded that an attempt is being made to doubly deceive their readers. Clearly, where the EU debate is concerned, this makes a mockery of any notion of a 'Fourth Estate' role in the cases of such papers.

As far as the overall Eurosceptic press is concerned, including the often grossly inaccurate *Mail*, it is all very well to say that in the multi-media age readers have a plurality of sources available to them to make up for any deliberate omissions and serious distortions in newspapers' coverage of the EU. The reality is that readership figures demonstrate that many voters still read the Eurosceptic press, despite the available alternatives (Greenslade 2002, 9), and that the size of its readership can enable it to be highly influential in helping to set the agenda for even the BBC amongst its broadcast rivals (McLeod 2003; Greenslade 2002, 9). For example, in October 2001 a senior EU Commission official informed the author that he rarely agrees to appear on BBC radio now because he assumes that more often than not the relevant programme item will be given a Eurosceptic bias and that his presence will be used merely to give it a bogus appearance of balance. The European Parliament's audio-visual officials told him during March 2000 of the near impossibility of persuading Independent Television News (ITN) to take an interest in positive aspects of parliamentary business. The *Daily Mail*'s owners have a 20% stake in ITN. There is no evidence to suggest that more than a small proportion of the overall electorate as yet regularly access the internet specifically for detailed news coverage of the EU.

While there is a debate within the literature as to what extent people actually believe what they read in the newspapers, what cannot be denied is that they can hardly weigh adequately the benefits against the costs of the EU if one side of the case is largely omitted from the information made available to them. The current modus operandi of much of the London-based Eurosceptic press is a serious problem for UK democracy for which no effective voluntary or compulsory regulatory solution seems seriously to be on the table as far as policy makers are concerned.

References

Anderson, Peter J. 2003. Patriots or Scoundrels? London's Eurosceptic Tabloid Dailies and the Nationalist Question. Paper available free of charge from the author.

Anderson, Peter J. and Anthony Weymouth. 1999. *Insulting the Public? The British Press and the European Union*. Harlow: Longman.

Black, Conrad. 1998. *Britain's Final Choice: Europe or America?* London: Centre for Policy Studies.

Fairclough, Norman. 1995. *Media Discourse*. London: Edward Arnold.

Fowler, Roger. 1991. *Language in the News: Discourse and Ideology in the Press*. London: Routledge.

Greenslade, Roy. 2002. Big is beautiful. *Media Guardian*, 14 January, 9.

McKie, David. 2000. Men of Feud Words. *The Guardian* November 16. www. guardian.co.uk, June 2002.

McLeod, Aileen. 2003. *An Analysis of the Impact of the United Kingdom's Print and Broadcast Media Upon the Legitimacy of the European Parliament in Britain*. PhD thesis. Preston: University of Central Lancashire.

Preston, Peter. 2002. Midsummer Madness. *The Observer*, 23 June. www.observer.co.uk.

Riddell, Peter. 2000. Over-reaction Reveals Opponents Stuck in the Past. *The Times*, November 23, 6.

Shawcross, William. 1992. *Murdoch*. London: Chatto and Windus.

Neil, Andrew. 1996. *Full Disclosure*. London: Macmillan.

EUROPEAN STUDIES 20 (2004): 171-191

IRISH EUROSCEPTICISM

Karin Gilland

Abstract

EU membership brought Ireland considerable economic gain, but also benefits of another kind. A radical view is that until 1973 Ireland's independence was vacuous due to the continued economic dependence on Britain. The year 2000 saw the start of a new relationship between Ireland and the EU: this was the year of the 'Boston-Berlin' debate, followed by the detrimental 'budget row' and Nice referendum in 2001. These events added nuance to the debate on Ireland's membership. However, opinion polls continued to show very high levels of public support for the EU throughout this time, and upon examination, the referendum results do not support the view that Euroscepticism has spread like wildfire, or even at all, among the Irish public. When confronted with decisive choices, political parties such as Fianna Fáil and the Progressive Democrats, whose prominent members had been making statements and taking positions that could be perceived as Eurosceptic, reassumed their conventional pro-European stance.

Ireland joined what was then the European Economic Communities in 1973. A decade later it was written, probably accurately, that in Ireland European integration was viewed much as 'democracy, peace, economic progress and happy family life – all were in favour in principle, only on matters of practice were there strong differences' (Hederman 1983, 183-184). In fact, until recently it may have been thought strange that a volume on Euroscepticism should even contain a chapter about Ireland. Opinion polls and referendums painted a picture of the Irish public as 'model Europeans', and consecutive Irish governments pursued essentially identical pro-European policies that had the support of major organisations in society such as trade unions, employers' organisations and groups representing the interests of farmers.

The truth was perhaps always more nuanced than that. Nevertheless, the broad, pro-European consensus appeared to come to an abrupt end in 2001, most spectacularly through the defeat of the Nice Treaty in a referendum but also in a number of other, less dramatic ways. Almost thirty years after joining the European Union Ireland's membership seemed to take a critical turn. Parties that had seemed wholly devoted to European integration suddenly made statements that challenged the EU in an unprecedented manner. Voters, who had voted Yes in four previous European-related referendums since 1972, did not ratify the Treaty of Nice in the 2001 referendum. Yet, there is a danger in overstating change: Ireland did not turn into a nation of Eurosceptics in one fell swoop at the beginning of the new millennium. The second referendum on the Treaty of Nice, in 2002, saw the parties reverting to their 'normal' positions – and voting behaviour, too, fell into line with voting behaviour in the referendums in the 1970s, 1980s and 1990s.

However, the early 2000s also signalled some potential long-term changes. The 2002 general election showed that some small, previously peripheral parties as well as the number of independent parliamentarians (TDs) are growing at the expense of the larger parties. Small, more or less left-wing parties and independents have been the voices of Irish Euroscepticism to date, and they are growing in significance and influence.

Ireland joins the Community

The Republic of Ireland gained independence from the United Kingdom in 1922, and spent the following decades defining its identity and character as an independent state. Éamon De Valera, the most dominant politician in post-independence Ireland, attempted to create an economically self-sufficient and externally neutral country. European integration clearly did not fit into this plan. Moreover, part of the reality of Irish independence was a continued dependence on the British economy. Britain had its own reasons not to participate in European integration, and Irish governments (ironically, given their obsession with independence) were loath to seek a relationship with Europe that was different from the UK's relationship with Europe. To boot, neutrality during 'the emergency' (as World War Two was known in Ireland) meant that Ireland did not suffer the destruction of many continental countries, and this further removed some of the rationale and need for integration (Maher 1986; Salmon 1989; Keogh 1990).

By 1961 Irish membership was nevertheless firmly on the political agenda, due primarily to the failure of Irish economic nationalism to sustain the population. Mass emigration had ensued, and from the mid-1950s Taoiseach (Prime Minister) Séan Lemass articulated the view that economic failure undermined political independence. An economic overhaul aimed to attract inward investment and to export Irish goods (primarily agricultural produce) followed, and it is in this context that the idea of Irish participation in European integration is most appropriately understood. Membership was sought (and promoted within the domestic setting) on the basis of rational calculations of how a small state with an overbearing neighbour might use its independence to its best advantage vis-à-vis stated national interests (in this case, to prevent the failing economy from undermining the political system).

The reason why it took over a decade before Ireland eventually joined was the continued dependence on the British economy. De Gaulle's famous veto on British membership in 1963 did not in principle prevent Ireland from continuing to advance its application, but the Irish government of the time did not choose to do so. Following De Gaulle's removal from European politics both the British and Irish applications were reactivated, and the two countries, together with Denmark, became members on 1 January 1973.

The good Europeans' 1973-2000

From 1973, successive Irish governments were spectacularly good at dovetailing Irish and Community interests. At home, the significant financial transfers Ireland received as a comparatively poor member state and region put integration in the same uncontroversial category of things as motherhood and apple pie. At the European level, the same transfers were cast in terms of promoting the single market as a level playing field; helping Ireland became equivalent to helping Europe.

The holding of referendums defined Ireland's participation in European integration from the very beginning, and an examination of the referendum campaigns as well as the results of the referendums reveals some interesting features of Irish attitudes toward Europe, both at the level of political parties and public opinion. Table 1 shows that a decisive majority supported accession. In subsequent referendums neither the 'Yes' vote nor turnout were ever as large again, the general (but not monotonic) trend being instead a decrease in the 'Yes' majority as well as in turnout. In this context, the outcome of the Nice Treaty referendum of June 2001 can be seen as a natural or logical part of a wider trend, albeit a trend that was reversed in 2002.

Table 1: European-related referendums in Ireland, 1972-2001

Referendum	Year	Yes %	No %	Turnout %	FF	FG	L	PD	DL	GP	WP	SF
Accession	1972	83	17	70.9	+	+	-	*	*	-	-	-
SEA	1987	70	30	44.1	+	+	±	+	*	-	-	-
Maastricht	1992	69	31	57.3	+	+	+	+	-	-	-	-
Amsterdam	1998	62	38	56.2	+	+	+	+	+	-	-	-
Nice	2001	46.1	53.9	34.5	+	+	+	+	+	-	-	-
Nice	2002	62.9	37.1	48.5	+	+	+	+	*	-	-	-

Sources: Sinnott 2001; Gilland 2002a, 2002b

FF = Fianna F; FG = Fine Gael; L = Labour; PD = Progressive Democrats; DL = Democratic Left; GP = Green Party; WP = Workers' Party; SF = Sinn Féin. + = Party favoured treaty; - = Party opposed treaty; ± = Party internally split; * = Party did not exist yet.

The *Eurobarometer* and other surveys concur with the argument advanced here that the Irish people have been broadly supportive of European integration since the early 1970s. In contrast to the referendum result trends, *Eurobarometer* strongly suggests that Irish public support for Europe has grown since 1973. The majority of the Irish public have consistently provided positive answers to all four of *Eurobarometer*'s most commonly repeated questions on support for integration.[1]

In contrast with the high levels of support for European integration measured in terms of the direction of attitudes, when it comes to the

---

[1] These trend questions are 'Taking everything into consideration, would you say that [your country] has on balance benefited or not from being a member of the European Union?'; 'Generally speaking, do you think that [your country's] membership of the European Union is a good thing, a bad thing, or neither good nor bad?'; 'If you were to be told tomorrow that the European Union had been scrapped, would you be very sorry, indifferent, or relieved?'; 'In general, are you for or against efforts being made to unify Western Europe? If for, are you very much for this, or only to some extent? If against, are you only to some extent against or very much against?'

salience of the EU a different picture of Irish public opinion emerges. That is, people do not care very much about Europe or know very much about it. An extensive study of Irish public opinion towards the European Union, carried out in 1995, concluded that there was a 'comprehension deficit' (Sinnott 1995, 28) in Irish public opinion vis-à-vis European issues. To probe salience further, we can look at a further question from the same *Eurobarometer*, asking people what they would be prepared to do to obtain more information.[2] It was found that 51.5 per cent would be prepared to telephone a 'specially reserved free-phone number', while 46.8 per cent would 'go to a public information office'. However, only 14.1 per cent would make a telephone call if they themselves had to pay for it, which suggests a rather low pain barrier in finding out about European issues.

At the level of political parties, the two main parties in Irish politics since the foundation of the state, Fianna Fáil and Fine Gael, have campaigned in favour of ratifying each European Treaty. Fianna Fáil was in government (either on its own or with a junior coalition partner) on the occasion of each European-related referendum, and from this fact alone one would expect Fianna Fáil to advocate ratification (for a government to oppose its own bill is surely unusual). What is more noteworthy is that Fine Gael, as the second largest party in Irish politics, has never tried to use the referendums as opportunities to score party political points off the Fianna Fáil (or Fianna Fáil-led) government of the day.

Between 1961 and 1989 the pro-European Fianna Fáil and Fine Gael routinely took a total of 70 per cent (sometimes exceeding 80 per cent) of seats in the lower house of parliament, the Dáil. Consequently, during this period the other Irish parties (some of which were rather critical of Ireland's membership) were much less influential forces when it came to European as well as other issues. The Labour Party deserves particular mention here: as suggested in Table 1, Labour opposed accession in 1972 and was too internally divided to take a position on the Single European

---

[2] 'In order to get such information [about the European Union], would you be prepared to: Call a specially reserved phone number and pay for it; Send a fax to a specially reserved number and pay for it; Call a specially reserved free-phone number; Send a fax to a specially reserved number free of charge; Write, send a letter to a person competent in this area; Go to an information office of the European Commission; Go to a public information office; Go to a journalist, who is informed about European affairs; Consult databases via a computer terminal located in your town/city/village; Consult databases via a PC, a computer at home'.

Act in 1987 (on both occasions it was the consequences of integration for Irish neutrality that was the main issue for Labour). This nuances the claim that until about the year 2000 the Irish political mainstream was solidly and unquestioningly pro-European. Yet, during this time Labour was never in government, Europe was not a salient issue in any of the elections in the 1970s or 1980s (or 1990s, for that matter), and election after election Irish European policy remained pro-European. Since 1989 coalition government has been the norm in Irish politics, but by then Labour had positioned itself close to the Fianna Fáil – Fine Gael position; Labour in coalition in the 1990s did not, therefore, add a different flavour to policy on Europe.

The norm of coalitions also raised the potential for small parties to enter government. Since small parties, particularly left-wing ones, have been the harbingers of Irish Euroscepticism, they might have been able to bring their views to bear on government policy in a coalition arrangement. However, to date this potential has remained theoretical, because the smaller parties that have been in government coalition with either Fianna Fáil or Fine Gael or both (e.g., Labour, Democratic Left, the Progressive Democrats) have espoused a pro-European line. This may have been either out of a genuine belief that a given Treaty was 'good' or in order not to expose splits within the government coalition. Either way, the point to note is that until 2001 European integration was not a divisive issue in Irish politics. Moreover, neither Fianna Fáil nor Fine Gael has ever been in coalition with the Green Party, Sinn Féin, or the Socialist Party.

The European project has not been politicised in Ireland, if politicisation is understood as a process whereby an issue becomes controversial, salient and perhaps politically sensitive. Consecutive Irish governments have had a stated *communautaire* commitment to Europe since 1973, viewing integration as a win-win situation in which even (limited and carefully selected) national concessions could be viewed as long-term gains inasmuch as they advanced collective interests which happened to correspond with narrower Irish interests. The incremental development of the Union's structural instruments to create a level playing field in the single market allowed Irish governments to wrap the national interest in arguments about European solidarity and redistribution. Irish governments thereby managed to make Ireland appear as 'a good European' through its commitment to major European projects, while at the same time acquiring very considerable benefits from Europe. Simultaneously, however, consecutive Irish governments' actual hesitation to take *communautaire* positions on key developments such as the Common Foreign and Security Policy and the Schengen Agreement (the removal of internal borders) qualifies Ireland's *communautaire* track record. The term 'conditionally integrationist', implying 'support for progressively closer integration, including political integration, provided the economic benefits will be fairly shared' (Scott 1994, 8) captures this approach, which successive governments pursued seamlessly.

While the mainstream parties were successfully managing to get Treaty changes ratified by referendum for the first twenty-five or so years of Irish membership, the much smaller, Eurosceptic parties and other non-party groups learnt to punch above their weight by changing the rules of the referendum game. The two main points of note with respect to the new regime pertain to government spending in referendum campaigns, and the allocation of airtime to political parties in referendum campaigns. With respect to the spending of public monies, Green Party MEP Patricia McKenna was the engine behind a court challenge, the outcome of which was that governments were no longer allowed to spend public monies to advocate their position on the issue at stake. The argument here was basically that if an issue was important enough to merit a referendum, then it was not right for a government to use public monies to tip the balance in favour of a particular outcome. The court challenge resulted in the Referendum Act (1998). Governments, and other parties and interested groups, were not precluded from using their own funds under the Act, which also established an ad hoc Referendum Commission whose remit was to:

> explain the subject matter of the referendum to the public at large, as simply and effectively as possible, while ensuring that the arguments of those against the proposed amendment to the Constitution and those in favour are put forward in a manner that is fair to all interests involved. (Referendum Commission 1998, 4).

The second point of note was that another court decision forced the public broadcaster Radio Telefís Éireann (RTÉ) to reformulate its criterion for allocating airtime between parties, groups or individuals representing different positions in a referendum campaign. Previously airtime had been allocated on the basis of the allocation of seats in the Dáil: if parties campaigning for a Yes held 90 per cent of the seats, then the Yes campaign was allocated 90 per cent of the airtime, and so on. This meant that pro-European messages were aired much more than anti-European ones, and also excluded a number of non-party groups in Irish society. The Amsterdam and Nice Treaty referendums took place under the new referendum regime.

The end of consensus? 'Boston versus Berlin' and the 'budget row'
The year 2000 saw the beginning of a sequence of events that signalled a change of climate in Ireland's relationship with the EU: the so-called 'Boston versus Berlin' debate, the 'budget row' between the Irish Minister for Finance and the European Commission, the failure to ratify the Nice Treaty in a referendum in 2001, and the general election of 2002 which made the twenty-ninth Dáil more likely than any previous Dáil to have a Eurosceptic voice. These events occurred on the back of the triumphant Irish economy of the 1990s, which was the result of a combination of domestic policy and EU membership. By the millennium, almost unimaginable economic growth brought Ireland to the point of disqualification from structural and regional transfers, which had become part of Ireland's expectations of the EU. Already in 1997 Ireland's GDP per capita was 102 per cent of the Community average; regionally within Ireland the border, midlands and western (BMW) region had 75 per cent per capita of Community GDP and the southern and eastern region 112 per cent per capita (Eurostat 2000). In other words, Ireland had surpassed the criteria for receiving funding, and stood poised to become a net contributor to the Community budget in the financial perspective beginning in 2007.

The 'Boston versus Berlin' debate was kicked off by Mary Harney, the Tanaiste (Deputy Prime Minister) and Minister for Enterprise, Trade and Employment, as well as the leader of the Progressive Democrats. The central message of her mildly critical speech was that, apart from the benefits Ireland has derived from its European partners and Ireland's geographical connection with Europe, spiritually Ireland is much closer to the United States. In particular, she admired the United States' economic model, based in the 'rugged individualism of the original frontiersmen, an economic model that is heavily based on enterprise and incentive on individual effort and with limited government intervention' (Harney 2000, 1). The European model, meanwhile, she characterised as based on strong concern for social harmony and inclusion to be achieved through high levels of taxation and regulation. The Tanaiste did not deny that

Ireland's membership of the European Union was a crucial part in Ireland's economic success, but highlighted the importance of being able to take key economic decisions nationally. On this basis she argued (unusually in the Irish context) that a more centralised or a federal Europe would not be in Ireland's interests:

> The fact is that Europe is not America and never will be. The people of Europe are not united by common language, common history and common tradition the way that Americans are. During the next five years, for instance, the process of enlargement is likely to add a further half-a-dozen working languages to the European Union (...) I believe in a Europe of independent states, not a United States of Europe (Harney 2000, 2).

The Minister for Arts, Heritage, the Gaeltacht and the Islands, Fianna Fáil's Síle De Valera, followed suit in a speech delivered at Boston College (Massachusetts). In fact, the speech was not particularly anti-European, but it is a measure of how ingrained the acceptance of pro-European statements had become in Ireland that a speech stating that the European Union 'is not the cornerstone of what our nation is and should be' (De Valera 2000, 1) nevertheless was treated as anti-European ranting.

Politicians from other parties responded publicly to the two speeches in the Irish print media. Fine Gael's Gay Mitchell TD, a former junior Minister for European Affairs, wrote in the *Irish Times* (23 September 2000) that through Europe Irish men and women 'have choices that are unprecedented in Irish history'. In contrast, in the 'good old days' Ireland had no say in decisions made by for instance the UK and Germany, but suffered the consequences all the same – in fact suffered them more, because a place at the European table means Ireland has influenced their decisions since 1973. Moreover, he pointed out that in his view integration is quite distinct from assimilation, which requires peoples to become uniform and indistinguishable; integration was about 'different traditions, religions, and cultures living side by side by agreement and with mutual respect (...) based on the reality that in our increasingly complex world we can tackle certain issues only by working more closely together'. The same issue of the *Irish Times* carried an article by the President of the Labour Party and Member of European Parliament, Proinsias De Rossa. He agreed with Minister De Valera that more vigilance in Ireland regarding developments in Europe would be positive, but ruled out any distancing from Europe on Ireland's part:

As Europe evolves and as Ireland's role within it changes, we need to be much more thoughtful and proactive about how best our interests are articulated and advanced. For Sile De Valera (and Mary Harney) to string together a set of simplistic clichés about a 'United States of Europe' and EU regulations impinging on Ireland's identity shows the extent to which this government is detached from European thinking and cannot be relied upon to represent Ireland's interests in Europe (*Irish Times*, 23 September 2000).

In these exchanges the EU began to be a more politicised issue in Irish politics. A matter of months later, the European Commission criticised and ultimately reprimanded the Fianna Fáil-Progressive Democrat government's December 2000 budget. Commissioner Pedro Solbes advised the Irish Minister for Finance, Charles McCreevy, to rewrite his budget to take money out of the Irish economy. The Irish response was curt: the Commission should mind the limits of its competencies, and rather than reprimanding Ireland, the Commission might instruct other member states to follow the Irish example for outstanding economic performance.[3] The *Irish Times* (26 January 2001) reported an opinion poll taken after the Commission storm had started to blow, to the effect that 71 per cent of the Irish people thought the budget was 'good for the country'. The Irish government did not concede that 'the ECB and the Commission had both a right and a responsibility to comment' (Fitzgerald 2002, 17) on the contents of the Irish budget, despite the fact that in each of the three years prior to the budget row the Irish government had signed up to broad economic guidelines which they subsequently ignored in the national budgets. The real significance of the budget row was that it highlighted Irish double standards towards the European Union. On the one hand, Irish governments have rarely missed an opportunity to remind their fellow EU members of their duty and responsibility vis-à-vis regional development, but on the other hand within Ireland the notion that Ireland has any duty vis-à-vis Europe appears anathema.

Nice I

Arguably, even if the Commission was within its rights to make an example of Ireland, doing so did not show much political savvy given that an

---

[3] The headlines in the press at the time give the flavour of the national reaction: 'McCreevy Says EU Critics are Jealous' (*Irish Times*, 26 January 2001); 'Mild-Mannered Pedro is Not for Turning' (*Irish Independent*, 27 January 2001); 'EU Censure Beggars Belief' (*Sunday Business Post*, 28 January 2001); 'Last Thing We Want is a Slagging Match with EU' (*Irish Independent*, 2 February 2001).

Irish referendum on the Nice Treaty was to follow a few months later; creating an 'us versus them' mentality among the Irish public was almost certainly not helpful especially at a time when it was well-known that Ireland was about to become a net contributor to the Community budget.

The Treaty of Nice (2000) began to resolve some of the issues facing the European Union with respect to enlargement. At this juncture perhaps the biggest challenge facing Ireland was to balance the need for institutional reform and the undeniable attractions of flexibility (enhanced co-operation) with the risk that a large state *directoire* would become established as a consequence of institutional reform and flexibility provisions.

The Nice Treaty referendum took place on 7 June 2001. Among political parties a familiar configuration launched 'Yes to Nice' campaigns: the two government parties Fianna Fáil and the Progressive Democrats came out in favour of it, along with Fine Gael and Labour[4] and the main social and economic interests. Their case in favour of the Treaty was a two-stranded argument about EU enlargement. The first strand presented Nice as the sine qua non of the historic opportunity not to say moral imperative finally to unite Europe. The rationale advanced here was simply that by having a place at the decision-making table of 15, 20, 27 or more countries Ireland can shape its own future much more effectively than would otherwise be the case. Part of this argument was also that many of the applicant countries seek to emulate Ireland's European experience, and that the Irish people should not stand in the way of that aspiration by voting no. The second strand of the argument was that although Ireland will become a net contributor to the Community budget, many benefits would accrue to Ireland from having access to an enlarged market.

An equally familiar constellation of parties and veteran anti-European integration campaigners were united in opposition to the Treaty. They had two prominent slogans: 'No to Nato, No to Nice' and 'You Will

---

[4] Incidentally, in the week after the Treaty was negotiated in December 2000 spokespeople for both Fine Gael and Labour were highly critical of the Treaty in the Dáil (the lower chamber of the Irish parliament). Then Fine Gael leader John Bruton said that 'This is one of the weakest negotiating outcomes achieved by an Irish government in the European Union (...) That is a very bad day for Europe' and Fine Gael foreign affairs spokesperson Jim O'Keeffe said that the Treaty was 'achieved at very considerable cost to this country.' In the same debate, Labour leader Ruairi Quinn called Nice a 'disaster (...) It is an appalling setback.' (Reported in *Sunday Business Post*, 27 May 2001).

Lose. Money, Power, Influence'. Anti-Nice parties and groups included the Green Party, Sinn Féin, the Socialist Party, the National Platform, the group 'No to Nice' and the pro-neutrality umbrella organisation the Peace and Neutrality Alliance. Anti-Nice campaigners did not see themselves as insular or necessarily anti-European or indeed opposed to enlargement, simply critical of the EU model of European integration as advanced in this Treaty. In this vein, the Green Party's position paper on the Treaty spelt out that the party said 'Yes to Europe – No to Nice'.

The No campaign's arguments pertained to touchstones in Irish politics and Irish political culture, as well as to a particular perception of Ireland's national interest. Fears for the future of Ireland's tradition of military neutrality, and fears that the Treaty would open the door to liberal abortion laws were long-standing concerns in the context of EU membership (Gilland 2001). These fears were not abated by the fact that Common Foreign and Security Policy provisions were peripheral in this Treaty, and that the Charter of Fundamental Rights and Freedoms, which was the focus for anti-abortionists' criticisms, was not legally binding on the signatories and in any case had nothing to do with the ratification of the Nice Treaty (the Charter simply happened to be signed at the same Council meeting as the one at which the Treaty was negotiated). With respect to the suggested loss of power and influence, anti-Treaty parties and groups felt that the Treaty would facilitate a *directoire* of large member states that would diminish Ireland's influence.

The 'No' result in the referendum (Table 1) should not be automatically read as a sign of Euroscepticism taking hold in Ireland, especially since the number of 'No' votes to Nice (529,478) was lower than the number of 'No' votes to the Amsterdam Treaty in 1998 (578,070; *Irish Times*, 25 May 1998). Survey evidence collected after the referendum corroborates this point. As the dust began to settle on the referendum result, it became increasingly clear that Nice was partly lost to Euroscepticism and partly lost to a general sense of indifference that for one thing meant that 65.5 per cent of the electorate did not vote. Indifference not only manifested itself in a low turnout, but also in the high proportion of 'No' voters (39 per cent) who cited 'lack of information' as their reason to vote 'No'. Other reasons to vote 'No' included 'loss of sovereignty/independence' (16 per cent), 'neutrality, military issues' (12 per cent), 'bad idea in general' (7 per cent), and 'influence of political party' (6 per cent). Reasons to vote 'Yes' included 'generally a good idea, development of existing commitments' (44 per cent), 'enlargement a good thing' (22 per cent), 'influence of government, political party, politician, TV debate' (14 per cent). Non-voters cited 'lack of understanding/lack of information' (44 per cent), 'not interested/not bothered' (22 per cent), and 'on holiday/away from home' (15 per cent) as their reasons for not voting (Gilland 2002a).

In the wake of the referendum the Irish government's coherence started to fall apart. One minister revealed that he had voted against the Treaty, and Finance Minister Charlie McCreevy (he of the budget row) called the referendum result a 'remarkably healthy development' (*Sunday Business Post*, 17 June 2001). The Taoiseach swiftly announced a National Forum on Europe, whose composition and terms of reference were modelled on a previous forum experience, the Forum for Peace and Reconciliation.[5] The terms of reference were 'to facilitate a broad discussion of issues relevant to Ireland's membership of an enlarging Union, and to consider the range of topics arising in the context of the debate on the future of Europe [e.g., the proposed 2004 intergovernmental conference]' (Ireland 2001). Fine Gael decided not to participate in the Forum on Europe (but joined it later, under a new party leader) since it believed the appropriate place for such debate was the Oireachtas, which continued the politicisation of Europe.

General election 2002

By this time the political parties were beginning to gear up for a general election that was certain to take place within a matter of months. In the course of events, 'Europe' turned out to be the dog that did not bark in this election. On the one hand this might be somewhat surprising, given that one of the most pressing issues that any incoming government would have to deal with was what, if anything, to do about securing Irish ratification of the Nice Treaty.

---

[5] The National Forum on Europe was to consist of members of the two houses of the Oireachtas, MEPs from the Republic and Northern Ireland, and a special observer pillar including the social partners, registered Northern Irish political parties and parties in the Republic not currently represented in the Oireachtas, and other groups that had campaigned both for and against the Treaty.

Table 2: First preference votes and seats, 1997 and 2002[6]

Party	First Preference Votes 1997 (%)	Seats 1997	First Preference Votes 2002 (%)	Seats 2002
Fianna Fáil	39.3	77	41.5	81
Fine Gael	27.9	54	22.5	31
Labour	12.9	21	10.8	21
Prog. Dem.	4.7	4	4.0	8
Green Party	2.8	2	3.9	6
Sinn Féin	2.5	1	6.5	5
Other, Ind.	9.4	7	11.0	14
Total	100	166	100	166

Sources: Marsh et.al. 1999; www.ireland.com

Reversing the Nice result would depend greatly on an increased turnout in a second referendum, and one way of ensuring this would have been to let 'Nice II' coincide with the general election. However, the government promised that if returned to office they would hold 'Nice II' in October 2002, probably out of fear that 'No' voters may not vote for parties campaigning for a 'Yes'. In the event, the promise of a referendum 'later' defused the Nice issue in the general election.

The small amount of space allocated to Europe in the parties' election manifestos also suggests an unwillingness to make it an election priority. In Fianna Fáil's ninety-four page manifesto, only two and a half pages were allocated to 'Ireland's role in the European Union'. Here the party promised to submit a 'suitable' declaration (on Irish neutrality) to be attached to the Treaty, and subsequently to hold a second Nice referendum in the autumn of 2002 and (importantly) to campaign vigorously for a 'Yes' result. Every other issue on the European agenda for the years ahead that appears in this manifesto (including enlargement, Commission reform, UN-sanctioned Petersberg tasks, subsidiarity and the 'community method', and the Euro) receives Fianna Fáil's support. Moreover, in its contribution to the Constitutional Convention Fianna Fáil will 'insist on a model [of the EU] that respects as well as pools the sovereignty of Nation States'. Strengthened parliamentary scrutiny of EU business was

[6] Note: Figures for Democratic Left in 1997 have been included in the figures for Labour in 1997, since Democratic Left merged with Labour in 1999.

also promised (and delivered, after the election). The junior coalition party, the Progressive Democrats, also favoured a second Nice referendum, promised parliamentary scrutiny of EU business, eulogised the Euro, and in general advocated strong Irish participation in all aspects of integration.[7]

Fine Gael devoted two of thirty-eight manifesto pages to 'Playing a full part in Europe'. With a dig at the outgoing government, a Fine Gael-led Ireland would 'once again play a full and active role in Europe, both in day-to-day matters and in shaping the EU's future development.' A key part of Fine Gael's statement refers to the need to secure a 'Yes' vote in a second Nice referendum. Further issues raised include democratising the European Commission, some institutional innovations, pursuing European economic, social and political solidarity, and support for 'full Irish involvement in EU decisions on peace and security, participating in appropriate missions but reserving the right to decide on a case by case basis whether to participate.'

Labour, the only sizeable party in Ireland with a 'natural' European party family, only mentioned the EU briefly twice: once to say that if elected, Labour would 'strengthen Ireland's international commitment – within Europe, by facilitating enlargement of the EU and contributing to the reform of its institutions', and once to say that they would also 'work with our EU partners to promote corporate responsibility in developing countries.'

Sinn Féin and the Green Party provided the only audible Eurosceptic voices. Both opposed the holding of a second Nice referendum, branding this a corrupt attempt to manipulate the Irish people. Sinn Féin's further election promises regarding Europe consisted of enshrining Irish neutrality in the constitution to ward off any threat to it from the 'EU army', retaining a Commissioner per member state and the right to veto (e.g. decision-making by unanimity), as well as ensuring that member states 'be able to relate to the rest of the world on their own terms and not as part of a giant EU state', and ending the democratic deficit. In a similar vein, the Greens (who acknowledged that 'the greatest achievement of the EU has been the creation of structures for the development of peaceful, mutually beneficial relations between states') also singled out the EU's foreign, security and defence capabilities for particular criticism, with

---

[7] This and other references to party manifestos are taken from www.ireland.com/ focus/election_2002/parties/.

reference to the perceived negative impact on Irish neutrality. The Greens favoured enlargement, demanded greater Oireachtas powers for scrutinising EU business, and opposed flexibility provisions in European-level decision-making.

The Socialist Party, the Socialist Workers' Party, the Workers' Party and the Christian Solidarity Party also contested the election, along with many independents.[8] These parties had campaigned against the Nice Treaty in 2001 and in the 2002 election they opposed the holding of a second referendum (as did many of the independent candidates).

The election returned to office the outgoing centre-right coalition between Fianna Fáil and the Progressive Democrats, but there were several more interesting, unexpected and perhaps in the long term more important 'stories' to tell about this election from the perspective of how European issues may play out in Irish politics for the foreseeable future. For instance, Fine Gael, historically the second largest party in Irish politics and arguably the Irish party with the most genuine, long-term commitment to European integration, suffered an electoral meltdown. It not only lost 23 seats, but this included ten out of 16 members of the Fine Gael front bench (consisting of the party's most senior and experienced parliamentarians). This development might mean that one of the strongest and most persistent forces for European integration in Ireland is significantly undermined and weakened. It is noteworthy that the new party leader who took over Fine Gael after the election ended the party's self-imposed exile from the Forum for Europe.

Another major point of note in this election was the success of Sinn Féin, who increased their representation from one to five seats on the basis of a platform based on the ideal of a united, independent, socialist Irish republic. Sinn Féin's perception of Irish independence makes it a 'soft' Eurosceptic party, recognising the European arena as one where the party's objectives can be advanced but nonetheless rejecting suprana-

---

[8] The Socialist, Socialist Workers' and Workers' parties combine Marxism/Socialism and Irish republicanism in different ways. The Socialist Party was formed out of Labour in the 1980s. The origins of the Workers' Party is that it is a transmuted off-shoot from Sinn Féin. The Socialist Workers' Party is a Trotskyist group. The Christian Solidarity Party is primarily concerned with Catholic doctrine on the four issues of supporting natural life from birth to death, supporting the traditional model of the single income family, regeneration of the West of Ireland, and democracy questions including the question of how the EU impinges on national democracy.

tional developments especially in any area of policy with perceived implications for Irish military neutrality.

From the perspective of European issues, the rise and rise of Sinn Féin is nevertheless only one of two potentially crucial developments arising out of the 2002 election, the second one being the success of the Green Party. The Green Party increased its seat share from two to six, thereby becoming potentially 'coalitionable' from a strictly arithmetic point of view. However, the Greens had in effect ruled themselves out of a potential coalition by making a pre-election commitment to only entering a coalition if the major coalition party (most likely Fianna Fáil) undertook to reopen the Nice Treaty – something which would be beyond the control of any Irish party (assuming they would wish to do so in the first place), since doing so would require the acquiescence of the other 14 EU governments.

The final major story of the 2002 election was the dramatic increase in the number of independents. The twenty-eighth Dáil had witnessed the disproportional influence a pivotal independent can wield and 13 independents were elected to the twnety-ninth Dáil, on issues ranging from health and disability rights to the location of mobile phone masts. From the perspective of European issues it is difficult to foretell what the effects of the increase in the numbers of independents will have, but there is at least the potential that some of them might be effective Eurosceptic voices.

After the election, the deputies belonging to the Green Party, Sinn Féin and eleven of the independents (a total of 22 out of 166 deputies) formed a 'technical group' to maximise their impact in the Dáil. The motivation was not one of ideological common ground, but a strategic move to obtain rights under the Dáil's standing orders to, for example, question the Taoiseach and other ministers on policy issues. A political grouping requires seven deputies to qualify as a party in terms of obtaining these rights, as well as material and practical resources in their parliamentary work. In practise, this would increase their ability to voice their point of view in the Dáil. However, most immediately, this did not make a difference to the eventual ratification of the Treaty of Nice.

Nice II

The returned Fianna Fáil – Progressive Democrat government took the first significant post-election step towards Irish ratification of the Nice

Treaty at the Seville European Council (21-22 June 2002) by succeeding in getting the other 14 EU governments to accept an Irish declaration that spelled out the so-called triple lock on Irish participation in EU activities of a military nature. The triple lock (UN mandate; cabinet approval; Dáil approval) was nothing new, and moreover the declaration had no legal status, so this measure on the part of the Irish government must be understood as a political signal aimed primarily at the Irish electorate. In response to the Irish declaration, the European Council issued a declaration of its own, recognising the right of all member states to decide in accordance with national constitutions and laws whether and how to participate in any activities under the European Security and Defence Policy (Ireland 2002; European Union 2002).

The Irish declaration was subject to hard criticism and ridicule from parties opposed to the Nice Treaty in the first place and who also opposed the holding of a second referendum. 'If it were a cheque it would bounce' according to Mr John Gormley of the Green Party, when he spoke in the Dáil on 25 June 2002 (*Dáil Éireann Official Report*). The declaration's legal standing, the fact that it added no new safeguards for neutrality and the question of constitutionally enshrining neutrality as an alternative to the weak declaration were issues that were aired, as well as the democratic probity of holding a second Nice referendum.

The government, Fine Gael and Labour campaigned in favour of the Treaty together with the major trade unions (Irish Congress of Trade Unions, Irish Farmers' Association, Irish Business and Employers' Confederation) and other groups such as the Alliance for Europe and Irish Co-operative Organisation Society. Their central arguments focused on preparing the EU for enlargement, and that enlargement would be beneficial for Ireland in addition to being something of a moral obligation to show solidarity to the people of Central and Eastern Europe who had suffered under Soviet rule and subsequently spent 10 years trying to democratise.

The No campaign consisted of political parties (the Greens, Sinn Féin, Socialist Party, Workers' Party) and a number of other organisations (Immigration Control Platform, National Platform, and Afri (Action from Ireland)) who worked under a shared umbrella, the No to Nice campaign. Their central claim was that the Nice Treaty was not about enlargement at all, which they claimed could take place under the provisions of the Amsterdam Treaty (at least for five more countries to join).

They also argued that Nice would make the EU even more undemocratic and militaristic, and 'You will still lose: Power. Money. Freedom'.

There were three significant differences between the 2001 and 2002 referendums. The three differences are inter-related. The first and most obvious difference was the result: the 2002 referendum decisively overturned the No vote of 2001. In 2002 62.9 per cent of people cast a Yes vote, as against 37.1 per cent casting No votes. The second difference was turnout. Turnout was 14 percentage points higher in 2002 than in 2001 (Table 1). The third difference was that the Yes vote doubled (453,461 votes in 2001; 906,202 in 2002) while the No vote stayed roughly the same (529,478 in 2001; 534,887 in 2002). To simplify the complex story of voting behaviour that underlies these figures, a large segment of the Irish electorate that was inclined to support the Nice Treaty did not vote in 2001, but were activated in 2002. The No campaign, in contrast, seems to have reached the limits of its potential support base in 2001.

In light of these figures, reading the 2001 Nice referendum as a manifestation of a wave of Euroscepticism sweeping over Ireland emerges as an over-simplification. There is certainly a group of Eurosceptic voters, but they are significantly outnumbered by the rest of the electorate who are positively inclined – when they can be bothered about it.

Conclusion

From 1973 until 2000 Irish governments were very clever at advancing Irish national interests by saying that it was in the European Union's interest to support Ireland, as part of the single market's efficient functioning. But the single market has meant more than economic gain in Ireland: a radical view is that until 1973 Ireland's independence was vacuous due to the continued economic dependence on Britain. Accordingly, the argument goes, both countries' accession to the Treaty of Rome (1957) in 1973 rather than the Anglo-Irish Treaty (1921) made Ireland independent (Halligan 2000).

The year 2000 saw the start of a new relationship between Ireland and the EU: this was the year of the 'Boston-Berlin' debate, followed by the detrimental 'budget row' and Nice referendum in 2001. These events added nuance to the debate on Ireland's EU membership. However, opinion polls continued to show very high levels of public support for the EU throughout this time, and upon examination, the referendum results do not support the view that Euroscepticism has spread like wild-

fire, or even at all, among the Irish public. When confronted with decisive choices, political parties such as Fianna Fáil and the Progressive
Democrats, whose prominent members had been making statements and
taking positions that could be perceived as Eurosceptic, reassumed their
conventional pro-European stance.

The 2001 Nice referendum is arguably not the most noteworthy development of this time period, despite the drama surrounding it. Instead,
the 2002 general election signals a number of gradual, more long-term
changes. The EU was not a big issue in this election but Eurosceptic
parties did better than ever, while pro-European Fine Gael and Labour
had a bad election. The Greens and Sinn Féin might not overtake either
of them anytime soon, but as far as the arithmetic of coalition-building
goes, they have become realistic partners in a future government lead by
either Fianna Fáil or Fine Gael.

References

Dáil Éireann Official Report. 2002. Dublin: Government Stationary Office.
De Valera, Síle. 2000. Speech Delivered at the Launch of *The American Irish* by
    Kevin Kenny. Boston College, Massachusetts, 18 September 2000.
European Union. 2002. Declaration of the European Council, 21 June.
Eurostat. 2000. *Statistics in Focus: General Statistics, Theme 1-1/2000.* Luxembourg:
    Office for Official Publications of the European Communities.
Fitzgerald, Rona. 2002. *Close Encounters of an EMU Kind: Ireland and the EMU
    Reprimand.* Newsletter No. 9, The Jean Monnet Centre, University of Aarhus.
Gilland, Karin. 2001. Ireland: Neutrality and the International Use of Force. In
    Public Opinion and the International Use of Force, eds. Philip Everts and
    Pierangelo Isernia, 141-162. London: Routledge.
Gilland, Karin. 2002a. Ireland's (First) Referendum on the Treaty of Nice.
    Journal of Common Market Studies 40: 527-535.
Gilland, Karin. 2002b. Europe and the Irish General Election of May 2002.
    Royal Institute of International Affairs/Opposing Europe Research Net-
    work Election Briefing No. 2. www.sussex.ac.uk/Units/SEI/oern/Election
    Briefings/Paper2Irish.pdf
Halligan, Brendan. 2000. What Difference Did It Make? Setting the Scene. In
    Europe: The Irish Experience, ed. Rory O'Donnell, 18-31. Dublin: Institute of
    European Affairs.
Harney, Mary. 2000. Remarks by Tanaiste, Mary Harney, at a Meeting of the
    American Bar Association in the Law Society of Ireland.' Blackhall Place,
    Dublin on Friday 21 July.

Hederman, Miriam. 1983. *The Road to Europe: Irish Attitudes 1984-61*. Dublin: Institute for Public Administration.

Ireland. 2001. Government Press Release on the National Forum on Europe, 10 October.

Ireland. 2002. National Declaration by Ireland on the Treaty of Nice.

Keogh, Dermot. 1990. *Ireland & Europe 1919-1989: A Diplomatic and Political History*. Cork: Hibernian University Press.

Maher, Denis. 1986. *The Tortuous Path: The Course of Ireland's Entry into the EEC 1948-73*. Dublin: Institute of Public Administration.

Marsh, Michael and Paul Mitchell, eds. 1999. *How Ireland Voted 1997*. Boulder, Co.: Westview Press.

Referendum Commission. 1998. *Report on the Referendum on the Eighteenth Amendment of the Constitution – Consequential on the Amsterdam Treaty*. Dublin: Referendum Commission.

Salmon, Trevor C. 1989. *Unneutral Ireland: An Ambivalent and Unique Security Policy*. Oxford: Clarendon Press.

Scott, Dermot. 1994. *Ireland's Contribution to the European Union*. Dublin: Institute for European Affairs.

Sinnott, Richard. 1995. *Knowledge of the European Union in Irish Public Opinion: Sources and Implications*. Dublin: Institute for European Affairs.

Sinnott, Richard. 2001. *Attitudes and Behaviour of the Irish Electorate in the Referendum on the Treaty of Nice*. Report on Flash *Eurobarometer* Survey commissioned by the European Commission (Directorate-General for Press and Communication).

EUROPEAN STUDIES 20 (2004): 193-205

SWEDISH EUROSCEPTICISM:
DEMOCRACY, SOVEREIGNTY AND WELFARE

Milena Sunnus

Abstract

In 1995 Sweden joined the European Union in the face of considerable national opposition. Since entry Euroscepticism appears to have
been reinforced, with many Swedes claiming that Brussels is meddling
with internal affairs and declaring themselves against the euro. Drawing on interviews with various Swedish public figures, this article
shows that Swedish Euroscepticism is largely of a cultural nature and
based on perceptions of national superiority, especially in the fields of
gender equality, protection of the environment and control of alcohol
abuse. It is widely thought that things are better in Sweden and that
the 'cultural flow' from Brussels should be stemmed or even counter-
acted by a crosscurrent of 'Nordic' values. Over time, these perceptions of superiority will, however, almost certainly diminish, as increasing transnational contacts moderate the forces of isolationism.
Originally quite determined to protect Sweden's 'Nordic' values, the
Swedish Prime Minister, Göran Persson, recently declared that these
are in fact part of a European 'family of values'.

In 1996, one year after Sweden's accession to the European Union, Prime
Minister Göran Persson defined four main achievements of Swedish
political culture: welfare for all, education, transparency, and protection
of the environment. He also talked about social justice and equality,
which he considered central concepts of Swedish democracy (Persson
1996).[1]

---

[1] See also his Statements of Government Policy, 2000 and 2001: 'The equality of all
humans is the basis of democracy' (Persson 2000), and 'Sweden shall be a country of
social justice and security' (Persson 2001).

With its deep rooted 'passion for equality', the Swedish welfare state has been regarded as a 'model' for a long time (Graubard 1986). It is characterised by a comprehensive social security system, high taxation, a very low rate of unemployment and a relatively 'calm' labour market.[2] It has been received opinion that the democratic welfare system is founded on strong collective values and the idea of social homogeneity, and that in Sweden economic differences are less marked and social inequalities less pronounced than elsewhere in Europe (Eduards 1991). The basis of Swedish political culture may be described, in anthropological terms, as 'egalitarian individualism' (Gullestad 1992), with social equity and equal citizenship as the most fundamental values (Graubard 1986).

However, as of the 1990s these notions of 'Swedishness' have been debated intensely (Daun 1998; Ehn, Frykman and Löfgren 1993). An economic crisis and changes in social policy triggered speculation about 'the end of the welfare state' (Henningsen and Stråth 1995), and made many Swedes uneasy about their cultural self-awareness. This was mirrored in newspapers and magazines: 'Today we are a nation without self-confidence. We have lost the ground under our feet', claimed a literary journal (*BLM* 1995). Another magazine detected political disorientation and published an issue entitled 'The left? Which left? Sweden? Which Sweden?' (*Arena* 1995).

A crucial question in the Swedishness debate is to what extent this nation is or should become 'European'. When the country joined the European Union in 1995, public opinion was hostile. Today this situation has not changed. Eurosceptic themes appear to have found a deep resonance in the national political culture.[3] Often the debate focuses on the cultural dimension of European integration and on how Swedish values and, by extension, 'Nordic values' are threatened.

Various anthropologists have commented on the cultural dimension of European integration, using concepts such as 'mobility', 'boundaries' and 'cultural flows' to examine the transnational processes affecting national, regional and local identities (Daun and Jansson 1999; Daun 1997; Borneman 1997). A cultural flow, as it is described by the Swedish an-

---

[2] The absence of wage conflicts is due to the fact that the Swedish Confederation of Trade Unions (LO) and the Swedish Employers' Confederation (SAF) negotiate collective agreements (Henningsen 1986; Meidner and Hedborg 1985).

[3] According to *Eurobarometer* results published in spring 2001, for example, 54% of Swedes thought that that their country had not benefited from EU membership, as against only 31% who thought that it had benefited.

thropologist Ulf Hannerz, usually runs from the centre to the periphery, diffusing ideas and values. Such processes obviously play a role in European integration and 'Europeanisation'. Thus, the idea of 'cultural flows' may offer a helpful model to explore the meaning and use of the term 'Euroscepticism'. Cultural flows, however, are not necessarily centrifugal. They can flow from the periphery to the centre, allowing the former 'to talk back' (Hannerz 1992, 265). They may diminish cultural and national boundaries within the EU, but some policies provoke flows that may enhance Euroscepticism and produce fragmentation rather than integration.[4] This article aims to highlight some cultural aspects of the Swedish EU debate, concentrating on perceptions of democracy, sovereignty and welfare, and demonstrating how these issues are essential to Swedish Eurosceptics as they 'talk back'.

The primary source material is a series of interviews with twenty-four political actors in Stockholm and Jämtland (a highly Eurosceptical region in the Northwest of Sweden) during February-April and June-August 2000 (cf. Sunnus 2003; Sunnus and Sifft 2003). The interviewees are allowed to speak for themselves. Their thought processes are revealed, rather than rigorously examined or 'measured'. Thus, the reader is invited to be a co-interpreter of Swedish Euroscepticism and of its culturally constructed core concerns, such as the desire to safeguard the 'Nordic' sense of equality.

Democracy and Sovereignty

'Will Sweden survive as an independent nation?' This question, which was debated at a public meeting in Stockholm's *ABF House* on 8 April 2000, sums up the essence of the public's anti-EU sentiment. The issues of national sovereignty and democracy were also intensively debated in Parliament (the *Riksdag*) at the time of the referendum on Sweden's membership in 1994.[5] Whereas opponents of Swedish membership feared for

---

[4] Another model analysing the connection between cultural and political processes is presented by Appadurai (1996), who examines the tension between homogenisation and heterogenisation in multiple centres and peripheries of global interactions.

[5] Although Swedish governments had long steered towards membership (Stråth 1993), the referendum divided public opinion and party positions. The debate on European integration intensified after 1990, when the Social Democratic government announced its intention to apply for membership (Twaddle 1997). The political elite was supportive, whereas the majority of the people (including party members) regarded European integration as problematical (Widfeldt 1997).

the country's sovereignty, those favouring accession stressed the benefits of the common market and the desirability of having a direct say in EU decision-making. The pro/anti divide broadly coincides with the traditional right/left cleavage, with the Swedish left-wing parties showing the greatest propensity for Euroscepticism and warning most consistently against the loss of self-determination. As the EU correspondent of Sweden's biggest newspaper *Dagens Nyheter* put it: 'The EU debate in Sweden is about sovereignty, about the loss of sovereignty and the fear to lose it. And it's about democracy, and the fear to lose democracy. It is also about bureaucracy, about the feeling that the bureaucrats in Brussels meddle with everything. This is what people are concerned about' (*Dagens Nyheter*'s EU correspondent, 6 April 2000).

Many Eurosceptics question the democratic legitimacy of the EU, claiming a discrepancy between the Swedish notion of democracy and the practices of EU.[6] Transparency is a key concern, which is obvious from *Eurobarometer* data. Results from 2001 show that a majority of Swedes believe that the EU and its institutions must be simplified and become more open in order to achieve broader public support. In the words of a Swedish MEP: 'People don't feel connected with the EU. I voted against Swedish membership because I thought it essential to have grass-root support. The EU is imposed from above. For me democracy is a bottom up affair' (Social Democratic MEP, 20 June 2000).

The Swedish concern for the democratic quality of the EU seems not just determined by political or moral ideas and norms, but also by geography. The 1994 referendum showed a significant gap between rural and urban attitudes. The big cities Stockholm, Göteborg and Malmö voted in favour of the EU membership, while in the country, and especially in the Northern regions, public opinion was very sceptical (Kaiser et al. 1995; *Eurobarometer* 1996). 'Probably Swedish Euroscepticism has to do with distance', a representative of the Swedish trade union *HTF* claimed. 'I mean, you have this loss of control. The closer you are to issues, the easier it is to exert influence. You lose this ability when you move a lot of issues to Brussels' (14 March 2000). An MP from Värmland, a region in the mid-west of Sweden added, 'the EU is too far away. A lot farmers in Värmland say "no" to the EU because they don't want the EU to say "you should do your things in such and such a manner." They think that

---

[6] This view may be found a wide range of literature, e.g. Johanson and Svensson 1994; Gilljam and Holmberg 1996; Johansson, et al 1999.

Stockholm is far away, but Brussels?' (Swedish Labour Party MP representing the *Socialdemokratiska Arbetarepatiet*, 6 April 2000). A Swedish
MEP agreed, arguing that the north of her country is too far from
Brussels. She added, however, that geography cannot be the only explanation. Political and social distance is just as important: 'The surprising
thing is that scepticism has risen instead of decreased since we joined. My
feeling is that people find that Europe is not doing anything that relates
to their personal problems, like unemployment, day care centres, social
security' (Social Democratic MEP, 20 June 2000).

A former Swedish EU Commissioner showed irritation over these
arguments, which she stamped as irrational. Distance there may be, but
people should be outward looking: 'I am from the north of Sweden. My
father was a paper mill worker. The Swedish trade unions have always
been very outward looking, because they knew that it is not enough for a
paper mill worker if we [the Swedes] buy their paper. You also have to be
a good exporter. And Sweden is one third dependent on exports. Particularly the north, where you have all these industries. And they are the most
negative! We are a little bit out-of-touch in the north, a little bit isolated.
This is also because of our neutrality policy. Politicians have been telling
people that we can manage everything ourselves' (Swedish EU Commissioner, 11 August 2000).

Neutrality and being a 'small state'

Neutrality is at the heart of Sweden's encounter with Europe. As one of
the interviewed politicians put it: 'The main issue determining my vote
against Sweden's membership was the danger joining a federal Europe
with a common defence (Social Democratic MEP, 20 June 2000). It is
often suggested that Sweden's non-combatant status lies at the heart of
the country's hesitant attitude (Stråth 1993). Whereas the horrors of war
motivated the wishes of the founding countries, Sweden has enjoyed a
long period without serious conflicts. Because of that, European integration is regarded with less urgency: 'Sweden hasn't had war in over a hundred years, people here don't know what war is like. I believe that the
idea of the EU as a peace project doesn't affect them. People can't identify with this. They don't see the gains. They only see that the EU says:
you can't do that, you have to do this, and so on (Christian Democratic
MP representing the *Kristdemokratiska Samlingspartiet*, 22 March 2000).

Just as 'neutrality' is an important part of the Swedish self-image, so is
the idea that the country is a 'small state'. Europe is seen as the play-
ground of the 'big four': Germany, France, Great Britain and Italy. Where
pro-Europeans argue that adopting the euro would increase Sweden's
influence, Eurosceptics claim that such a move would only further diminish Sweden's sovereignty, making it into a yet smaller member state,
unable to finance its much cherished social welfare policies. Opinion
polls show that less than three in ten people are in favour of the euro
(*Eurobarometer* 2001). In January 2000, a few days after the Social Democratic government had pronounced in favour of joining EMU in 2005 or
2006,[7] a cross-party-alliance of opponents uttered their scepticism, claiming that 'opposition against the single currency is growing all over Sweden. We, who are living in Sweden, are convinced that the euro is neither
good for Sweden, nor for Europe' (*Dagens Nyheter*, 24 January 2000).
'Well, this is what people are saying', commented a former Swedish EU
Commissioner. 'They want an independent Swedish economic policy.
Then I say: when do you think Sweden was economically independent
the last time? That was at the beginning of the eighteenth century. After
that we have been selling iron and steel (...) and we have imported people
that have helped us develop this society and industry. But still, people go
on saying that we need a special independent economic policy (Swedish
EU Commissioner, 11 August 2000).

In the recent past, several events have contributed to the Swedish self-
image of being 'small' and suffering from the unequal distribution of
power in Europe. The EU decision not to allow a merger between Scania
and Volvo was a case in point: 'When Volvo and Scania wanted to merge
and the EU said "No!" people were very, very angry. They can't understand why we can't decide ourselves what we want to do. We come from
a small country and why aren't we allowed to create a big industry. We,
the Swedish people, don't want federations, we are concerned about our
country and our own Swedish issues' (Christian Democratic MP representing the *Kristdemokratiska Samlingspartiet*, 22 March 2000). A local left-
wing politician from Stockholm added: 'When the EU said "no, Volvo
cannot form one company with Scania, because they will dominate the
market in Sweden", I am sure that 90% of the Swedish population was

---

[7] Actual membership is made dependent on whether enlargement of the EU takes
place, on the economic circumstances in 2005 or 2006, the effects on Sweden's fiscal
policy and a referendum which is to be held in 2003.

very upset. How can our small companies compete with Volkswagen, Mercedes, Fiat?' (29 March 2000).

The inequality of federalism
Many of the interviewees identified the EU with federalism and saw this as the main source of Swedish Euroscepticism. A Green MP (from the *Miljöpartiet*) complained that European decisions 'make the countries the same. We don't feel comfortable with laws that don't respect national and cultural differences.' A majority of Swedes associate federalism with a lack of transparency and a surplus of bureaucracy: 'The EU should only concern itself with issues that *have* to be solved on the European level. The different member states and the local governments, people themselves, should decide on all other issues. The problems are not the same all over Europe, and therefore the solutions cannot be the same either. The EU tends to meddle with "tiny" issues, and that makes people laugh. But when it comes to major issues, for instance foreign affairs, the EU has no coherent policy' (Liberal politician representing the *Folkpartiet Liberalerna*, 15 March 2000). The Green politician who was quoted above added, however, that even decisions which, on the face of it, are rightly taken at the European level (such as directives on the environment) could go against the preferences and traditions of individual member states: 'There is one question where we should act more across borders, and this is pollution, because pollution has total freedom of movement. But it is still important not to coerce countries. Otherwise we might be forced to tone down our existing environmental laws, and that is a big danger.' In the debate prior to the 1994 referendum, environmental issues also played an important role. Eurosceptics argued that Sweden would lose its ability to develop strong and effective environmental regulations. In general, people were and are concerned that EU membership will compromise the country's high standards in such fields as the environment or welfare.

Another field where Swedish and EU norms are seen as incompatible is the sale of alcohol, which in Sweden is a state monopoly. The Union has demanded an end to this practice, which means that Sweden can no longer pursue its own alcohol policy as of 2003. Due to the European freedom of movement of goods Swedish citizens will be allowed to import much higher quantities of alcohol and tobacco. Many see this as a challenge to sovereignty and a regression which will endanger public health: 'We have a very difficult discussion about how much alcohol we can bring into Sweden. We want to have our own policy to keep alcohol away from our children and youngsters and to combat alcohol abuse. But now the EU tells us that Sweden has to conform to the other countries. People are allowed to take more and more alcohol into the country. This will increasingly cause problems. We will have to lower our alcohol duties in Sweden and we don't like that' (Christian Democrat MP representing the *Kristdemokratiska Samlingspartiet*, 22 March 2000).

The alcohol debate shows that Swedish Eurosceptics see themselves as defenders of a political culture which assigns a strong protective role to the nation state. According to this view, it is the state's duty to preserve the *folkhem*, a protective home for the people. Europe is seen as an outside force, shooting holes in the walls of this Swedish home. 'It is now easier for alcohol and drugs to cross our borders', said *Dagens Nyheter*'s EU correspondent. 'Travelling is easier now and borders are penetrated by crime and drugs. This means our protection is being compromised' (6 April 2000).

Gender equality and social welfare

In Sweden, gender equality is conceptualised around the cultural notion of 'equality as sameness' (Gullestad 1992), meaning that attention is also paid to the role of men in society. There is a high public awareness of family issues, which focuses increasingly on the part played by men. Almost all party programmes contain a section on 'men and gender equality'. Because the majority perceive Swedish gender politics as very advanced, Sweden's EU membership is often seen as an obstacle to women's opportunities. This was manifest in the referendum, when a majority of women (52%) voted against EU membership (Oskarsson 1996). *Dagens Nyheter*'s EU correspondent commented: 'In Sweden people tend to see the Union as a market driven project. Therefore it is a threat to social life and the Swedish welfare system which has strengthened the position of women by making childcare widely available' (6 April 2000).

As was noted earlier, in Sweden Euroscepticism is usually associated with the parties of the left. One explanation is that gender equality and the protection of the welfare state are traditionally left-wing issues: 'Criticism of the EU comes from the left, and women in Sweden tend to be more left-wing than men, that's an obvious gender gap in politics. It is probably related to the fact that lots of women work in the public sector, and the left tends to be a defender of the public sector and the welfare system in general' (Social Democrat MP representing the *Socialdemokratiska Arbetarepartiet*, 28 March 2000).

So, according to this argument, European integration is seen as the antithesis of the egalitarian principle of the Swedish welfare model, which is believed to be based on 'Nordic values' such as the freedom of all citizens to realise their capabilities through political, welfare and labour market institutions (Bergquist 1999; Eduards 1991): 'The Nordic countries have organised good daycare, and that is a path I would like Europe to take, for the sake of women. We see what happened to women in Eastern Europe, when the new economic system took away all the daycare centres, their jobs and the protection of their children. Women are victims of unemployment, victims of bad social security, the lack of daycare centres and care for the elderly. When I talk to Swedish women I understand that these are core issues. It is all about children, social security, jobs, and they don't think that the EU will solve these problems for them. This is the basis of their Euroscepticism' (Social Democratic MEP, 20 June 2000).

This Euroscepticism is enhanced by the unequal representation of women in EU institutions (Hoskyns 1996; Abels 1998), which is often seen as confirmation that the EU is male dominated and has no eye for women's wishes and needs (Lundström 1999): 'It has all to do with the question of who governs the EU? If you switch on your TV you see that the EU is run by men, and that makes some women think: "why should we be a member of this?" In Sweden about 40% of the government consists of women. Why should we revert to an organisation run by men? It is, moreover, obvious that European gender policies have been very focused on women, giving them equal rights. But they have not been focused on giving equal rights to men, for instance when it comes to taking care of the children. It's not enough to give women more rights, you also have to push men into the family and childcare.' And as far as the European institutions are concerned women only seem allowed to handle social welfare issues. "Oh let the women take care of that", they say, and we men will concentrate on the big issues, like EMU' (local Liberal councillor representing the *Folkpartiet Liberalerna*, 15 March 2000).

Conclusion

Swedish Euroscepticism is largely inspired by a positive national self image. The Swedish 'model', which stresses democracy, equality and social welfare, is believed to be besieged by backward European laws and directives. Thus the European Union functions as the 'significant other', confirming and enhancing a complacent sense of Swedishness and invoking a nationalist, defensive 'cultural flow'. As the governor of Jämtland argued: 'Euroscepticism has to do with the Swedish self image of being special, more liberal, more social, equal and better than the rest of Europe. This image was established in the 1960s, and then there was some truth in it. But people do not realise that things changed in the 1980s and 90s. Sweden is not so special any longer. However, during this debate about membership the image of "being better" was widely propagated and created this reluctance towards EU. I think many people still live by these ideas' (Governor of Jämtland, 15 August 2000). In a similar vein *Dagens Nyheter*'s EU correspondent concluded: 'Sweden is like Britain, it sees itself as a "better" and "different". It is an old and proud nation state that sees itself as isolated from the rest of the world; it has practically never been invaded. I mean, we had wars, but we have almost never been occupied. So, people are proud of their national sovereignty and seem to be saying "we are doing very nicely on our own, thank you very much." These emotions lie at the root of Swedish Euroscepticism' (6 April 2000).

It should be noted that the Swedish sense of being different and isolated has not affected its attitude towards enlargement. On the contrary, enlargement is the only European topic which is supported by all *Riksdag* parties, as well as by a majority of the population. In this case European integration does not seem to provoke a fear of losing cultural values and national achievements. Since many of the new member states are geographically near Sweden, it is hoped that enlargement will regulate cross-border traffic and bring a good relationship with Russia. While the EU is often seen as a threat to the Swedish welfare system, gender equality and national sovereignty, membership of the Baltic States is a matter of considerable interest. Next to environmental issues and employment, enlargement was therefore prioritised during Sweden's EU presidency in the first half of 2001. In the words of the Prime Minister: 'Enlargement of the EU is our generation's opportunity to secure peace and freedom, democracy and prosperity in the whole of Europe. Sweden will be pro-active in carrying the enlargement negotiations forward, with the aim of achieving crucial progress during our presidency. Enlargement will have a greater impact on our immediate neighbourhood than anything else. The combination of mature welfare states and young, rapidly growing democracies round the Baltic Sea opens unique opportunities for development in our part of Europe' (Persson 2000).

Although Swedish EU membership has triggered a considerable cultural flow of feelings of national pride and exceptionalism, there is no need to exaggerate Swedish Euroscepticism. According to one MP, convincing the Swedes of the benefits of EU membership is proving an uphill struggle: 'Very large groups of the population see the EU as the cause of all negative things that have happened the last couples of years. The problem for those of us who are more favourable to the EU is that we know that a lot of good laws have been introduced (in the area of employment policy for instance). But it has proved difficult to get this through to the public (Social Democratic MP representing the *Socialdemokratiska Arbetarepartiet*, 28 March 2000). This and the other above-quoted interviews, however, are 'snapshots' taken at the beginning of the 21st century. Europeanisation is an ongoing process, running parallel with political, economic and cultural flows of globalisation and transnational contacts. The time factor should therefore be taken into consideration. In due course, cultural flows, running from the centre to the periphery, and *vice versa*, will stimulate cross-national thinking, diffuse ideas and adjust national self images and prejudices. An indication of change is provided by a shift of opinion in the Swedish Prime Minister's statements on Europe. In 1996 he appeared protective about Sweden's achievements: 'Sweden is a rich country. We have a good environment, a high level of competence, advanced gender equality and considerable openness. These qualities must be safeguarded and further developed' (Persson 1996). Five years later, however, he was much less focused on championing these 'Nordic values', declaring the entire European Union 'a family of values of democracy and pluralism, respect for human rights and solidarity', and celebrating 'the social cohesion brought by a well-functioning market economy' (Persson 2001).

References

Abels, Gabriele. 1998. *Engendering the Representational Democratic Deficit in the European Union*. Berlin: Wissenschaftszentrum für Sozialforschung.

Appadurai, Arjun. 1996. *Modernity at Large: Cultural Dimensions of Globalization.* Minneapolis: University of Minnesota Press.

Arena. Politikens, kulturens & idéernas. 1995. *Vänstern? Vilken Vänster? Sverige? Vilket Sverige?*

Bergquist, Christina et al., eds. 1999. *Equal Democracies? Gender and Politics in the Nordic Countries.* Oslo: Scandinavian University Press.

BLM, Bonniers Litterära Magasin. 1995.

Borneman, John. 1997. Europeanization. *Annual Review of Anthropology* 26: 487-514.

Daun, Åke and Sören Jansson, eds. 1999. *Europeans: Essays on Culture and Identity.* Lund: Nordic Academic Press.

Daun, Åke. 1998. *Svensk mentalitet: ett jämförande perspektiv.* Stockholm: Rabén.

Daun, Åke. 1997. *Den europeiska identiteten: Sverige och Italien, EU och framtiden.* Stockholm: Rabén.

Eduards, Maude.1991. The Swedish Gender Model: Productivity, Pragmatism and Paternalism. *West European Politics* 14, no. 3: 166-181

Ehn, Billy, Jonas Frykman and Orvar Löfgren. 1993. *Försvenskningen av Sverige.* Stockholm: Natur och Kultur.

European Commission. 1996. *Eurobarometer: Public Opinion in the European Union* 45. Brussels: European Commission.

European Commission. 2001. *Eurobarometer: Public Opinion in the European Union* 55. Brussels: European Commission.

Gilljam, Mikael and Sören Holmberg. 1996. *Ett knappt ja till EU: Väljarna och Folkomröstningen 1994.* Stockholm: Norstedts Juridik.

Graubard, Stephen R.. ed. 1986. *Norden: the Passion for Equality.* Oslo: Scandinavian University Press.

Gullestad, Marianne. 1992. *The Art of Social Relations: Essays on Culture, Social Action and Everyday Life in Modern Norway.* Oslo: Scandinavian University Press.

Hannerz, Ulf. 1992. *Cultural Complexity: Studies in the Social Organization of Meaning.* New York: Columbia University Press.

Hannerz, Ulf. 1997. *Flows, Boundaries and Hybrids: Keywords in Transnational Anthropology.* Published in Portuges as Fluxos, fronteiras, híbridos: palavars- chaves da antropologia transnacional. *Mana* 3, no. 1: 7-39.

Henningsen, Bernd. 1986. *Der Wohlfahrtsstaat Schweden.* Baden-Baden: Nomos.

Henningsen, Bernd and Bo Stråth.1995. Die Transformation des Schwedischen Wohlfahrtsstaates – Ende des Modells? *Jahrbuch für Politik* 2: 221-246.

Hoskyns, Catherine. 1996. *Integrating Gender. Women, Law and Politics in the European Union.* London: Verso.

Johansson, Karl Magnus, ed. 1999. *Sverige i EU.* Stockholm: Studieförbundet Näringsliv och Samhälle (SNS).

Johanson, Kjell E. and Jörn Svensson. 1994. *EU och alternativen.* Stockholm: Carlsson.

Kaiser, Wolfram et al. 1995. *Die EU-Volksabstimmungen in Österreich, Finnland, Schweden und Norwegen: Verlauf, Ergebnisse, Motive und Folgen.* Wien: Institut für Höhere Studien, Reihe Politikwissenschaft.

Lundström, Karin. 1999. *Jämlikhet mellan Kvinnor och Män i EG-rätten. En feministisk Analys*. Göteborg: Iustus.

Meidner, Rudolf and Anna Hedborg. 1985. *Modell Schweden*. Frankfurt: Campus Verlag.

Oskarsson, Maria. 1996. Skeptiska Kvinnor – Entusiastiska Män. In *Ett knappt ja till EU. Väljarna och folkomröstningen 1994*, eds. Mikael Gilljam and Sören Holmberg, 211-224. Stockholm: Norstedts Juridik.

Persson, Göran. 22 March 1996. Statement of Government Policy Presented by the Prime Minister to parliament. www.statsradsberedningen.regeringen.se.

Persson, Göran. 19 September 2000. Statement of Government Policy Presented by the Prime Minister to Parliament. www.statsradsberedningen. regeringen.se.

Persson, Göran. 18 October 2001. European Challenges: A Swedish Perspective. www.whi-berlin.de/persson.htm.

Stråth, Bo. 1993. *Folkhemmet mot Europa. Ett historiskt perspektiv på 90-talet*. Stockholm: Tiden.

Sunnus, Milena. 2003. EC Challenges to the Pioneer in Gender Equality: The Case of Sweden. In *Between Diversity and Equality: Reframing Europeanisation*, ed. Ulrike Liebert. Brussels: Peter Lang: 223-253.

Sunnus, Milena and Stefanie Sifft. 2003. Euroskeptizismus und Wohlfahrtsprotektionismus in Dänemark und Schweden. In *Bürgerschaft, Öffentlichkeit und Demokratie in Europa*, ed. Ansgar Klein. Leverkusen: Leske + Budrich: 273-292.

Twaddle, Andrew.1997. EU or not EU? The Swedish Debate on Entering the European Union 1993-1994. *Scandinavian Studies* 69. no. 2: 189-211.

Widfeldt, Anders. 1997. *Linking Parties with People? Party Membership in Sweden 1960-1994*. Göteborg: Department of Political Science.

EUROPEAN STUDIES 20 (2004): 207-225

AUSTRIAN EUROSCEPTICISM:
THE SHIFT FROM THE LEFT TO THE RIGHT

Anton Pelinka

Abstract

Austria was a latecomer to the European Union amongst the prosperous European liberal democracies. The reason for this delay was Austria's permanent neutrality. During the years of the Cold War, Austria preferred to abstain from European Community membership due to its specific geopolitical position. When the coalition of the centre-left SPÖ and the centre-right ÖVP decided to apply for EC membership in 1989, most of the opposition came from the left, which considered neutrality and EC membership not to be fully compatible. During the 1990s, this situation changed – the left (notably the Green Party) progressively lost its earlier Euroscepticism, while the right (especially the FPÖ) increasingly identified itself with Eurosceptic positions. This was underlined by the Austrian response to the 'sanctions' imposed on the Austrian government in 2000 by the governments of the 14 other EU member states as a response to the inclusion of the FPÖ in the government. Moderate voters on both the centre-right and centre-left, as well as supporters of the Greens, retained their 'Euro-optimistic' attitudes, in contrast to the rightist voters of the FPÖ.

This article understands the term 'Euroscepticism' as a relative position on a scale, representing a point nearer to a notional zero than to a notional one hundred when measuring positive attitudes towards the European Union. Understood in these terms, there is no significant 'fundamentalist' Euroscepticism in Austria, as all major actors maintain a distance from the notional zero point. Nevertheless, on this Euroscepticism scale, there are significant differences between the various actors in Austria.

In order to arrive at a full understanding of Austrian Euroscepticism, one must examine the underlying conditions which account for the existence of both Eurosceptical and Euro-optimistic tendencies in the country. Both specifically Austrian factors and the impact of more generally applicable factors must be examined. The specifically Austrian conditions accounting for different positions on the Euroscepticism scale are as follows:

Delayed EU membership: despite an economically and 'ideologically' western orientation (as expressed in Austria's participation in the Marshall Plan), Austria had not tried to join the European Communities prior to 1989. Austria signed its accession treaty in 1994, some 37 years after its most important trading partners (Germany and Italy) had signed the Rome Treaties that established the EEC.

Permanent neutrality and its interpretation: Austria's neutrality, declared in 1955, was perceived to be of the Swiss kind. Switzerland (but also Sweden and Finland) defined their neutrality, differently from Ireland, as necessitating an abstention from too close an involvement not only in the sphere of Western military co-operation, but also in that of West European economic integration.

Austria's geopolitical situation: the country occupied a 'front-line' position between the East, defined as the Warsaw Treaty Organisation (WTO) and the West, defined as the North Atlantic Treaty Organisation (NATO). During the Cold War, two of Austria's neighbours belonged to the Warsaw Pact (Czechoslovakia and Hungary) and two to NATO (Germany and Italy). Both Soviet and American troops were stationed on Austria's borders.

Various other, non-specific factors have determined (and still determine) Austrian attitudes to European integration, in ways similar to that seen in other EU member states. Two factors are of particular importance. First, attitudes towards European integration differ significantly according to political and ideological position, and party preference. Second, one must account for the impact of education, class, generation, and gender. These classic lines of social cleavage, which more generally correlate to distinctive patterns of political (and especially electoral) behaviour, also play a significant role in influencing attitudes towards European integration.

Austrian attitudes towards the European Union and towards the direction of the two major 'logics' of European integration – 'widening' (enlargement) and 'deepening' (a strengthening of the Union's federal potential) – will presently be analysed by using the following differentials (Baun 2000; van Oudenaren 2000):

'Elite' vs. 'mass' – education, linked to social position and income, can be considered the most important variable explaining an 'elite' position and has an impact on interests and attitudes, including views on European integration. Education influences social mobility, vertically as well as horizontally.

'Right' vs. 'left' – any political perspective is linked to party preference, and political parties can be seen traditionally on a right-left scale. In Austria, the four parties represented in the *Nationalrat* (the first and directly elected chamber of the Austrian parliament) are clearly distinguishable on this scale. Running from left to right, they are the Greens, the Social Democrats (SPÖ), the conservative Austrian People's Party (ÖVP), and the Freedom Party (FPÖ) (Pelinka 1998, 33).

'Moderates' vs. 'extremists' – political attitudes within the mainstream parties of the moderate right (ÖVP) and the moderate left (SPÖ) – the two parties primarily responsible for the direction Austria took after 1945 – may differ significantly from attitudes within the parties on the fringes of the political spectrum, independently from positions on the right-left scale.

'Modernisation winners' vs. 'modernisation losers' – social groups and individuals who see their own future in optimistic terms and expect to benefit from 'modernisation' tend to see European integration differently from those who have a generally more pessimistic view of how future changes will affect them.

Historical background
Austria's European and international position after 1945 was defined by national political elites with special regard for the specific geopolitical situation in which the country found itself, on a fault line in the East-West conflict. In this immediate post-war period, Austrian public opinion did not play much of a role in defining the country's international position beyond signalling a clear, basic preference. The outcome of the general elections of November 1945 clearly indicated a strong anticommunist sentiment that led to the isolation of the small Communist Party

of Austria (KPÖ) and shaped the approach of the two major parties, the conservative Austrian People's Party and the Socialist (later Social Democratic) Party. The election result – the ÖVP got 50% of the votes, the SPÖ 45%, and the KPÖ 5% – reinforced the already existing anticommunist orientation of the major political elites represented by the ÖVP and the SPÖ.

The Austrian people had thus set the course: a choice against Soviet-style Communism and for the West. Taking this basic decision into account, the political elites of the two moderate mainstream parties formulated a specific Austrian response to the process of West European integration, which started with the Marshall Plan in 1947 and with the foundation of NATO in 1949.

The Marshall Plan, which led to the formation of Organisation for European Economic Co-operation (later the Organisation for Economic Co-operation and Development), was the beginning of Austria's western orientation on the European level. Like most other European countries, Austria was invited in 1947 by the US government to participate in the European Recovery Program (ERP). However, unlike countries which were already in the orbit of the USSR, Austria was willing and able to accept the invitation (Bischof 1999). As a result, Austria's economic outlook became western, its trade relations and its economy became increasingly enmeshed in the post-war structures of western interdependence.

The North Atlantic Treaty Organisation did not and could not invite Austria to join. The reason was the unique Austrian position between East and West. As was the case with Germany, Austria was divided into four occupation zones. However, differently from Germany, Austria was governed by a single national government, based on a western-style liberal democracy. When NATO was established, one third of Austrian territory was militarily controlled by Soviet troops, while the other two thirds were controlled by American, British, and French troops. Austria, moreover, did not have armed forces of its own. Under these conditions, an invitation to join NATO was not an option for the western military alliance – and asking for NATO membership was not an option for Austria either (Schlesinger 1972).

Austria was 'western' with regard to its political system and economic orientation. But in military terms the country belonged to neither the West nor the East. This pattern became even more pronounced in 1955, when Austria made a deal with the major powers. It was in this year that the State Treaty was signed, providing for the withdrawal of the four allied powers from Austrian territory, on the condition that the state become neutral in accordance with the Swiss model. This model included the understanding that Austrian neutrality would be an armed one and that the country would be completely free to adopt any political system of its choosing (Stourzh 1998).

Austria defined its neutrality carefully. In 'ideological' terms, it opted for 'western democracy', as it had done since 1945. In military terms, neutrality prevented Austria from joining any military alliance, which, in effect, meant 'not joining NATO despite being Western'. In economic terms, it did not prevent the country from joining the 'soft' versions of West European integration, but it was taken to preclude Austrian participation in the 'hard' versions. The 'hard' version of integration was that represented by the European Economic Community, established in 1957. Two major reasons were responsible for Austria's decision to abstain from EEC membership. First, the EEC consisted only of NATO members and, second, the EEC had a clearly supranational agenda. This agenda implied the need to transfer some aspects of national sovereignty to the European Communities (Bischof and Pelinka 1993; Luif 1994, 275-280). In this regard, Austria acted like the other European neutrals – especially like Switzerland, but also like Sweden, Finland, and Ireland. In all these cases, economic reasons would have spoken for EEC membership, but the political reasoning was against it. The 'soft' version of integration was that represented by the European Free Trade Association (EFTA), established in 1960. EFTA lacked any kind of supranational agenda, it was a pure trade association. Together with three of the other neutrals, Iceland, Sweden and Switzerland, Austria was among the founding members of EFTA. One of the roots of Austrian Euroscepticism thus came to be planted at this time. Supranational organisations of the 'hard kind', which aimed at political union, were seen as incompatible with neutrality. Neutrality and EEC membership were seen as antithetical. It became one of the major rallying points for all Austrians who did not want Austria to join the EEC (later EC/EU).

Originally the brainchild of a very pragmatic political elite consisting of moderate rightists (ÖVP) and moderate leftists (SPÖ), neutrality progressively acquired a more widespread resonance in Austrian society. Initially, neutrality had been conceived as an instrument; it was simply the price to be paid for getting rid of the liberating and occupying powers. The idea, however, gained in popularity, largely for reasons which had nothing to do with the 'Swiss model' of permanent neutrality. Neutrality was perceived as a pragmatic version of pacifism; it seemed to allow Austria to avoid the kind of militarisation which the Cold War forced upon the western as well as the eastern part of Europe.

After 1955, neutrality became more and more a 'leftist' topic. The right-wing League of Independents (VDU), established especially to reintegrate former members of the Austrian NSDAP into post-1945 Austria, had voted against the Neutrality Act in the Austrian parliament. It was the VDU which declared a preference for joining the EEC, against the policy designed by the two mainstream parties, the ÖVP and the SPÖ. The FPÖ, founded in 1956 as the successor party of the VDU, followed the same line. At least initially, it supported EEC membership, while opposing neutrality.

The ÖVP and SPÖ agreed in principle that EEC membership and neutrality were not compatible. But in the 1960s, the attitudes of these two parties started to diverge. The ÖVP was not completely satisfied with Austria's EFTA membership, especially after the United Kingdom (the leading partner within the Free Trade Association) had applied for EEC membership. The ÖVP developed the concept of an 'association' with the EEC, coming as close as possible to the status of membership, but stopping short of actual accession. The SPÖ opposed this orientation, influenced in part by its perception of the EEC as a club ruled by conservatives (reflecting the ascendancy, at the time, of French Gaullists together with German and Italian Christian Democrats). This split between the ÖVP and the SPÖ fitted into the left-right-divide where right-of-centre interests tended to be much more pro-EEC (Schneider 1990).

The EEC did not accept a special Austrian status as an 'associated' member. However, when the UK, Ireland and Denmark joined the EEC in 1973, Austria and the other remaining EFTA members signed a Free Trade Agreement with the EEC (Luif 1994, 280-283). This agreement seemed to fulfil the major objective of the ÖVP's association strategy. Austria had almost free access to the Common Market, without its sovereignty and neutrality being compromised.

The left-right divide became visible once more in the 1980s. Opposing the SPÖ, the ÖVP argued for full EC membership, based on the assumption that the EC's Single Market project would significantly reduce the benefits which Austria derived from its free trade status. In 1987, however, when the SPÖ and the ÖVP returned to government in a new 'grand coalition', the SPÖ accepted the ÖVP's position. It should, however, be underlined that it was clearly the moderate right, the conservative ÖVP, which had started the new move towards the EC (Schaller 1994). This move of the 1980s was accompanied by a shift in the interpretation of neutrality. Permanent neutrality and membership of a supranational community like the EC was less and less seen as a contradiction. It began to be argued that neutrality and EC membership were compatible (Hummer and Schweitzer 1987). Besides the single market argument deployed by the ÖVP, both mainstream parties realised that the climate of détente and disarmament of the Gorbachev era made neutrality less of an issue. In July 1989, the coalition government of SPÖ and ÖVP applied officially for EC membership. Thus Austria spearheaded a trend which the other European neutrals (Sweden, Finland, Switzerland) were to follow (Luif 1995).

In the 1990s Austria's geopolitical position had changed dramatically. Instead of being between two blocs in a bipolar European system the country found itself on the fringes of a western Europe that had lost its counterpart. The USSR, which had had a strong interest in preventing Austria from joining the community of its most important trading partners, had ceased to exist. There was no countervailing political power to balance the economic interest which clearly pushed the country towards the EC.

At the same time, the left-right divide was transformed into a centre-periphery divide. The rightist FPÖ became an outspoken opponent of Austria's entry into the EU, and the newly established Green party, considered to be to the left of the SPÖ, also opposed Austria's application for membership. The governing parties of the moderate right and of the moderate left, which favoured membership, were thus confronted with opposition from both ends of the political spectrum. This was a significant shift of the cleavage between Eurosceptics and Euro-optimists. Previously, the political left had been marked by a preference for neutrality and against EC membership, in opposition to the political right which had tentatively opposed neutrality, while moving towards EC membership. This left-right divide had now become an opposition between a Euro-optimistic centre and Eurosceptic fringes of the right as well as the left.

Euroscepticism since 1994

Austria signed its accession treaty with the EU in 1994, together with Sweden, Finland, and Norway. In Austria, 66.6% of those voting in the accession referendum backed EU membership. This contrasts with 57% in Finland and 52.2% in Sweden. In Norway, of course, a 'No vote' was recorded, with 52.2% of the electorate voting against EU membership. The Austrian referendum result can thus be seen as a democratic legitimation of the SPÖ/ÖVP coalition government's policy.

The Austrian referendum of 12 June 1994 exposed significant differentials in the relative propensity of the major segments of Austrian society to adopt Eurosceptic or Euro-optimistic positions (table 1).

Table 1: Voting behaviour in the Austrian EU-referendum, June 1994, according to gender, generation, education. Public opinion poll (exit poll by phone), n = 7000.

Should Austria join the EU? (%)

	Yes	No	Difference
Men	70	30	+40
Women	62	38	+24
Younger than 30 years	55	45	+10
30 – 44 years	64	35	+29
45 – 59 years	68	32	+36
60 years and older	70	30	+40
minimal education	60	40	+20
medium education	65	35	+30
higher education	70	30	+40

Source: Plasser and Ulram 1994, 97.

With the sole exception of farmers, all major groups in Austrian society had voted 'yes' when asked whether Austria should join the EU (Plasser and Ulram 1994, 97). But there were some important differences in this overall Euro-optimistic attitude. Lower levels of support were found amongst younger voters, women, and less educated voters.

The generational divide is a reflection of the differences between the parties (table 2). The two parties which in 1994 opposed Austria's membership (the FPÖ and the Greens) attracted at this time a significant number of young voters (Plasser, Ulram and Sommer 2000). The two governing parties (the SPÖ and the ÖVP), which were both responsible for Austria's application, were significantly stronger among older voters.

Table 2: Voting behaviour in the Austrian EU referendum, June 1994, according to party preference. Public opinion poll (exit poll by phone), n=7000.

Should Austria join the EU? (%)

	Yes	No
SPÖ voters	73	27
ÖVP	66	34
FPÖ	41	59
Greens	38	62
LIF[1]	75	25
Voters without declared party preference	60	40

Source: Plasser and Ulram 1994, 99.

Te educational gap reflects the divide between the elite and masses. It is obvious that well educated Austrians are less Eurosceptic. They may be classified as 'modernisation winners', who see European integration not as threatening but as providing opportunities. The gender gap is more difficult to explain. Austrian women are more Eurosceptic than men, yet the Eurosceptic FPÖ is significantly under-represented among female voters (Pelinka 1998, 36). Apparently the gender gap is not related to political preference.

In June 1994, the major divide which explained Euroscepticism was not the difference between left and right, but rather that between moderates and extremes, as well as that between the elite and the masses. However, after Austria's entry into the EU this situation changed, with Euro-optimism moving to the left. The Greens rather quickly became less Eurosceptic, and the difference between centrist (moderate) and non-centrist (extreme) party preferences ceased to define Euroscepticism. Within the party system, Euroscepticism became more and more a phenomenon of the right, with the FPÖ acquiring a monopoly. The Eurosceptic direction which the FPÖ took can be illustrated thus (Hummer and Pelinka 2002, 508–510):

---

[1] LIF: Liberal Forum – a party which broke away from the FPÖ in 1993. The LIF, which represented a strong pro-EU outlook, was in the Austrian parliament as an opposition party between 1993 and 1999. In 1999, the LIF failed to reach the 4 percent threshold of the Austrian electoral system.

1994: The Freedom Party officially asked its MPs to vote against the ratification of the treaty which the Austrian government had signed with the EU.

1997: The FPÖ published a new party platform which opposed the trend towards a federal ('deeper') EU.

1998: The FPÖ organised a popular initiative (*Volksbegehren*) against Austria's participation in Economic and Monetary Union (EMU).

1999: The FPÖ used the campaign before the general elections to underline its scepticism regarding EU enlargement.

The Greens had opposed Austrian EU membership for two reasons in particular: they feared for Austria's neutrality and they saw the EU as a decisive factor in the globalisation of the world's economy. In 1991, they had backed a popular initiative to force the government to hold a referendum on Austria's entry into the European Economic Area (Schaller 1994, 196-200). In 1994, most Greens declared their intention to vote 'No' in the EU accession referendum. But soon after, as the Greens were able to use the EU and especially the European Parliament as a platform, their attitude became visibly more pro-European.

The shift of Euro-optimism to the left and of Euroscepticism to the right can be explained by the different interests and attitudes of 'modernisation losers' and 'modernisation winners'. The FPÖ of the 1990s had become the party of a less educated, young, male, and blue collar electorate. The Greens, conversely, had largely drawn support from a better educated electorate since their entry into the party system in the 1980s (Pelinka 1998, 30-36; figure1). The Greens' move towards a more pro-European position may thus be understood in terms of their need to remain in step with the attitude of their younger and better educated voters, who could be placed (and who place themselves) among the 'modernisation winners'. The FPÖ, as the party of younger and less educated voters, reflects the anxieties of Austrians who have reason to be afraid of a Europe without borders.

Figure 1: Austrian parties and their supporters at the end of the 1990s.

| | | Age | |
		Young	Old
Education	High	Greens	ÖVP
	Low	FPÖ	SPÖ

The SPÖ and the ÖVP, jointly responsible for the direction Austrian politics took in 1989, did not waver in their pro-EU orientation (Pollak and Slominski 2002). The two mainstream parties were, however, separated on one major issue, to do with the implications of EU membership for Austria's neutral status. Austria had applied for EC membership in 1989 on the understanding that the country could and would join the European Community as a neutral state. The case of Ireland – until 1995 the only non-NATO country in the EU – provided a precedent for such a possibility (Luif 1995). Yet, when Austria joined the EU in 1995, it joined the EU of the Maastricht Treaty, i.e. a Union with a Common Foreign and Security Policy (CFSP). By accepting the CFSP, by becoming an observer in the West European Union (WEU), and by joining NATO's Partnership for Peace, Austria accepted that EU membership had some consequences for the international status of even a neutral country.

The ÖVP saw more changes on the horizon. The People's Party argued that in the long run Austria's neutrality would just disappear in the CFSP and that the CFSP cannot be seen separately from NATO. The SPÖ hesitated and – like the Greens, who became Euro-optimistic but were still very eager to defend Austria's neutrality – insisted on maintaining the 1989 formula of EU membership plus neutrality. This difference remained unresolved in the SPÖ-ÖVP coalition cabinet in the 1990s.

Although the two mainstream parties were divided by on the issue of neutrality, they were united in their views on the EU's 'Eastern Enlargement'. Shortly before Austria joined the EU, the European Council had decided at the 1993 Copenhagen Summit that the post-communist 'reform states' of Central and Eastern Europe would be welcome as EU members after fulfilling certain political and economic conditions (Baun 2000). The SPÖ and the ÖVP, despite some internal opposition (for instance by representatives of organised labour within the SPÖ), openly favoured this process of enlargement.

It was the FPÖ, speaking for the 'modernisation losers', which tried to block the enlargement process, while the Greens joined the SPÖ and ÖVP in supporting enlargement. Austrian public opinion was rather sceptical at the beginning of the negotiations with the EU candidates, which started during Austria's first presidency of the Council of Ministers in 1998. This scepticism, however, has weakened, while optimism about enlargement has grown (table 3).

Table 3: Attitudes in Austria concerning Eastern enlargement, 1998-2002. Public opinion polls, n = between 1,000 and 1,500.

	for	against	difference
Third Quarter 1998	43	52	-9
First Quarter 1999	51	46	+5
Second Quarter 1999	41	56	-15
Third Quarter 1999	45	51	-6
Fourth Quarter 1999	47	48	-1
First Quarter 2000	52	45	+7
Second Quarter 2000	53	42	+11
Third Quarter 2000	53	41	+12
Fourth Quarter 2000	50	45	+5
First Quarter 2001	50	44	+6
Second Quarter 2001	50	44	+6
Third Quarter 2001	49	46	+3
Fourth Quarter 2001	55	41	+14
First Quarter 2002	60	34	+26
Second Quarter 2002	53	43	+10

Source: Ulram 2002, 77.

The predominantly negative view concerning EU enlargement had been replaced by a predominantly positive view. But the general picture is not completely stabilsed. The majority in the Austrian case welcoming EU enlargement is volatile. Nevertheless, in this particularly sensitive field of the EU's development, Austrian Euroscepticism has been in retreat since the end of the 1990s.

The impact of the 'sanctions' of 2000

The coalition between the traditionally pro-European ÖVP and the FPÖ, which had been the only consistently Eurosceptic party in the Austrian parliament after 1994, resulted in a pro-enlargement majority. The FPÖ, which had opposed enlargement, signed a coalition agreement with the ÖVP in February 2000. In this agreement, the Freedom Party and its leader, Jörg Haider, accepted the position of the People's Party. In the declaration explaining the agenda of the new government, Haider and People's Party leader Wolfgang Schüssel stated that Austria's future lies in the 'deepening and in the widening of the Union' (Hummer and Pelinka 2002, 175). The FPÖ had officially exchanged its Eurosceptic position for the Euro-optimistic position of the ÖVP.

Due to the specific character of the right-wing Freedom Party and its entry into the Austrian government, the governments of the other EU members (hereafter the 'EU 14') declared a diplomatic boycott of the Austrian government as regards bilateral contacts outside of formal EU meetings. This boycott was lifted in September 2000 after a committee of 'Three Wise Men' had declared the measures justified and productive in the short run, but counterproductive in the long run (Hummer and Pelinka 2002, 388-420).

Many Austrians saw the boycott as 'sanctions' not only against the government, but against the whole country. Hence, the measures of the EU 14 could have had a negative impact on Austrian attitudes towards the EU. Such a backlash, however, was not visible. In March 2000, when the dispute regarding the 'sanctions' was especially vivid, a huge majority of Austrians said that joining the EU had been the right decision and that leaving the EU would be wrong (table 4).

Table 4: Public opinion in Austria, March 2000 (party affiliation). Public opinion poll, n = 998.

From today's perspective, was the Austrian decision to join the EU right or wrong?
right: 68%   wrong: 27%   do not know, no answer: 6%
Percentage of the answer 'right' among the voters of the following parties:
Greens: 79 %
ÖVP: 74 %
SPÖ: 71 %
Should Austria stay in the Union or leave it?
stay: 76%   leave: 19%   do not know, no answer: 5%
Percentage of the answer 'stay' among the voters of the following parties:
Greens: 88 %
ÖVP: 82 %
SPÖ: 78 %

Source: Hummer and Pelinka 2002, 350 ff.

The results of this poll were remarkable for two reasons. First, it under-lined that Green voters had completely followed the shift of their party from Euroscepticism to Euro-optimism. Second, it stressed that the traditionally Euro-optimistic ÖVP voters had not wavered in their atti-tude despite the conflict between the ÖVP-FPÖ coalition government and the EU 14. Although a huge majority (82%) of ÖVP followers de-clared themselves to be 'outraged' by the 'sanctions' (Hummer and Pelin-ka 2002, 353), this was not transformed into a negative view of the EU. This picture was confirmed in a poll three months later. This second poll also considered the special attitude of the FPÖ voters (table 5).

Table 5: Public opinion in Austria, June/July 2000. Public opinion poll, n = 1000.

Should Austria remain a member of the EU or leave?

	SPÖ	ÖVP	FPÖ	Greens	all voters
stay:	78%	76%	39%	93%	71%
leave:	17%	16%	53%	6%	22%
do not know, no answer:	6%	8%	7%	2%	7%

Source: Hummer and Pelinka 2002, 354.

The perception of the two governing parties' followers (that the sanctions were unjustified and an outrageous intervention into Austria's domestic affairs) did not shift the ÖVP ranks towards the FPÖ's Eurosceptic position. The FPÖ's strong criticism of the 'sanctions', which the EU 14 had taken and justified with reference to the 'right wing, xenophobic nature' of the FPÖ itself, fitted into the Freedom Party's more general Eurosceptic position (Hummer and Pelinka 2002, 184ff.). The ÖVP, however, seemed able to distinguish between a disapproval of the 'sanc-tions' and a still positive view of the EU in general.

The diplomatic boycott of the EU 14 did not change the general picture of the late 1990s. Three parties (the SPÖ, the ÖVP and the Greens) were Euro-optimistic, while one party (the FPÖ) was Euroscep-tic. The crisis between the Austrian government and the EU 14 did not create a split within the informal alliance of Euro-optimistic parties. The public opinion polls taken during the period of this crisis also suggested that younger Austrians, who had voted 'yes' in June 1994 to a lesser degree than older Austrians (see table 1), had become more Euro-optimistic. The gender difference, however, remained largely the same (table 6).

Table 6: Public opinion in Austria, March 2000 (social profile). Public opinion poll, n = 998.

From today's perspective, was the Austrian decision to join the EU right or wrong?	
	right
all Austrians	68%
men	76%
women	61%
age 24 or younger	76%
the higher educated	79%

Question: 'Should Austria stay in the Union or leave?'	
	stay
all Austrians	76%
men	83%
women	70%
age 24 or younger	80%
the higher educated	85%

Public opinion poll, n = 998

Source: Hummer and Pelinka 2002, 351.

The coalition between chancellor Wolfgang Schüssel (ÖVP) and vice chancellor Susanne Riess-Passer (FPÖ) was a coalition between two parties with contradictory attitudes towards the European Union. This contradiction did not change. Despite the outrage within the coalition about the boycott, the ÖVP stuck to its pro-European position, and, despite having signed a coalition agreement which favoured the enlargement process, significant sectors of the FPÖ did not follow this agenda. The result was the collapse of the coalition in September 2002. The Euro-optimistic attitude of the ÖVP and the Euroscepticism of the FPÖ were not reconciled. However, the elections of November 2002 weakened the FPÖ and strengthened the ÖVP. Consequently, the re-established ÖVP-FPÖ coalition did not block the enlargement procedures of 2003.

Contemporary Austrian Euroscepticism has a name: the FPÖ. The Freedom Party is against EU enlargement, against 'deepening' and against migration as a consequence of integration. It is sceptical with respect to the lifting of any kind of borders within the Union and seeks a more general rethinking of Austria's EU membership. The FPÖ gives voice to that segment of Austrian society most likely to hold Eurosceptic attitudes, reflecting the anxieties of those with lower levels of education.

Conclusion

Some aspects of Austrian Euroscepticism are more stable than others. Better educated Austrians will probably remain less Eurosceptic than their lesser educated compatriots. The fact that Euroscepticism is mainly a phenomenon of the Austrian right can change very easily, and must be considered one of the more flexible aspects of the present situation. Developments such as enlargement, the outcome of the deliberations of the European Convention, and the further implementation of the CFSP will continue to influence Austrian attitudes towards the EU.

Contemporary Austrian Euroscepticism reflects an anti-elitist and anti-centrist opposition from the right alone, and not, as was previously the case, from both the left and the right. Austria's EU membership was the result of the combined efforts of the moderate parties of the political centre. It was backed by the well-educated elite and it was initially opposed by the parties on the periphery of the political spectrum. This has now changed. At the beginning of the twenty-first century, Euro-optimism is still a quality of the centre and of the elite, but it has also become a quality of the left, represented not only by the SPÖ, but also by the Greens.

The present situation of Austrian Euroscepticism reflects the history of Austria's delayed entry into the EU and the experience of eight years of membership. It is the result of dynamic changes: the end of the East-West conflict; the functional decline of Austria's neutrality; a shift from the left to the right; and the measures of the EU 14 against the Schüssel and Riess-Passer government in 2000.

Austrian Euroscepticism is not unique. It has some specific roots and some specific qualities, but the general picture within the other member states is not so different (Büthe, Copelovitch and Phelan, 2002). In the near future, the most important factor shaping Austrian Euroscepticism will be enlargement. No other EU member will be affected as much as

Austria, because only Austria borders on four of the ten candidate states. Other factors, however, will also be important. The further development of the CFSP and the possible end of Austrian neutrality is likely to figure prominently in the national political debate. Any moves towards an increased redistributive role for the EU are also likely to be a source of concern for a 'net payer' such as Austria. Both the presence and the volatility of Austrian Euroscepticism thus appear set to continue in the future.

References

Baun, Michael J. 2000. *A Wider Europe: The Process and Politics of European Union Enlargement.* Lanham, MD: Rowman and Littlefield.

Bishof, Günter. 1999. *Austria in the First Cold War 1945-1955: The Leverage of the Weak.* Basingstoke: MacMillan.

Bischof, Günter and Anton Pelinka, eds. 1993. *Austria in the New Europe. Contemporary Austrian Studies*, vol.1. New Brunswick, NJ: Transaction Publishers.

Bischof, Günter, Anton Pelinka and Michael Gehler, eds. 2002. Austria in the European Union. *Contemporary Austrian Studies.* Vol. 10. New Brunswick, NJ: Transaction Publishers.

Büthe, Tim, Mark Copelovitch and William Phelan. 2002. The Domestic Politics of European Integration: Public Opinion, Referenda, and EU Membership. Paper prepared for presentation at the annual convention of the International Studies Association. New Orleans, 24-27 March.

Hummer, Waldemar and Michael Schweitzer. 1987. *Österreich und die EWG. Neutralitätsrechtliche Beurteilung der Möglichkeit der Dynamisierung des Verhältnisses zur EWG.* Vienna: Signum.

Hummer Waldemar and Anton Pelinka. 2002. *Österreich unter 'EU-Quarantäne'. Die 'Maßnahmen der 14' gegen die österreichische Bundesregierung aus politikwissenschaftlicher und juristischer Sicht. Chronologie, Kommentar, Dokumentation.* Vienna: Linde Verlag.

Luif, Paul. 1994. Die Integrationspolitik der europäischen Neutralen. In *Ausweg EG? Innenpolitische Motive einer außenpolitischen Umorientierung*, eds. Anton Pelinka, Christian Schaller and Paul Luif, 271-305. Vienna: Böhlau.

Luif, Paul. 1995. *On the Road to Brussels: The Political Dimension of Austria's, Finland's, and Sweden's Accession to the European Union.* Vienna: Braumüller.

Neisser, Heinrich and Sonja Puntscher Riekmann, eds. 2002. *Europäisierung der österreichischen Politik? Konsequenzen des EU-Mitgliedschaft.* Vienna: WUV Universitätsverlag.

van Oudenaren, John. 2000. *Uniting Europe: European Integration and the Post Cold War World.* Lanham, MD: Rowman and Littlefield.

Pelinka, Anton, ed. 1994. *EU-Referendum. Zur Praxis direkter Demokratie in Öster-reich.* Vienna: Signum.

Pelinka, Anton. 1998. *Austria: Out of the Shadow of the Past.* Boulder, CO: Lynne Rienner.

Pelinka, Anton, Christian Schaller, and Paul Luif, eds. 1994. *Ausweg EG? Innenpolitische Motive einer außenpolitischen Umorientierung.* Vienna: Böhlau.

Plasser, Fritz and Peter A. Ulram 1994. Meinungstrends, Mobilisierung und Motivenlage bei der Volksabstimmung über den EU-Beitritt. In *EU-Referen-dum. Zur Praxis direkter Demokratie in Österreich,* ed. Anton Pelinka, 87-119. Vienna: Signum.

Plasser, Fritz, Peter A. Ulram and Franz Summer, eds. 2000. *Das österreichische Wahlverhalten.* Vienna: Signum.

Pollak, Johannes and Peter Slominski. 2002. Die österreichischen Parteien und die europäische Integration: Stillstand oder Aufbruch? In *Europäisierung der österreichischen Politik? Konsequenzen des EU-Mitgliedschaft,* eds. Heinrich Neisser and Sonja Puntscher Riekmann, 177-200. Vienna: WUV Universitätsverlag.

Schaller, Christian. 1994. Die innenpolitische EG-Diskussion seit den 80er Jahren. In *Ausweg EG? Innenpolitische Motive einer außenpolitischen Umorientierung,* Anton Pelinka, Christian Schaller, and Paul Luif, eds., 27-269. Vienna: Böhlau.

Schlesinger, Thomas O. 1972. *Austrian Neutrality in Postwar Europe: The Domestic Roots of a Foreign Policy.* Vienna: Braumüller.

Schneider, Heinrich. 1990. *Alleingang nach Brüssel. Österreichs EG-Politik.* Bonn: Instituts für Europäische Politik.

Stourzh, Gerald. 1998. *Um Einheit und Freiheit. Staatsvertrag, Neutralität und das Ende der Ost-West-Besetzung Österreichs, 1945-1955.* Vienna: Böhlau.

Ulram, Peter A. 2002. Einstellung der Österreicher zur EU. In *Europäisierung der österreichischen Politik? Konsequenzen des EU-Mitgliedschaft,* eds. Heinrich Neisser and Sonja Puntscher Riekmann, 81-100. Vienna: WUV Universitätsverlag.

EUROPEAN STUDIES 20 (2004): 225-245

AN AWKWARD NEWCOMER?
EU ENLARGEMENT AND EUROSCEPTICISM
IN THE CZECH REPUBLIC

Petr Kopecký

Abstract

This article analyses opposition to Europe in the Czech Republic, both on the mass and the elite level. It offers a precise definition of Euroscepticism, based on the distinction between diffuse and specific support for European integration, and considers how the exigencies of the EU enlargement process may fuel anti-EU stances. On the basis of an analysis of both mass attitudes and party political stances, the article argues that a major anti-EU mobilisation is unlikely in the Czech Republic, regardless of the relatively strong undercurrent of Euroscepticism that now exists in the country. However, current expressions of Euroscepticism should be understood as potentially defining characteristics of Czech (elite) attitudes in the soon to be enlarged EU.

Now well into the second decade of post-Communism, the Czech Republic is on the verge of joining the European Union (EU). Gaining full EU membership will mean achievement of the highest foreign policy goal of all successive Czech governments since the fall of Communism in 1989. Already in 1990, the Czechoslovak government signed a treaty dealing with mutual trade and economic relations between Brussels and the then federal state. In 1993, the newly established Czech Republic first re-negotiated and then signed the association treaty with the EU, which had been prepared by the previous Czechoslovak federal authorities. Finally, the Czech government, under the leadership of Prime Minister Václav Klaus, officially applied for full EU membership in 1996. The successful completion of entry negotiations, which started in 1998, was

achieved at the December 2002 Copenhagen Summit, with full membership in prospect for May 2004.

The issue of European integration in general, and the country's EU
membership in particular, had very little salience in Czech political discourse in the first half of the 1990s. Until then, it was subject to a positive, if only romantic and illusory, consensus among the political elites
and the public alike to become part of Europe. The 1989 regime changes
in Central Europe were commonly interpreted by the vast majority of
domestic political actors as a 'return to normality', which meant a 'return
to Europe' (Kumar 1992; Pontes Resende and Tanasoiu 2001). There was
an expectation of the return of the post-Communist countries to the
family of liberal democracies. EU membership was perceived as a logical
consequence of this 'return to normality'. Moreover, enlargement was
seen by many as automatic – a technical process rather than a political
problem – and a matter of time. Indeed, it was the question of NATO
membership that proved politically more divisive at that time than the
question of European integration.

The country's Euro political debate has nevertheless evolved, perhaps
inevitably, together with both the daunting reality of complicated and
long-drawn enlargement negotiations, and of course the approaching date
of entry. The abstract and broad geopolitical terms in which the consensus on European integration was initially gauged have been replaced by
more nuanced, concrete and, most importantly, somewhat more salient
debate about what EU membership actually entails, what its potential
costs and benefits are, and what Europe the Czech Republic would like
to join. Indeed, the 2002 general elections witnessed a first attempt by a
major political party to make European integration and EU membership
a key campaign issue. This, moreover, finds its place in a country that has
for some time now been known as (allegedly) one of the most 'Eurosceptic' in the post-Communist region.

This article analyses opposition to Europe in the Czech Republic,
both on the mass and the elite level. The first section provides a contex-
tual background by looking into how the exigencies of the enlargement
process may fuel opposition to European integration in the candidate
countries. The second section looks in more detail at how opposition to
Europe can actually be conceptualised and offers the definition of
Euroscepticism that guides the subsequent analysis of (elite) attitudes in
the Czech Republic. Mass support of EU membership is analysed in the
third section, while the fourth section offers an analysis of elite attitudes
to European integration, specifically looking at stances of major political

parties. EU membership retains broad support in the Czech Republic, regardless of the relatively strong undercurrent of Euroscepticism that now exists in the country. However, current expressions of Euroscepticism should be understood as potentially defining characteristics of Czech (elite) attitudes in the soon-to-be enlarged EU.

Exigencies of enlargement

Before we can proceed with the analysis of attitudes towards European integration in the Czech Republic, several comments are necessary to understand the context in which these attitudes are formed. Domestic political context – be it the dynamics of a government/opposition divide, constituency interests, the strength of extremist parties or parties' electoral strategies – is crucial to our understanding of Euroscepticism (see Taggart 1998; Taggart and Sczcerbiak 2001; Sitter 2001; Batory 2002). In other words, the issue of European integration is rarely just an international issue, uncoupled from both present-day domestic politics and the broader historical context of national political cultures.

Indeed, the way European integration was perceived in the Czech Republic and elsewhere in Central Europe in the early 1990s, after the fall of Communism, is a good example of the cultural framing of European integration related to the experience of the immediate past. As indicated above, Europe, then, had a strong normative meaning. For most, especially from the anti-Communist opposition, it was an embodiment of the good; Europe and the EU were perceived as the bastion of democracy and civil liberties, and as the place of existence of modern affluent societies. Becoming part of the EU thus became an important political statement, because it encapsulated a burning desire to disassociate the country from the evil Communist system, allegedly rooted in eastern civilization. It also meant, specifically in the Czech Republic, a radical rejection of the Communist past as an experiment that had plunged the country into a morass of underdevelopment, which would never have happened had it not been for the external imposition of a Soviet-style socialist system.

As we shall also see later, some of the present-day anxieties and ideological positions on European integration also strongly relate to the so-called 'German question', which represents something of an evergreen in any debate on Czech national identity and Czechs' place in Europe. Indeed, the so-called Beneš decrees – a set of laws passed by the Czechoslovak government after World War II, which ordered the expulsions of the (large) German and (smaller) Hungarian minorities and the confiscation of their property – emerged as a focal point for these debates in the post-Communist period. However, of equal importance to the dynamics of Euroscepticism, in the candidate countries in general and in the Czech Republic in particular, is the nature of the enlargement process itself. There are several issues to mention in this respect.

Firstly, as Karen Henderson (2002) reminds us, it is important to realise that the Czech Republic's experience of the EU, like that of its other counterparts in the post-Communist region, has not been that of a member state. This has had potentially significant repercussions for the formulation of positions towards European integration, because the overarching aim of attaining membership may have muted, at least temporarily, any potential ideological critique of the process, or it may have softened positions on several controversial policy issues that formed part of the enlargement negotiations. The EU has enjoyed, in this sense, a strategically strong position vis-à-vis those attempting to gain membership, especially given the comparatively lower levels of economic performance which characterise the candidate states. One other consequence of this strategic situation is that it may occasionally be difficult to distinguish between what is a genuine opposition to (certain aspects of) European integration and what has been merely an irritation with the exigencies of the enlargement process, because of the temptation for political actors in the candidate countries to see the reality of the EU through the reality of EU enlargement.

This has been exacerbated by the practical nature of association negotiations as conducted between the EU and the aspirant states. From the very start, the EU used various forms of conditionality to influence the processes of political and economic change in the aspirant countries, specifying the obligations that candidate states must fulfill, and the laws they must adopt, as prior conditions of membership. In June 1993, these conditions were laid down for the first time by the Copenhagen European Council and, in due course, candidate states have been required to adopt the full *acquis communautaire*.

The extensive size of the *acquis* – currently standing at some 9,000 pieces of legislation – is of course in itself a test case of resolve for any proponent of European integration in the candidate countries. It is also a convenient source of inspiration for those opposing the EU on the grounds that it introduces a set of meaningless and extensive directives resembling the bureaucratic system under the Communist regime. Moreover, the vast amount of legislation represented by the current *acquis* must be reconciled with the relatively low institutional capacity of candidate states to transpose them into their legal system. One way of coping with the need to absorb the *acquis* by the candidate countries has been to introduce fast-track legislative procedures. On the one hand, these procedures allow post-Communist governments to treat EU-related laws speedily, as a legislative priority. However, on the other hand, they also frequently fuel the critique of the EU as the procedures both distort the deliberative process that is expected of parliamentary debates and undermine the creation of indigenous norms and procedures of governance.

This brings us to the final point, namely that the current enlargement process does not just represent an adjustment to a relatively limited set of rules, as was arguably the case of previous enlargements both in Southern Europe and, more recently, in Scandinavia. Rather, from the view point of current candidate countries, it is something of an adoption of a complete system. As Heather Grabbe (2001) argues, EU impact on the development of governance in Central and Eastern Europe extends well beyond the competencies in the existing member states. She hereby correctly implies that the tight conditionality applied to the candidate countries goes beyond merely ensuring that EU norms, procedures and institutions are transplanted to the post-Communist world. Nowhere has this been more apparent than in the so-called Progress Reports. These reports, issued yearly by the European Commission since 1997, not only assess the progress of candidate countries in adopting the extensive *acquis*, but also address many other political issues, for example the treatment of minorities, which the EU would hardly address in relation to the existing EU member states.

Under such pressing conditions, and considering the strong perception in Eastern Europe of the unequal position between the two bargaining sides, the resentment towards the EU can find a strong breeding ground. This is especially true if we also realise that the aspirant states from post-Communist Europe have just liberated themselves from the yoke of a hegemonic system. Arguably, anti-Communist revolutions were as much about national independence from the Soviet Union as they were about democracy. In addition, the suppression of national specificities in the name of internationalism and working class solidarity has led everywhere in the region to the search for a national identity after the breakdown of Communism. These projects of nation-building have obviously been applied with various degrees of urgency and with different political consequences across Eastern Europe. The region as a whole nonetheless represents a fertile ground for political forces that might exploit national awakening and pursue anti-integration rhetoric.

To be sure, EU pressures for large scale reforms have had a positive impact on Eastern Europe, much as EU conditionality aided the consolidation of new democracies on the Iberian peninsula in the late 1970s. Indeed, given the generally positive mass attitudes towards EU membership in the candidate states, Eastern European governments have often skillfully introduced painful reforms or controversial policy measures arguing they are inevitable if the country wants to join the rich club. However, doing the precise opposite is a perfectly possible scenario, especially for opposition parties, who can blame the EU for everything that is going wrong in the reform process.

What is Euroscepticsm?

The above has given us some indication as to how to understand potential opposition to European integration in the EU candidate states of Eastern Europe. The sensitivity to the political context of enlargement should of course not imply that the phenomenon of Euroscepticism cannot be meaningfully compared across national boundaries. Rather, it means that any explanatory or analytical framework must rely on a precise definition of what actually constitutes opposition to Europe in general, and Euroscepticism in particular. Indeed, academic studies and the popular political discourse concerning European integration have been plagued by a whole range of terms used to capture opposition to these processes. 'Euroscepticism' has been the most frequently used term in this respect, but alternative and complementary terms, such as Eurorealism, Europragmatism or Europhobia, are commonplace as well.

I follow in this analysis the definition of Euroscepticism elaborated in earlier collaborative work (see Kopecký and Mudde 2002; for alternative definitions see Taggart 1998; Taggart and Szczerbiak 2001), in which we provided a two-dimensional conceptual map for the study of various party positions on the question of European integration. We distinguished between diffuse and specific support for European integration. By *diffuse* support we meant support for the general *ideas* of European integration that underlie the EU; i.e. institutionalised co-operation on the basis of pooled sovereignty (the political element) and an integrated liberal market economy (the economic element). By *specific* support we denoted support for the general *practice* of European integration; i.e. the EU as it is (developing).

We then specifically defined *Eurosceptics* as those parties and groups who support general ideas of European integration underlying the EU, but are sceptical about the EU as a system that best reflects these ideas, or as a system that is developing in the direction that best embodies these ideas. In contrast, we also identified: a) *Euroenthusiasts*, as parties or groups that support the general ideas of European integration and also believe that the EU is/will soon become the institutionalisation of these ideas; b) *Eurorejects*, who ascribe to neither the ideas underlying the process of European integration nor the EU and c) *Europragmatists*, who do not support the general ideas of European integration underlying the EU, nor do they necessarily oppose them, yet they do (often for purely pragmatic reasons) support the EU.

Figure 1: Typology of party positions on Europe

SUPPORT FOR EUROPEAN INTEGRATION

		Europhile	Europhobe
S U P P O R T	EU-optimist	Euro-enthusiasts	Euro-pragmatists
F O R E U	EU-pessimist	Eurosceptics	Eurorejects

Source: Kopecký and Mudde 2002

Several caveats are necessary at this point to clarify the definition of Euroscepticism that will be used in the subsequent analysis. Firstly, not all Eurosceptics will necessarily object to EU membership. This is a particularly important point with respect to the candidate countries, where the decision on EU membership is yet to be taken. Rather than rejecting membership, some Eurosceptic parties or groups will simply consider the current EU to be a serious deviation of (their interpretation of) the founding ideas of European integration. However, as they do support these ideas, they might hope to change the EU in such a way that it becomes a more true reflection of them.

Secondly, not all who express some criticism of either the EU or certain policies of the EU will qualify as Eurosceptics. Indeed, given the now extensive influence of EU over many elements of the political, economic and social policies of both member and candidate member states, conceivably all parties, including the most Euroenthusiastic formations, will have been critical about some aspect of the EU. However, as soon as such parties or individuals accept the current EU overall, they should not be considered as Eurosceptics.

Finally, it is important to emphasise that Euroscepticism can take different forms and shapes, following from different visions of European integration and different interpretations of the EU. Euroscepticism should therefore not be defined in rigid terms. However, I concur with Tiersky (2001, 3) that all Eurosceptics are essentially in favour of European integration: 'Euro-skeptics are not against what they see as realistic advantageous cooperation among various groups of European states for greater peace and prosperity'.

Public opinion

Czech public opinion has been showing weaker levels of support for EU membership than many other candidate states. In aggregate form, the majority of Czechs have consistently been of the opinion that the country should attempt to join the EU. Yet, asked how they would vote in a referendum on EU membership (if held tomorrow), which is a standard question used by polling agencies surveying mass opinion towards the EU, the attitudes of Czechs appear slightly more lukewarm: for example, only 40% would have voted in favour in April 2002.[1] Long-term data suggest that the pro-vote hovers above 50%, with between 15% and 20% of Czechs indicating opposition to membership, and about 30% undecided.[2]

Surveys by various local polling agencies point to a number of characteristics in public attitudes towards the EU. Firstly, there is a certain level

---

[1] See the research by the Centre for Public Opinion Research (CVVM) published at: http://ihned.cz (May 2002).

[2] See research/data by CEORG (2000), Česal (2002), STEM (www.stem.cz), Sofres-Factum (www.tnsofres.cz), IVVM (www.ivvm.cz) and *Eurobarometer* (http://europa.eu.int/comm/public_opinion/).

of unease with the EU. For example, the Czechs do not strongly believe the EU is interested in admitting the country as a new member. According to CVVM research, 40% do believe so, while around the same number of respondents said they believed the opposite and 17% could not answer. In addition, the number of those who see the mutual relationships between the EU and the Czech Republic as negative has been increasing over the years as well (see Česal 2002).

Secondly, European integration remains rather low down on the list of problems troubling Czechs. According to research by STEM, almost 50% consider EU entry a marginal issue. Similar research by CVVM shows that 35% are interested in the Czech preparations to join the EU, while 39% have little interest in them, and 25% do not care about them at all. On both accounts, there appears to be a correlation between both the level of education and political affinity and interest in membership, with the higher educated and supporters of right-wing parties more interested and concerned than people with lower education and a left-wing orientation. Interestingly, a similar pattern typifies support for EU membership, with younger, higher educated and right-wing supporters in favour of EU membership and speedy accession, while the opposite attitudes are more prevalent among left-wing sympathisers, pensioners and those with lower education.

Thirdly, EU membership is not expected to bring any major benefits. For example, according to CVVM, the Czechs think that EU entry would bring more advantages than disadvantages to state officials. On the other hand, many Czechs think it would cause more complications for private businesses, industry and farmers. The most frequent answer on the likely benefits of EU is nevertheless that it would not bring about any change. However, certain patterns emerge also in this aspect of public opinion. Entrepreneurs and higher earners see more advantages than disadvantages in joining the EU, while workers and, increasingly, also farmers, belong to the opposite category (see Franzen 2002).

Overall, there seems to be an agreement among observers that public attitudes towards the EU continue to be positive, but shallow (see Hartl 2000). They reflect a general symbolic pro-western orientation, but are little rooted in a deeper understanding of the pros and cons of EU membership. However, there is also an agreement that a more structural discontent has developed in some social groups, like farmers, in light of the progress and results of the entry negotiations. Furthermore, public opinion with respect to EU membership has been subject to short-term swings in the popular mood. For example, support for EU membership decreased when, in late 1998, the Czech government fought with the EU over the export quotas for agricultural commodities. A similar situation occurred at the beginning of 2002, when the issue of the Beneš decrees was (again) hotly contested by (some of) the EU members and the Czech political elite.[3]

This does not, however, suggest scope for a major anti-EU mobilisation from within civil society. Even farmers' organisations remain rather weak in terms of their mobilising potential,[4] while public anti-EU activities have so far been confined only to minor (usually extreme right) fringe groups. However, there is scope for political party mobilisation, because it is parties that have virtually monopolised the sphere of representation in the country. In other words, if any mobilisation in the Czech Republic is to carry weight, it must involve major political parties.

It is therefore of utmost importance to locate the support for EU membership among the supporters of political parties. Here the picture corresponds with the aggregate data presented above. According to long-term trends (see Mišovič 2000), the supporters of right of centre parties – the Civic Democratic Party (ODS) and the Freedom Union (US) –remain in the large majority supportive of EU membership (above 75% in both cases). Around 60% of voters of the centrist Christian Democratic Union – Czech People's Party (KDU-ČSL), which has a strong constituency in rural areas, also support membership, but there is also a large group of about 30% undecided. The supporters of left of centre parties, however, appear more sceptical: support for the EU hovers around 50% in the case of the Czech Social Democratic Party's (ČSSD) electorate, with a sizable

---

[3] In January 2002, the (sudden and inexplicable) comments by then Prime Minister Miloš Zeman, who described the Sudeten Germans as 'traitors' with whom no reconciliation was possible, led to strong reactions from Austrian and German politicians, as well as from the then Hungarian Prime Minister Viktor Orbán. In the subsequent political exchanges, the issue of the Beneš Decrees became linked with Czech EU accession and, in April 2002, the ODS and KSČM proposed a parliamentary resolution asserting that the Decrees were an inalienable part of Czech law. The resolution was passed unanimously in the parliament.

[4] The farmers organised several rallies in Prague in December 2002, among other things, protesting against the deal offered by the EU as part of the enlargement negotitations. However, the protest showed that a) the farmers are divided on the issue; b) the protest was as much against the EU as it was against the agricultural polices of the Czech government; and c) while the public sympathises with the farmer's demands, it does not consider their grievances sufficient reason to reject EU membership.

group of some 20% of their supporters against membership. A clear Eurosceptic, or even Euroreject, electorate typifies the Communist Party of Bohemia and Moravia (KSČM), where about 60% of supporters oppose membership, while only about 20% back accession.

Political (party) elites

The Czech Republic has always had a strong pro-integration and pro-European representation in the parliament.[5] This has, most notably, included the KDU-ČSL, Civic Democratic Alliance (ODA), the US, as well as the ČSSD; all Euroenthusiast parties which have had experience with government. The ČSSD, KDU-ČSL and US have formed the government following the 2002 elections; the ČSSD governed alone in a minority government between 1998 and 2002; the KDU-ČSL and ODA governed with the ODS (see below) between 1992 and 1996, and between 1996 and 1997; the former was also involved in the caretaker government between 1997 and 1998. Taken together, as Figure 2 shows, these parties polled 40.88% of the votes and controlled 92 seats (out of 200) in (the lower chamber) of parliament after the 1996 elections; 49.91% of votes and 113 seats after the 1998 elections; and 44.97% of votes and 101 seats after the 2002 elections.[6]

To be sure, the Euroenthusiasm of these parties stems from slightly different ideological standpoints. The ČSSD supports the ideas of the Socialist International and sees the EU as a venue for the advancement of the modern social democratic project, i.e. a federalist Europe with a social market economy. The KDU-ČSL is an associated member of the European People's Party and, in foreign policy at least, has adopted many (pro-integration) ideas from the German CDU (see Chalupa 2001). Like the liberal US, the party supports the idea of a federalist Europe, though both parties are also seemingly determined to formulate and defend interests of smaller EU member states. It is important, however, that on the domestic political scene all three parties have always argued for EU

---

[5] Beyond the parliament, former President Václav Havel has also been a strong supporter of the EU and European integration, arguing for a federal Europe, with a bicameral parliament and a ('short and clear', 'symbolic') EU constitution, much along the lines of, for example, the proposal of German Foreign Minister Joschka Fischer.

[6] It is important to note that the data in Figure 2 are only an indication of the electoral and parliamentary strength of different Czech political parties. I do not claim here that the electoral results are related to these parties' positions on European integration/enlargement.

membership and for European integration and presented them not only as the country's strategic necessity, but also as something that is compatible with the cultural and normative orientation of the Czech people.

Figure 2: Classification of main Czech political parties by position on Europe and their (combined) electoral and parliamentary strength (votes and seats*)

SUPPORT FOR EUROPEAN INTEGRATION

		Europhile	Europhobe
	EU-optimist	Euro-enthusiasts CSSD, KDU-ČSL, ODA, US 2002: 44.97% (101) 1998: 49.91% (113) 1996: 40.88% (92)	Euro-pragmatists
	EU-pessimist	Eurosceptics ODS 2002: 24.47% (58) 1998: 27.74% (63) 1996: 29.62% (68)	Eurorejects KSČM**, SPR-RSČ (RMS) 2002: 19.48% (41) 1998: 13.93% (24) 1996: 18.34% (40)

S U P P O R T — F O R — E U (vertical label at left)

*   Seats for lower chamber only; n=200
** This party is difficult to classify, as it hovers between two types

Nevertheless, the Czech parliament has also housed a significant Euroreject and Eurosceptic segment of the political elite (see Figure 2). This included the extreme right Association for the Republic-Republican Party of Czechoslovakia (SPR-RSČ), the Communists from KSČM, and the largest right of centre party, the ODS. The former two parties have never been involved in government and both remain pariahs of the party system in which they operate, though KSČM is far from marginal in the parliament. The ODS was involved, as the largest party, in two coalition governments between 1992 and 1997; it also acted as an external support party for the ČSSD government between 1998 and 2002. Taken together, these parties polled 47.96% of votes and controlled 108 seats after the 1996 elections; 42.67% of votes and 87 seats after the 1998 elections; and 43.95% of votes and 99 seats after the 2002 elections.

Of the three parties, the SPR-RSČ are clearly the least stable political formation. In fact, the party split several times and finally went bankrupt in 2000. It contested the 2002 elections under a different name, the Republicans of Miroslav Sládek (RMS), but polled far less than 1% of the vote. Until the mid-1990s, however, the SPR-RSČ were the most clear, if rather inconsistent, example of a Euroreject party in the Czech Republic. Owing to its nationalist and fierce anti-German stands, the 'Republicans' rejected the founding ideas of European integration, and were clearly anti-EU. When the party was in parliament (1992-1998), its critique of the EU focused mainly on the alleged sell-outs of Czech industry and property to Western (read: German) companies. It claimed that these 'sell-outs' were embraced by the 'traitorous' Czech elite, and by the EU's integration policies, and that they were designed to reinforce the domination of the Czech Republic by the interests of 'multinational capital'.

Since 1998, the KSČM – considered domestically as a left extremist and anti-system party – has become the sole flag-bearer of the Euroreject cause in the Czech parliament. However, the party is very difficult to classify as it hovers between a Euroreject and a Europragmatic position. On the one hand, various documents published on the party website (see www.kscm.cz), as well as the party programmes from 1996 and 1998, suggest that the KSČM is not only highly ambiguous about EU membership, but also that its criticism of European integration bears all the hallmarks of a Euroreject party. The Communists associate the current process of European integration with exploitative multinational capitalism, with the dictatorship of the large countries over the small ones, and with the domination of bureaucracy. The accession process itself is seen as dominated by, and protective of, (German) economic interests, at the expense of the welfare of candidate countries. It can therefore be said that KSČM rejects both the economic and political foundations underlying European integration and the EU itself, thus belonging to the group of Euroreject parties.

On the other hand, the party has not categorically ruled out EU membership. This may stem from an ideological schism in the Communists' feelings towards European integration: whether to see it as a (positive) realisation of internationalism, or as a (negative) product of imperialism (Mareš 2000). Most importantly, it also derives from the division that exists between (and also within) the party leadership and the party membership (see Hanley 2001). Many leaders are either keen to accept EU membership (a sort of Europragmatic position), mainly in order to gain broader acceptance within the domestic and international political establishment, or are actually Euroenthusiastic, in a similarly ideologically oriented way as are the Social Democrats. However, as we have seen above, the members appear much truer to the party's declared ideological (op)position and, in majority, oppose EU membership. Indeed, the intra-party tensions were demonstrated in the aftermath of the 2002 elections, in which the KSČM polled its highest share of 18.51% of votes in the post-Communist period, when several leaders of regional party branches sharply criticised two party vice-chairmen over their declared support for EU membership. In the ensuing conflict, the party executive eventually decided to back the two vice-chairmen.

However, it is interesting to note that the Communists' 2002 electoral programme was far less critical of the EU as such, instead focusing on specifying conditions under which the Czech Republic should join. This indicates, firstly, that accession is now seen as (accepted) reality by the party (leadership). The focus is now on getting the best deal for the country from the accession negotiations and, consequently, on heavily criticising (all) governments and other parties for not doing so. Secondly, together with the increasing frequency of (light) pro-integration speeches by the party leadership, it is also indicates that the party bosses are finally willing to lead an intra-party campaign that might eventually mute the opposition to European integration among both the party members and, possibly, also the party voters. Interestingly, a similar campaign within the ČSSD, conducted after the 1998 elections, resulted in a wider acceptance of the EU and EU membership among the party membership.

The largest right of centre party, the ODS, is therefore the only unambiguously Eurosceptic party in the Czech Republic. In the context of the region, it is perhaps also the most outspoken and consistent Eurosceptic formation. Indeed, Václav Klaus, the party's former long-serving leader, has for long been known as the most vocal critic of EU-related matters not only in the country, but also in the region as a whole. The ODS's Euroscepticism is two-fold. On the one hand, the party displays a strong pro-European orientation in a cultural and historical sense in that it considers the Czech Republic to belong to the sphere of Western (European) values. Moreover, the ODS and its leader have been consistently in favour of EU membership, and they accept a certain loss of national sovereignty resulting from the process of accession. Indeed, it was during the ODS-led coalition government that the Czech Republic officially applied for EU membership.

On the other hand, the ODS sees the project of European integration primarily as a means to enlarge markets and to further deepen *economic* co-operation. Therefore, the party is deeply unimpressed by the post-Maastricht direction of EU development. It has criticised many aspects of the current EU from standpoints similar to like-minded parties in Western Europe, most notably the British Conservative Party (see further Hanley 2002). The EU bureaucracy, perceived as vast and unaccountable, is at the centre of its critique. Other bones of contention are the allegedly excessive EU regulations, as well as the overly welfarist dimension of EU policies. Enhanced political integration and trends towards supranationalism or federalism are not welcomed by the ODS either (see Klaus 1997; 2000). The party supports the intergovernmentalist vision of European integration, advocating limiting the powers of both the European Parliament and the European Commission, and the strengthening of the European Council.

The ODS's position on European integration has been consistent over years. However, it has become far more articulated in the late 1990s, after the party went into opposition. Perhaps most importantly, the Eurosceptic critique of the EU is no longer confined to the speeches and proclamations of Klaus, but has also been taken up by a significant group of (younger) ODS politicians, who became more powerful within the party following both its split in 1997, and the 1998 elections. Indeed, the most extensive internal party document dealing with the question of European integration, the so-called *Manifesto of Czech Eurorealism*[7] (see www.ods.cz), has been drafted by a commission under the guidance of party vice-chairman and foreign policy spokesmen, Jan Zahradil. In addition, the party's Euroscepticism has also seemingly radicalised, at least in that the rhetoric of defending 'Czech national interests' against a 'self-interested EU', and of defending 'natural entities' like nation-states against 'empty Europeanism', has enriched what was previously almost

---

[7] Interestingly, the ODS prefers to refer to its position as 'Eurorealist'. As Karen Henderson (2002, 14) argues, it suggests that it embodies the one, real truth, rather than some vague doubts, about EU integration. It is also stems from the fact that, in Czech political discourse, the term 'Eurosceptic' is usually used to depict those who are against EU membership. We have seen that the ODS is, despite its reservations towards the EU, committed to Czech EU membership.

solely a critique of the post-Maastricht EU developments from a neo-liberal perspective (associated with Klaus).

Sean Hanley (2002) has argued that such radicalisation should be seen as a response to the party's ideological and organisational crisis, whereby radical Euroscepticism represents an attempt at the party's programmatic renewal and the creation of a unifying ideological outlook. However, it should also possibly be seen in the context of both the changed position of the Czech Republic on the European (and international) scene, and the reality of accession negotiations. The ODS's initial Euroscepticism was predicated on a feeling of Czech superiority towards both the EU and the other Central European states; a feeling that was partly fed by the western perception of the Czech Republic as a model case of post-Communist transformation.[8] This sort of optimism had evaporated in 1996, however, after the fall of Klaus's second government and the realisation that the Czech 'miracle' economy carried far more problems than was generally seen to be the case. Concurrently came the detailed and sharply critical annual evaluations by the EU Commission, as well as hard negotiations over such matters as the size of EU subsidies for applicant states' farmers. At this time the ODS's Euroscepticism became more defensive which, in turn, partly explains the more prominent place assumed by a rhetoric of national interests in the party's position on European integration. In addition, the 'defence of national interests' as defined by the ODS most often refers to the defense of the (economic) interests of the state (in negotiations with other states), rather than to the promotion of distinct ethnic, national or cultural traits. In that, the rhetoric does not differ much from the vocabulary used especially in the Anglo-Saxon world and, in that sense, also does not represent any dramatic radicalisation of the ODS's position.

In any case, it is important to realise that the ODS's attempts to make European integration one of the key themes of its 2002 electoral campaign did not reap any noticeable benefits. Not only did the party obtain its lowest share of votes ever (24.47%), but the economic and social issues, long dominant in structuring the patterns of competition in the Czech party system (e.g. Vlachová 1997; 1999), proved to be far more

---

[8] A good example here is a heated exchange at the meeting of the World Economic Forum in Davos in 1995, where the then EU commissioner Hans van den Broek insisted that the Central European candidates should adapt their agricultural sectors to EU standards and was rebuffed by Klaus, who said that if anything needed to be changed, it was the agricultural policies of the EU.

decisive to the outcomes of elections than the issue of European integration. In this context, it is also important to repeat that the ODS's voters, though possibly not its local politicians (see Perron 2000), are the most enthusiastic supporters of EU membership among the Czech electorate.

Conclusion

The Czech Republic has often been marked out, amongst EU candidate states, for its relatively high level of Euroscepticism. Yet, these reservations have not acted as a brake on the country's move towards EU accession. Public support for EU membership remains relatively high. The Czech Republic, moreover, now has the most pro-European, in fact Euroenthusiastic, coalition government in its post-Communist history, committed to making a success of accession, of course under the patronage of the parties that form the government. There are no anti-EU groups in civil society strong enough to trigger an anti-EU mobilisation. In addition, the two Eurosceptic (Euroreject) political parties – the ODS and the KSČM – are, for ideological and strategic reasons, unlikely to co-operate in a concerted fashion. Czech Euroscepticism does, however, continue to pose the question of what kind of new EU member the country will become. Careful analysis suggests that, to borrow from Stephen George (1994), the country might easily become an 'awkward partner'. There are several reasons for this. First, regardless of its changing nature, the ODS's Euroscepticism has been an integral part of the party identity and, like the party itself, is unlikely to go away. Secondly, the current Euroenthusiastic block is far from uncritical about the EU; in fact, much of its open Euroenthusiasm, especially in the case of both KDU-ČSL and US, relates to strategic attempts to create a sense of difference with their main electoral opponent, the Eurosceptic ODS. What will therefore happen with the Euroenthusiastic bloc after the accession, once the strategic constraints of entry negotiations are lifted, is very much an open question.

To be sure, the real impact of the awkwardness of any EU state depends to a large extent on the weight the country has within the EU institutions. In that, the Czech Republic certainly does not carry the same potential as large countries like Britain. However, the Czech Eurosceptic parties already anticipate entering alliances within the EU to reform it along their preferred lines: the ODS desires co-operation with the (probably Eurosceptic) forces in the UK and Scandinavia; the KSČM aims to join the United European Left in the European Parliament. The KDU-ČSL is already affiliated with the European People's Party, though in terms similar to those used by the ČSSD it has constantly reiterated its wish to promote and protect the interests of small countries within the EU. This, together with both the more deeply seated Czech distrust of large powers and oppressive international regimes, and the feelings of humiliation stemming from the long-drawn and unequal accession process, may well become the defining characteristics of Czech (elite) attitudes in the newly enlarged Europe.

Postscript

The Czech referendum on EU accession, which took place on 13 and 14 June 2003, after this article was finished, largely confirmed the expectations expressed above. The Czechs overwhelmingly supported EU accession: 77.33% voted in favor of EU membership, while only 22.67% voted opposed it. The turnout, at 55.21%, was higher than expected. However, those voting in favour represented only 41.73% of the total electorate, one of the lowest percentages among all accession referendums held so far.

The 'Yes' campaign was very well organised and financed. Both government coalition parties, together with NGOs and other civil society organisations at the regional and local levels, were involved in running the pro-membership campaign. One of the central messages of this campaign was a focus on 'bread and butter' issues, stressing the advantages which EU membership would bring in daily life, such as lower prices and free travel. In addition, the campaign was heavily centred around the (positive) experiences of foreigners (read Westerners) with the EU. Although the 'Yes' campaign was probably excessively positive about the EU membership and thus too one-sided, it at least created an awareness among the electorate that an important decision was to be taken. In contrast, the 'No' campaign turned out to be weak and isolated. This was partly attributable to the limited access which the 'No' side had to the media. However, in large part, it was also because the 'No' campaign, at least its most visible and vocal part, was dominated by a loose alliance of radical right-wing groups and activists.

Crucially, all the major Czech political parties asked their voters to support EU membership. However, in the case of the Eurosceptic ODS, the endorsement came only shortly before the polling booths were due to open; several top ODS politicians and MPs also openly declared they would vote against EU membership. In addition, much controversy surrounded the position of the former ODS leader, and now Czech President, Václav Klaus. In the month preceding the referendum, he aired his well-known Eurosceptic views, among other things arguing that Czech EU membership was a marriage of convenience rather than a love match. He also criticised the government's 'Yes' campaign for failing to launch any serious debate concerning EU membership. Although Klaus urged the electorate to participate in the referendum, he neither openly supported the 'Yes' campaign, nor did he disclose his own voting intentions.

The KSCM was nevertheless the only parliamentary party and major political player which explicitly did not recommend EU membership to its electorate. After much internal discussion, the KSCM executive opted for a 'No' because of the allegedly unfavourable terms of entry. Indeed, KSCM supporters were also most likely to reject membership on the day of the referendum – with only 37% voting in favor of joining the EU. In contrast, 92% of US, 86% of ODS, 84% of KDU-CSL and 82% of CSSD participating supporters voted 'Yes' in the referendum.

References

Batory, Agnes. 2002. Attitudes to Europe: Ideology, Strategy and the Issue of European Union Membership in Hungarian Party Politics. *Party Politics* 8, no. 5: 525-540.

Chalupa, Kamil. 2001. KDU-ČSL a Evropská unie. *Integrace* 6. www.integrace.cz/.

CEORG. 2000. Trends in EU, Czech, Hungarian and Polish Public Opinion on Enlargement: Implications for EU Institutions and Industry. Report for the European Parliament, 17 October. Brussels.

Česal, Jiří. 2002. Názory naší veřejnosti na vstup České republiky do Evropské unie. *Integrace* 2. www.integrace.cz/.

Franzen, Wolfgang. 2002. Podpora evropské integrace v České republice – Zpráva Útavu pro empirickou sociální ekonomiku v Kolíne nad Rýnem o veřejném mínění ve Střední Evropě. *Integrace* 12. www.integrace.cz/.

George, Stephen. 1994. *An Awkward Partner: Britain in the European Community*. Oxford: Oxford University Press.

Grabbe, Heather. 2001. How Does Europeanization Affect CEE Governance? Conditionality, Diffusion and Diversity. *Journal of European Public Policy* 8, no. 6: 1013-1031.

Hanley, Sean. 2001. Towards Breakthrough or Breakdown? The Consolidation of KSČM as a Neo-Communist Successor Party in the Czech Republic. *Journal of Communist Studies and Transition Politics* 17, no. 3: 96-116.

Hanley, Sean. 2002. Party Institutionalisation and Centre-Right Euroscepticism in East Central Europe: the Case of the Civic Democratic Party in the Czech Republic. Paper presented at the twenty-ninth European Consortium for Political Reseach Joint Sessions of Workshops, 22-27 March. Turin.

Hartl, Jan 2000. Evropská unie v zrcadle veřejného mínění'. *Integrace* 2. www.integrace.cz/.

Henderson, Karen. 2002. Exceptionalism or Convergence? Euroscepticism and Party Systems in Central and Eastern Europe. Paper presented at the twenty-ninth European Consortium for Political Reseach Joint Sessions of Workshops, 22-27 March. Turin.

Klaus, Václav. 1997. Obhajoba zapomenutých myšlenek. Prague: Academia Praha.

Klaus, Václav. 2000. Evropské sjednocování a rozdělování. *Integrace* 4. www.integrace.cz/.

Kopecký, Petr and Cas Mudde. 2002. The Two Sides of Euroscepticism: Party Positions on European Integration in East Central Europe. *European Union Politics* 3, no. 3: 297-326.

Kumar, Krishan. 1992. The 1989 Revolutions and the Idea of Europe. *Political Studies* 40: 439-461.

Mareš, Petr. 2000. České politické strany a Evropská integrace. *Integrace* 1: 15-20.

Mišovič, Ján. 2000. Podpora vstupu do EU podle jednotlivých sociálních skupin. *Integrace* 4. www.integrace.cz/.

Perron, Catherine. 2000. Views of Czech Local Politicians on European Integration. European University Institute Working Paper RSC 2000/39.

Pontes Resende, Madalena and Cosmina Tanasoiu. 2001. The Change of Fate of a Political Symbol: 'Europe' in Post-Communist Central and Eastern Europe. Paper presented at the Annual Meeting of the Political Studies Association, 10-12 April. Manchester.

Sitter, Nick. 2001. The Politics of Opposition and European Integration in Scandinavia: Is Euro-Scepticism a Government-Opposition Dynamic?. *West European Politics* 24, no. 4: 22-39.

Taggart, Paul. 1998. A Touchstone of Dissent: Euroscepticism in Contemporary Western European Party Systems. *European Journal of Political Research* 33: 363-388.

Taggart, Paul and Alex Szczerbiak. 2001. Crossing Europe: Patterns of Contemporary Party-Based Euroscepticism in EU Member States and the Candidate States of Central and Eastern Europe. Paper presented at the Annual Meeting of the American Political Science Association, 29 August-2 September. San Francisco.

Tiersky, Ronald. 2001. Introduction: Euro-skepticism and 'Europe'. In *Euro-skepticism: A Reader*, ed. Ronald Tiersky, 1-6. Lanham, MD: Rowman & Littlefield.
Vlachová, Klára. 1997. Czech Political Parties and their Voters. *Czech Sociological Review* 5, no. 1: 39-56.
Vlachová, Klára. 1999. *The Crystallization of Political Attitudes and Orientation. In Ten Years of Rebuilding Capitalism: Czech Society after 1989*, eds. Jiří Večerník and Petr Matějů, 251-272. Prague: Academia.

EUROPEAN STUDIES 20 (2004): 247-268

POLISH EUROSCEPTICISM IN THE RUN-UP
TO EU ACCESSION[*]

Aleks Szczerbiak

Abstract

Recent years have seen increasing Polish cynicism about the EU that has led to a significant fall in support for membership and the emergence of a sizeable bloc of anti-EU public opinion. Support was bound to fall once it became apparent that conforming to EU norms would involve negative economic and social consequences as well as benefits. Even more significantly, the crack in the previously overwhelming pro-EU elite consensus and the subsequent politicisation of the debate on EU membership have also chipped away at public support. However, support for Polish EU membership appears to have stabilised at a relatively high level. Even though parties critical of or even opposed to EU membership performed well in the most recent September 2001 parliamentary election it would be wrong to interpret this as a kind of Eurosceptic backlash given that, by virtually any measure, the EU was not a salient campaign issue.

Until recently Poland enjoyed one of the highest levels of public and elite support for EU membership among the Central and East European candidate countries. However, as the largest of the post-Communist applicant states it was always going to be one of the most difficult for the

---

[*] The present article was completed prior to the Polish EU accession referendum of 7-8 June 2003. A brief postscript presents the results of that referendum, in the context of the overall pattern of pre-accession politics detailed in the main text of the article.

EU to accommodate. Once the accession negotiations began in March 1998, the issue of EU membership began to develop a relatively higher political profile. At the same time, the term Polish Eurosceptic, previously considered something of an oxymoron, began to enter into the political lexicon. As in other countries, the term was used in an inclusive and somewhat imprecise way to encompass both those who opposed Polish EU membership in principle, as well as those who were critically supportive, although these softer Eurosceptics often preferred to call themselves Eurorealists. The latter generally tended to be critical of the EU (or the Polish government) stance in the accession negotiations and the kind of membership package that Poland was likely to secure rather than the substance of the European integration project as such.

This paper examines the emergence and development of Polish Euroscepticism, particularly current debates on EU membership and the state of the parties exemplified by the most recent September 2001 parliamentary election. It begins by examining and accounting for changing patterns of public support for Polish EU membership over the last few years. It shows that support for Polish EU membership declined steadily since the accession negotiations began in 1998, with the emergence for the first time of a sizeable bloc of Eurosceptic public opinion. It then moves on to consider the reasons for this decline, arguing that increasing cynicism towards EU membership was partly due to the fact that earlier polling data may have artificially overstated the true levels of support for Polish EU membership. Even more significantly, the opening of the accession negotiations also marked the politicisation of the Polish Euro-debate with the emergence, for the first time, of an organised Eurosceptic lobby and divisions among the pro-EU parties over the terms of Polish membership and the kind of EU that Poland would join. Opposition to EU membership was rooted in fear of the possible negative socio-economic consequences rather than in ideological 'nationalist' themes. However, public support for Polish EU membership appears to have stabilised at a fairly high level from around the middle of 1999. The paper then goes on to consider the signifcance of the most recent September 2001 parliamentary election. Even though parties critical of or even opposed to EU membership performed well, it would be wrong to interpret the results as representing some kind of Eurosceptic backlash.

Changing patterns of support for Polish EU membership

Until a couple of years ago Polish EU membership was the subject of an overwhelming political elite consensus and enjoyed extremely high levels of public support. However, in the late 1990s, Poland saw a significant fall in support for EU membership.[1] The number of Poles supporting EU membership declined steadily from 77% in June 1994 (the year that Poland formally submitted its application) and a peak of 80% in May 1995 to only 55% in March 2002.[2] At the same time, a significant segment of anti-EU opinion began to emerge with the number of opponents increasing from only 6% in 1994 to 29% in 2002. However, it is striking that from mid-1999 onwards public support began to stabilise at around 55-60% in favour while the number of opponents has fluctuated between 22-30%. Precise figures vary between different polling organisations but the overall trend in terms of support for EU membership has clearly been one of steady decline and then subsequent stabilisation (CBOS 2002c).

Perhaps even more significantly, beneath the surface of what remained relatively high levels of public support there were a number of potentially significant indicators suggesting that the prospect of EU membership provoked considerable anxieties even among the pro-EU majority. In particular, the decline in overall support was also reflected in increasing uncertainty about whether or not (and by how much) Poles would actually benefit from EU membership compared with current member states. Having fallen from 41% in July 1993 to only 19% in June 1996, the number of Poles who believed that existing EU member states would derive the greatest benefit from Polish accession increased steadily to 59% in February 2002. At the same time 19% of Poles believed that accession would be equally beneficial to both Poland and the EU while

---

[1] For a full analysis of this see Szczerbiak (2000 and 2001a). For other interesting accounts of how EU membership has impacted upon Polish domestic politics see Blazyca and Kolkiewicz (1999), Kolarska-Bobińska (1999) and Millard (1999).

[2] The analysis in this paper rests heavily on data published by the two leading Polish polling organisations, the Centre for Research on Public Opinion (Centrum Badania Opinii Społecznej: CBOS) and the Institute for Research on Public Opinion (Ośrodek Badania Opinii Publicznej: OBOP), and the Institute of Public Affairs (Instytut Spraw Publicznych: ISP) research institute. All the usual limitations of relying on such data are, of course, applicable. These include the margin of error arising from (in some cases) relatively small samples and the inability to subject the data to more rigorous statistical analysis, together with the fact that information is not always available in the precise form required.

only 7% cited their country as the main beneficiary (CBOS 2002a, 2002b).

Similarly, while most Poles continued to think that EU accession would bring their country more benefits than losses they were more uncertain when it came to whether they would benefit as individuals. For example, a March 2001 CBOS survey found that 56% of respondents said EU membership would benefit Poland and only 16% that it would be disadvantageous (10% said it would make no difference and 18% did not know). On the other hand, only 32% felt that EU membership would benefit them personally, while 50% said it would make no difference and 11% did not know (8% said that it would be disadvantageous) (CBOS 2001). Similarly, a June 2001 OBOP/Polityka survey found that 31% of respondents felt that EU membership would bring Poland more gains than losses while 27% thought the opposite (25% said that they would be equal and 17% did not know). However, only 21% felt that it would bring them more gains personally while 24% said that it would bring them greater losses and 23% said it would have no impact (18% said the effect would be neutral and 14% did not know) (Polityka, 7 July 2001).

Increasing anxiety about the possible impact of EU accession was confirmed by data on the effects that Poles thought that it would have on specific sectors of the economy and their living standards more generally. In February 2002, for example, 53% of Poles said it would have a negative effect on individual farms while only 26% said it would be positive (the analogous figures for June 1994 were 24% and 40% respectively). Similarly, 35% of Poles said that EU membership would have a negative effect on the functioning of public sector enterprises compared with only 33% who felt it would be positive (37% and 32% in 1994). Even the number who believed that EU membership would have a positive effect on the private business sector fell from 67% in 1994 to 42% in 2002 while those who said it would have a negative effect increased from 6% to 29% over the same period. The number who said that it would have a positive effect on their living standards fell from 57% in 1994 to 42% in 2002, while those who felt it would be negative increased from 10% to 23% (CBOS 2002c). Indeed, in an earlier analysis of changing Polish attitudes towards EU membership, I argued that the best way to characterise the state of public opinion was that Poles *consented* to the idea of EU accession but were not particularly *enthusiastic* about it.[3]

Explaining shifts in public attitudes

There are number of factors that account for these shifts in public attitudes towards the EU. Firstly, although there were always varying degrees of enthusiasm and nuances in their different approaches, the issue of Polish EU membership was, initially at least, the subject of an overwhelming consensus among the main political groupings and elites. No major political grouping openly questioned EU membership as a primary objective of Polish foreign policy. For example, all the parties and electoral blocs that won seats in the September 1997 parliamentary election declared their support for it.[4] Given the existence of such an overwhelming consensus among political elites, Polish Eurosceptics may have been reluctant to identify themselves as such and earlier polling data may have artificially overstated the true levels of public support for EU membership. In this sense, the more recent polling data are, it could be argued, simply a more accurate reflection of the true levels of support for Polish EU membership and, therefore, simply represented a kind of 'reality check'.

Secondly, given the existence of this elite consensus, there was also very little serious debate about the potential costs and benefits of EU accession and the issue had virtually no resonance in the day-to-day lives of individual Polish citizens. Rather, it was couched in very abstract and broad geopolitical or historical terms relating to general notions such as 'returning to Europe' and ending the post-war division of Europe into East and West. An August 1997 CBOS poll, for example, found that 41% of Poles felt that EU membership would bring Poland more good than harm. However, the number who said it would benefit them or their families personally fell to 27% while nearly one third (31%) did not know how the process would affect them (CBOS 1997). Consequently, the previous very high levels of support for EU membership may not have represented a conscious and considered declaration of support and were constructed on rather shaky foundations.

---

[3] One Polish commentator has characterised this as a 'shallow consensus' in favour of EU membership (Skotnicka-Illasiewicz 1998).

[4] See, for example, the useful survey of Polish parties' attitudes to EU membership in the run up to the September 1997 elections by the ISP (undated).

Thirdly, it was always likely that the beginning of the actual accession negotiations would reduce the level of support for Polish EU membership. As noted above, Poland will be a difficult new member for the EU to accommodate and, given the asymmetrical nature of the accession negotiations, there was always a danger that opponents of membership could argue that Poland would be admitted to the EU as a 'second class' member. Given the difficult issues that needed to be tackled, therefore, the accession negotiations themselves inevitably focused to a large extent on the concessions that had to be made by the Polish side. This, in turn, raised the profile of the European issue in Polish politics in a very negative way, with Brussels viewed increasingly as a focus for conflict and hostility.

Fourthly, although attitudes towards the two issues did not overlap completely, there was also some evidence that the painful and increasingly unpopular reforms associated with the socio-economic transition had become more linked to Polish EU membership in the popular consciousness (Roguska and Kucharczyk 2001, 20). In October 1999, for example, research undertaken by the ISP revealed that an equal number of Poles (38%) believed that economic and social reforms were being imposed on Poland as believed that they were essential to modernise the country whether the country joined the EU or not. However, among supporters of Polish EU membership a clear majority (58%) was convinced of the objective necessity of reforms and only a minority (28%) felt that they were being imposed. These proportions were reversed among EU opponents: 70% blaming the EU compared to 17% who saw the reforms as inevitable (ISP 1999).

Indeed, it was socio-economic arguments, particularly the fear that Poland would not be able to cope successfully with accession and have to pay huge social costs, that particularly struck a chord with the Polish public and provided the most fertile recruiting ground for the anti-EU camp. For example, a June 2000 ISP survey found that 56% of Poles believed that EU accession would mean the collapse of many small and medium sized enterprises and increased unemployment (28% disagreed). Similarly, although a majority felt that EU accession would mean more money for Polish farmers a substantial minority (40% to 44%) also felt that it would lead to a collapse of Polish agriculture when exposed to EU competition. Moreover, only 41% of Poles believed that their standard of living would increase when Poland joined the EU (Strzeszewski 2001, 108). Similarly, as table 1 shows, a February 2002 CBOS survey also revealed that the potentially negative impact of EU membership on the Polish economy was the most frequently cited motive for opposing accession.

Table 1: Motives for opposing Polish EU membership, January 2002

General disadvantages	18%
Impact of distance between Poland and EU countries	
Poland is unprepared, too weak to be an equal partner	20%
Loss of sovereignty, fear of becoming vassals	20%
General fear of second class membership	12%
Threats to specific areas	
Negative impact on agriculture	13%
Negative impact of the economy, industry, trade with the EU	13%
Negative impact on employment, opportunities to work abroad	6%
Negative impact on living standards	4%
Other factors	
Lack of information	10%
Disapproval of accession negotiations	6%
General lack of trust towards the EU	4%
General uncertainty, fear of the future	5%
Don't know	2%

Source: CBOS (2002b)

At the same time, it is worth noting here that the strategy adopted by some Polish Eurosceptics of stressing the threat to national sovereignty posed by EU membership made little headway with the majority of Poles. A June 2000 ISP report found that most Poles did not believe that EU membership would lead to a loss of independence (only 13% compared to 77%) nor a weakening of Polish traditions and culture (only 31% compared to 60%) (Strzeszewski 2001: 108). Similarly, as table 1 shows, only 20% of those opposed to Polish EU membership cited 'ideological' or 'nationalist' factors rather than economic ones.[5] One explanation for

[5] Obviously, it is difficult to completely separate economic issues from those relating to national sovereignty. However, it is possible to distinguish between those anti-EU Poles who are primarily motivated by fears of loss of sovereignty (and who, implicitly, would oppose EU membership even if they accepted that the net economic effects were beneficial) and those who are mainly fearful of the economic consequences rather than any loss of sovereignty *per se*. Polish opponents of EU membership are, I would argue, principally located in the latter category.

this phenomenon was the unambiguously pro-EU stance adopted by the Pope and Catholic Church hierarchy. This made it very difficult for Catholic nationalists, such as those clustered around the influential Radio Maryja (discussed below), to evoke the possible 'loss of national identity' as an argument against EU membership (Kucharczyk 2001, 9-10).

Fifthly, and perhaps most significantly, the period since the beginning of the accession negotiations saw a striking politicisation of the debate on Polish EU membership. Partly this was because a crack appeared in the previously overwhelming pro-EU elite consensus with the emergence of the first organised and potentially significant political forces to adopt an overtly anti-EU stance. The Polish Agreement party led by Jan Łopuszański was established in April 1999 by seven deputies associated with the Catholic nationalist right who left the parliamentary caucus of the governing Solidarity Electoral Action (Akcja Wyborcza Solidarność: AWS). One of the Polish Agreement's primary objectives was to oppose Polish EU (and NATO) membership (*Gazeta Wyborcza*, 26 April 1999). However, the derisory 0.79% of the vote obtained by Łopuszański in the October 2000 presidential election suggested that the Polish Agreement's political impact would be limited (Szczerbiak 2001b).[6]

A more significant development, therefore, was the way that the debate on EU membership began to be conducted among those political forces that were ostensibly pro-EU. This was not so much about whether or not the country should join *per se* but about the terms on which (and the kind of EU that) it should join. As one commentator has noted, this led to a tendency to turn political debates about EU membership into 'ideological' confrontations between the right-wing AWS led government and the ex-communist Democratic Left Alliance (Sojusz Lewicy Demokratycznej: SLD) opposition (Kucharczyk 1999b). One of the most important aspects of this politicisation of the Polish Euro-debate was the division of the pro-EU camp into those who (allegedly) favoured a 'soft' negotiating stance and those who (allegedly) favoured a 'tough' one. The former, it was argued, were prepared to 'give in' to Brussels while the latter placed numerous conditions upon and posited reservations concerning support for EU membership.

A prime example of this politicisation of the Polish Euro-debate was the rhetoric employed by AWS leader and presidential candidate Marian

---

[6] Although, as the September 2001 parliamentary election was to show, this did not really reflect the anti-EU Catholic-nationalist milieu's real electoral potential.

Krzaklewski, particularly in the early stages of the October 2000 election campaign in order to distinguish himself from the unequivocally pro-EU SLD-backed incumbent, Aleksander Kwaśniewski.[7] Krzaklewski contrasted what he saw as his own 'pragmatic' approach to European integration with the SLD's (allegedly) 'ideological' approach. AWS wanted Europe to be a 'community of free nations that remember their identity'. He wanted 'to participate in the building of a Europe of nations, John Paul II's Europe, and not a Europe of left-wing Utopias'. This approach contrasted with that of the SLD which saw EU membership as an 'ideological objective' and for whom the 'negotiation of the Polish political and economic interests (was) a second order matter'. The SLD were, he argued, motivated by the same opportunism that characterised them during the communist era and 'regard Brussels as a new Moscow, the European Union as a new Comecon and their policy as simply finding new protectors for their own careers'.

According to Krzaklewski, Poland faced 'challenges going beyond the dimension of ordinary politics'. He saw these two approaches to European integration as exemplifying and embodying a 'fundamental civilisational battle' that was taking place in Poland, with AWS on the side of whose who wanted to modernise Poland and open up to the West while simultaneously safeguarding her national identity. The outcome of this battle would determine, 'in what way and on whose side we will unite in the building and uniting of Europe. We are now deciding if Poland will take the place that belongs to it among free states that remember their national identity, or if we will become the subject of ideological experiments, whose objective was the formation of a new so-called European nation'. Krzaklewski also sought to portray himself as an advocate of a 'tough' negotiating stance in the EU accession negotiations and, in particular, a staunch defender of the interests of Polish farmers. As Krzaklewski argued, 'Polish politicians travelling to Brussels do not have the right to forget about the interests of Polish farmers, do not have the right to think and talk about Polish farmers as if they were an obstacle on our path to the EU. The Polish farmer should be supported in the same way as his colleague in the West is supported by their government and by the President of their country.' As one Polish commentator put it, the overall effect of this kind of rhetoric, that placed numerous conditions upon and

---

[7] All the quotations from Krzaklewski in this section are taken from Szczerbiak 2001b, 10-13.

posits reservations concerning support for EU membership, was to create the impression that Poland was negotiating with an enemy. EU membership was a regrettable necessity rather than something to be sought positively (Kucharczyk 1999a and 1999b). Obviously, this did not have the same impact as that of a major political grouping campaigning overtly against Polish membership. However, by implicitly arguing that the EU was attempting to undermine Polish national interests, it did chip away at the overall level of support for membership.

The September 2001 election: a Eurosceptic backlash?

In spite of the emergence of this significant bloc of anti-EU opinion, the European issue did not really feature as an issue in the October 2000 presidential campaign. Although, as the quotes from AWS candidate Marian Krzaklewski cited above indicate, there were clear differences of approach and nuance, the election did not produce a significant pro versus anti-EU cleavage among the main candidates. Some of the minor candidates, such as Łopuszański, were more openly anti-EU and did make it a major focus of their campaign but received a derisory share of the vote (Szczerbiak 2001b). The September 2001 parliamentary election, on the other hand, saw parties and political groupings that were critical of, or openly hostile to, Polish EU membership win significant support and a substantial bloc of parliamentary deputies. Of the six parties and groupings that secured representation in the Sejm (the more powerful lower house of the Polish parliament) two of them, winning 18.07% of the vote and 91 seats, might be described as having adopted a hard Eurosceptic stance of *de facto* outright opposition to EU membership.[8] This made some foreign commentators link the result to changing Polish attitudes towards the EU and interpret it as part of a broader Eurosceptic backlash.[9] In other words, it was argued that the increase in public opposition to EU membership that had emerged over the last couple of years had finally found expression in the party system, as some commentators had previously predicted that it would.[10]

---

[8] On the distinction between hard and soft Euroscepticism see Taggart and Szczerbiak (2002).

[9] See, for example, Reed (2001).

[10] See, for example: Kolarska-Bobinska (1998) and Bachman (2000). Cf: Grabowska (1999).

Table 2: September 2001 Polish parliamentary election results

	Votes (%)	Seats
Democratic Left Alliance-Labour Union (SLD-UP)	41.04	216
Civic Platform (PO)	12.68	65
Self-Defence (Samoobrona)	10.20	53
Law and Justice (PiS)	9.50	44
Polish Peasant Party (PSL)	8.98	42
League of Polish Families (LPR)	7.87	38

Source: Polish State Electoral Commission

The most openly and unambiguously anti-EU grouping was the League of Polish Families (Liga Polskich Rodziń: LPR), a coalition of various parties and organisations on the Catholic nationalist right that, as table 2 shows, won 7.87% of the vote and 38 seats. While accusing the EU of 'conducting a policy of economic colonialism towards Poland', in its election programme the LPR focussed its attention primarily on the need to renegotiate Poland's EU association agreement. This, it was argued, had led to a $10 billion trade deficit and created more than one million new jobs in EU countries at Poland's expense. With the connivance of previous Polish governments, who behaved 'as if some of them were directed by the interests of foreign capital', the association agreement also meant that, 'an important segment of our national assets has been given away while the remainder is (now) being taken over'.[11]

During the election campaign, however, LPR leaders were much less ambiguous about their outright opposition to EU membership. LPR chairman Marek Kotlinowski, for example, argued that 'for us the alternative to taking Poland into the EU is respecting the rights of sovereign states (...) We are for co-operation with everyone who wants to build social relations with Poland on a Christian basis' (*Gazeta Wyborcza*, 25 September 2001). Similarly, LPR vice-chairman Roman Giertych argued that, 'we did not fight for our independence for all those years only to now give away a portion of our sovereignty to some kind of supranational organisation' (*Wprost*, 28 October 2001). Ending all expenditure connected with preparing for EU membership would, he argued, save the country around 39 billion złoties (*Rzeczpospolita*, 30 August 2001). Another LPR leader Antoni Macierewicz argued that Poland should 'begin negotiations as quickly as possible on the subject of the development of

[11] Extracts taken from the LPR election programme.

ties with NAFTA' (*Gazeta Wyborcza*, 24 September 2001). The radical nationalist Solidarity trade union official Zygmunt Wrzodak, who stood as a parliamentary candidate on the LPR ticket, argued that 'we have to return to a Christian Europe of Nations. Only God stands above the nation, not some kind of communo-liberal European Union' (*Wprost*, 28 October 2001). Perhaps the most consistently vocal opponent of Polish accession among LPR leaders was Łopuszański (the PP was part of the LPR electoral coalition), whom one LPR leaflet described as 'personifying opposition to the EU'. Speaking at the LPR's July 2001 electoral convention, Łopuszański argued that, 'the effect of our entry into the EU will be the Polish state's loss of sovereignty. The objective of our programme is the defence of the Polish state as a sovereign state, which cannot hand over its newly won independence to another "international", this time with its headquarters in Brussels' (*Gazeta Wyborcza*, 24 September 2001).

Critical to the LPR's success was the backing of the Catholic nationalist broacaster Radio Maryja whose charismatic director, Father Tadeusz Rydzyk, had always used its airwaves to convey a strong anti-EU message. Radio Maryja had 2.7 million listeners and was closely aligned to the 'Our Daily' (*Nasz Dziennik*) newspaper with 600,000 readers (*Rzeczpospolita*, 11 December 1998). In a previous paper, I argued that the support of Radio Maryja was probably a necessary condition for the emergence of a significant anti-EU party in Poland. A good illustration of this was Łopuszański's October 2000 presidential bid when, in spite of a campaign that focussed heavily on opposing Polish EU membership, he failed to secure Radio Maryja's backing and received a derisory share of the vote (Szczerbiak 2001b, 16).

The other hard Eurosceptic political grouping that secured parliamentary representation was the radical-populist Self-Defence (Samoobrona) party led by Andrzej Lepper. Self-Defence came to public prominence at the beginning of the 1990s as a radical farmers' union engaged in direct action to prevent the enforcement of debt foreclosures (Sabbat-Swidlicka 1992). As Lepper faded from public view in the mid-1990s he performed progressively worse in successive parliamentary and presidential elections. However, he re-emerged as a public figure at the head of a campaign of farmers' road blockades at the beginning of 1999 and his relatively high 3.05% of the vote in the October 2000 presidential election gave a hint that Self-Defence was capable of garnering a more a sizeable electorate. Indeed, although opinion polls did not detect any significant levels of support for Self-Defence (nor, indeed, the LPR) until the last fortnight of the campaign, as table 2 shows, it eventually emerged as the third largest grouping in the new parliament with 10.2% of the vote and fifty-three seats.

Unlike the LPR, Self-Defence did not state explicitly that it was against Polish EU membership. Indeed, its election programme contained only one rather oblique (albeit very negative) reference to the EU. It argued that

> they (the SLD, PSL [Polish Peasant Party], AWS, UW [Freedom Union] and their chums in the [Civic] Platform) are implementing the same programme of making Poland dependent on the West, selling our national assets together with the liquidation of jobs. They have all gone mad about Brussels. But the truth is brutal - no one will give us something for nothing. It is the European Union that is exporting more than 16 billion US dollars worth of goods to us annually. Our total imports add up to 48 billion US dollars. It is we who are supporting two and a half million jobs in the West, jobs that we lack here' (Samoobrona 2001).

The Self-Defence website contained a short policy statement that set out its 'position on joining the EU' in more detail. Here the grouping argued that

> at the present moment we have, as a result of the (European) Union, reduced our production levels by around 50%. Partnership with the Union requires us to define the limits of our productive capacity, and this particularly affects farming, steel production, coal mining, copper, light industry. We must fight for our production limits, because in the European Union everything is subject to limits, everyone has production quotas. In this situation, if we do not have these (quotas), and we reduce our production every year, then our opposition to integration with the European Union is unambiguous (...) Self-Defence is opposed to integration with the European Union in the current form that it exists today' (Samoobrona 2001).

In other words, although it failed to spell out its position unambiguously, Self-Defence can be considered a *de facto* hard Eurosceptic, anti-EU party. While not opposing the idea of Polish EU membership in principle, Self-Defence made its support conditional upon securing an unachievable set of conditions (effectively exemption from the provisions of the Single Market).

Although they avoided opposing Polish EU membership in principle, two of the other four groupings elected to the Sejm, the Law and Justice party (Prawo i Sprawiedliwość: PiS) and the Polish Peasant Party (Polskie Stronnictwo Ludowe: PSL), also adopted a critical tone towards the EU in their election programmes and campaign rhetoric. For example, the leaders of both groupings failed to attend the signing ceremony of the 'Pact for Europe', an attempt to develop an all-party consensus in support of EU membership during the election campaign.[12] In fact, both parties were primarily concerned with highlighting the need for the Polish government to maintain a 'tough' negotiating stance. This kind of rhetoric did, however, contain an implicit message that the EU was attempting to exploit Poland and, therefore, often came close to shading into a kind of soft Euroscepticism.[13]

PiS was created as an attempt to construct a 'renewed right' from the remnants of the disintegrating AWS bloc and, as table 2 shows, emerged as the fourth largest grouping in the new parliament winning 9.5% of the vote and 44 seats in the Sejm. The original PiS party was formed in April 2001 to cash in on the popularity of Justice Minister Lech Kaczyński, who was by far the most popular member of the AWS government (although not a member of any AWS affiliated political party). The PiS party was later to form an electoral alliance with the Right-wing Agreement (Porozumienie Prawicy: PP) grouping. The PP was, in turn, also set up in April 2001 by defectors from two AWS affiliates: the Christian National Union (Zjednoczenie Chrześcijańsko-Narodowe: ZChN) and the Conservative People's Party (Stronnictwo Konserwatywno-Ludowe: SKL).[14] In the event, PiS adopted a broadly supportive if somewhat ambiguous position on Polish EU membership. The PiS election programme described EU membership as one of its two foreign policy priorities but went on to criticise a negotiating strategy based on attempting a secure a specific (early) target date for Polish accession. PiS argued that, 'striving for an appropriate position for Poland in the Union, in other words one worthy of a large European country, cannot be pursued effectively, when the method and speed of the negotiations are determined by successive, apparently unrealistic, entry dates. The quality of our membership, and

---

[12] PSL leader Jarosław Kalinowski had previously agreed to attend the ceremony while the PiS leadership had delegated their election organiser Ludwik Dorn to attend, but neither of them actually turned up (*Rzeczpospolita*, 23 August 2001 and *Gazeta Wyborcza*, 23 August 2001).

[13] Soft Euroscepticism can be defined as where concerns on one (or a number) of policy areas lead to the expression of qualified opposition to the EU, or where there is a sense that 'national interest' is currently at odds with the EU's trajectory (Taggart and Szczerbiak 2002).

[14] In fact, the latter were prompted to leave their party by the SKL's decision to withdraw from AWS in March 2001 and form an electoral coalition with the liberal Civic Platform grouping.

therefore a determined defence of our interests, is what is most important' (PiS 2001, 27). When asked directly (in an interview) if PiS was for or against Polish EU membership, Kaczyński said that he, 'would vote for accession, but as a politician would accept a different decision by the nation. I would vote against if Poland was to be a second class member' (*Rzeczpospolita*, 6 September 2001). Moreover, the PP element of the PiS election alliance comprised the former leaders of the soft Eurosceptic ZChN who had been most critical of the EU. PP and former ZChN leader Marian Piłka, for example, argued that 'Poland should oppose the bureaucratisation of the EU and prevent the liquidation of the nation-state formula' (*Rzeczpospolita*, 5 June 2001). Another ex-SKL PP leader, Kazimierz Ujazdowski argued that 'we want the EU to be a strong union of countries in solidarity with one another, and not a further tier in the careers of the ruling class, which is what the SLD, a party that regards the idea of European integration as a kind of new Comecon, wants' (*Rzeczpospolita*, 11 June 2001).

Another party that secured parliamentary representation and was highly critical of the EU was the agrarian PSL. As table 2 shows, the PSL won 8.98% of the vote and 42 seats and went on to become the former Communists' junior partner in the new coalition government.[15] The party's programme argued that, '(Poland's) relations with the EU should be based on strengthening (our) national interests as part of the process of integration, and not just passively joining a larger community. It is necessary to be aware that, in spite of the disproportion that exists in the levels of income among its member states, the EU is a "rich man's club" and not inclined to give in to the demands of the poor candidate states from the East'. The PSL further argued that the EU 'must also take into account our expectations and aspirations'. A pre-condition of this was 'the inclusion of Polish agriculture in the Common Agricultural Policy, from the moment when Poland joins the EU, (with Poland) entitled to the same direct payments and structural funds, on the basis of principles that have operated in the Union up until now' (PSL 2001a, 35-37). In its election declaration, the PSL criticised the previous AWS led government for creating 'a noticeable asymmetry in Poland's relations with European Union states to our disadvantage'. This, the PSL argued, had been one of the main factors accounting for why 'foreign firms (were) taking control

---

[15] This result was, however, somewhat below its expectations particularly because it unexpectedly secured less support than Self-Defence, its direct rival for the rural-agrarian vote.

of strategic segments of the Polish economy, the enormous deficit in trade and the emergence of a substantial lobby for foreign interests in Poland' (PSL 2001b, 4). Arguing that the party were 'Euro-realists', PSL Vice-President Marek Sawicki said that they supported EU membership but only 'on the basis of partnership' (*Rzeczpospolita*, 5 June 2001) and rejected an 'unqualified opening up' to the EU (*Gazeta Wyborcza*, 7 August 2001). In particular, the PSL supported the previous government's demand for an eighteen-year transition period before Polish land could be sold to foreigners (*Gazeta Wyborcza*, 7 August 2001).[16]

The September 2001 election outcome clearly meant that the new Polish parliament would contain a much larger bloc of deputies that were either critics or outright opponents of EU membership. However, it would be far too simplistic to interpret the September 2001 election as representing a kind of 'Eurosceptic backlash'. With opinion polls showing the emergence of an anti-EU segment of Polish public opinion of 25-30% of voters, one should not be too surprised that some openly anti-EU parties won seats in the Polish parliament. Moreover, even if one accepts Self-Defence as a *de facto* hard Eurosceptic party, the share of the vote won by the anti-EU parties (18.07%) still understated the levels of public opposition to EU membership. Indeed, it is easy to forget that the two most successful groupings in this election were the two who were the most supportive of Polish EU membership. As table 2 shows, these were the electoral coalition of the SLD and small Labour Union (Unia Pracy: UP) party and the liberal Civic Platform (Platforma Obywatelska: PO), that won 41.04% and 12.68% of the vote and 216 and 65 seats respectively. Although critical voices would be much more evident in the new parliament, there was still a strong consensus in favour of the principle of EU membership with the vast majority of parliamentarians broadly pro-EU. Perhaps more significantly, it was striking how, although EU membership had a much higher profile than in any previous parliamentary election, by virtually any measure it was, once again, not a particularly salient campaign issue. This was particularly noteworthy when one considers its significance as a Polish foreign policy choice of such historical proportions.

Firstly, most parties did not really give the issue much of a profile in their own election campaigns. A survey (conducted by the author) of the

---

[16] On another occasion Sawicki argued that the PSL supported transition periods until 'Polish purchasing power was comparable to the possibilities of citizens in other EU states' (*Rzeczpospolita*, 5 June 2001).

coverage of the six major parties and groupings on the main TV evening news during the last fortnight of the campaign found that all of them gave this issue a fairly low profile. The SLD-UP coalition made EU issues its main campaign theme on three occasions, the PSL twice and the PO and LPR only once. Moreover, Self-Defence did not once 'lead' on the EU as the main focus for its TV campaign for that day. Indeed, as noted above, it only warranted one oblique reference in this grouping's election programme.

Secondly, whatever Polish parties may or not have said about Polish EU membership during the campaign, polling evidence suggested that it did not attract much interest or attention from the voters themselves and was certainly not a key factor in determining voting behaviour. For example, a July 2001 Social Research Workshop (Pracownia Badań Społecznych: PBS) survey found that only 4% of respondents cited EU membership as one of the issues that would have the greatest impact when determining which grouping they would support, coming in seventh (last) place (*Rzeczpospolita*, 20 July 2001). Similarly, a July 2001 Pentor survey found that, when asked which election issues were important to them, only 7% chose EU membership, tenth out of the seventeen issues cited (voters were allowed to choose up to three) (*Wprost*, 19 August 2001).

Thirdly, as table 3 shows, polling evidence indicated that supporters of EU membership represented a majority among the voters of all the main parties and groupings represented in parliament except for the LPR (24% in favour and 52% against) but including Self-Defence (33% in favour and 29% against). This suggests that, although its stance on EU membership may not have put people off voting for it, misgivings about Polish accession were probably not the main reason why voters supported Self-Defence and were (at most) only one, relatively minor factor.[17]

Table 3: Support for EU membership by party, October 2001

	PO	SLD	PiS	Samoobrona	PSL	LPR
Yes	66	60	44	33	32	24
No	9	15	14	25	25	52
Don't know	8	11	14	13	13	2
Won't vote	18	15	28	29	29	22

Source: Roguska and Kucharczyk (2001, 13).

[17] See also: *Rzeczpospolita*, 21 November 2001.

In other words, while hard Eurosceptic anti-EU parties did relatively well in this election it was almost certainly not primarily as a result of their policy on the EU.[18] Only in the case of the LPR was it possible to credibly argue that opposition to Polish EU membership played any role in determining the grouping's level of electoral support. However, even in the LPR's case, electoral success was probably due more to the support of the 'religious right' electorate mobilised by Radio Maryja than its anti-EU stance as such (Szczerbiak 2002).

Conclusion

Recent years have seen increasing Polish cynicism about the EU that has led to a significant fall in support for Polish EU membership and the emergence of a sizeable bloc of anti-EU public opinion. A steady bloc of 20-25% of Poles are now opposed to EU membership and even the pro-EU majority appear to consent to the idea of membership rather than being particularly enthusiastic about it. We should not be too surprised by this. Support was bound to fall once it became apparent that conforming to EU norms would involve negative economic and social consequences as well as benefits. Indeed, it was primarily economic factors that provided the main basis for Polish anxieties regarding EU accession rather than ideological ones relating to loss of national sovereignty or identity. Moreover, the crack in the previously overwhelming pro-EU elite consensus and the subsequent politicisation of the debate on EU membership also chipped away at levels of public support. However, overall support for EU membership appears to have stabilised at a relatively high level.

Recent party debates, exemplified by the September 2001 election, illuminate both the nature of Polish Eurosceptic discourse and, in spite of the increased support for anti-EU parties and groupings, its still limited support. Two political groupings were openly hostile to the EU: the LPR opposed membership on ideological grounds arguing that it represented a loss of national sovereignty while Self-Defence made its support for accession conditional upon securing an unachievable set of conditions. Two other groupings, the PSL and PiS parties, were also highly critical of EU, primarily in relation to the kind of 'deal' that Poland was

---

[18] Indeed, most anti-EU voters actually voted for the SLD-UP coalition, the party that was perceived to have the most pro-EU policy! (Roguska and Kucharczyk 2001, 14-17).

likely to secure in the accession negotiations. However, it would be wrong to interpret this as representing a kind of Eurosceptic backlash given that, by virtually any measure, the EU was not a salient campaign issue. Most parties did not really give it much of a profile in their own election campaigns and EU membership was certainly not a factor in determining voting behaviour. Supporters of EU membership were a majority among the voters of all parties, except for the LPR whose electoral success was probably due more to other factors than its anti-EU stance as such.

Postscript

The Polish EU accession referendum was held over the weekend of 7-8 June 2003.[19] The SLD, UP and PO all ran vigorous and positive pro-EU campaigns. PiS and the PSL also called for a Yes vote, but ran more low key and reserved campaigns aimed more at reassuring their own supporters. After strongly criticising the progress of accession negotiations in the run up to the December 2002 Copenhagen Summit and even hinting that it might adopt an anti-EU stance, PiS eventually took a pro-EU stance following a special party Congress held in January 2003. The PSL also prevaricated for a long time and ended up linking its support for EU accession to the passage of a land turnover law that was approved just before Easter and campaigned on the rather half-hearted slogan 'Don't fear the Union. We are with you!'

The most high profile No campaign was run by the LPR and spearheaded by Roman Giertych. However, although the anti-EU campaign was quite visible, and a plausible case could be made that the terms of accession represented a 'second class membership' package', it never really made much of an impact. The LPR made a sensible tactical decision to focus primarily on anxieties about the potentially negative economic impact of Polish EU accession, either on particular sectors such as agriculture or on the macro-economic effects by, for example, arguing that prices would increase. They also stressed that a No vote would hasten the downfall of the unpopular SLD government, drawing attention to a pledge that Premier Miller gave in 2002 that he would resign if he lost the EU referendum. But the No campaign had difficulties in staying focused on its most powerful arguments and often fell back on less sa-

---

[19] For a more detailed analysis see Szczerbiak (2003).

lient emotional and ideological themes. Significantly, Self-Defence, ran a much less high profile anti-EU campaign than the LPR. Indeed, in spite of its leader Andrzej Lepper's often bitter anti-EU invective, Self-Defence argued that it was simply against the unfavourable accession terms negotiated by the government and campaigned on the rather enigmatic slogan, 'The Choice is Yours'. The No camp was also hamstrung by a lack of access to the public media. The only mass medium that gave strong backing to the anti-EU camp was Radio Maryja. However, the radical Catholic nationalist broadcaster came under intense pressure from the broadly pro-EU Church hierarchy to tone down its anti-EU coverage.

In the event, Poles voted overwhelmingly to join the EU by 77.45%% to 22.55%. More surprisingly, the 50% turnout required to make the referendum constitutionally valid was also comfortably reached, with 58.85% of Poles voting. Exit polling indicated that No voters were more likely to be found among the less well educated, those living in rural areas and the more conservative Southern and Eastern provinces. However, the best indicator of how people would vote appeared to be party allegiances. PO and SLD supporters voted Yes overwhelmingly by 91.7% and 90.3% respectively. PiS and PSL supporters voted Yes slightly less emphatically with majorities of 80.7% and 72.9% respectively. Self-Defence voters were evenly divided with a very narrow 50.3% majority voting in favour. The LPR was the only party where a clear 64% majority of its supporters voted No, although, interestingly, as many as 36% of them ignored party cues and opted for a Yes vote instead.

References

Bachman, Klaus. 2000. Historyczny kompromis inaczej. *Rzeczpospolita.* 9 June.
Blazyca, George and Marek Kolkiewicz. 1999. Poland and the EU: Internal Disputes, Domestic Politics and Accession. *Journal of Communist Studies and Transition Politics* 15, no. 4 (December): 131-143.
Centrum Badania Opinii Społecznej (CBOS). 1997. *Opinie o integracji z Unią Europejską.* Warsaw: CBOS. September.
Centrum Badania Opinii Społecznej (CBOS). 2001. *Przewidywane skutki integracji Polski z Unią Europejską.* Warsaw: CBOS. March.
Centrum Badania Opinii Społecznej (CBOS). 2002a. *Stosunek do integracji Polski z Unią Europejską po ogłoszeniu nowego stanowiska negocjacyjnego.* Warsaw: CBOS. January.

Centrum Badania Opinii Społecznej (CBOS). 2002b *Argumenty zwolenników i przeciwników integracji Polski z Unią Europejską.* Warsaw: CBOS. February.

Centrum Badania Opinii Społecznej (CBOS). 2002c. *Opnie o integracji Polski z Unią Europejską.* Warsaw: CBOS. March.

Centrum Badania Opinii Społecznej (CBOS). 2002d. *Poparcie dla wejścia Polski do Unii Europejskiej i opinie o konwencji Europejskim.* Warsaw: CBOS. March.

Grabowska, Mirosława. 1999. Przyszłość polskiej sceny politycznej – stabilność i zmiana. In *Przyszłość polskiej sceny politycznej,* Instytut Spraw Publicznych (ISP), 39-66. Warsaw: ISP.

Instytut Spraw Publicznych (ISP). undated. *Political Parties Towards Prospects for European Integration: 'Yes, and Furthermore No'.* Warsaw: ISP.

Instytut Spraw Publicznych (ISP). 1999. *Poparcie Polaków dla integracji z Unią Europejską w październiku 1999.* Warsaw: ISP.

Kolarska-Bobińska, Lena. 1998. Co innego będzie dzielić Polaków. *Rzeczpospolita.* 26 November.

Kolarska-Bobińska, Lena, ed. 1999. *Polska Eurodebata.* Warsaw: ISP.

Kucharczyk, Jacek. 1999a. *European Integration in Polish Political Debates 1997-1998.* Warsaw: ISP.

Kucharczyk, Jacek. 1999b. Porwanie Europy. *Rzeczpospolita.* 4 March.

Kucharczyk, Jacek. 2001. Club Class Europe? The Examination of Socio-political Conditions for a Eurosceptic Backlash in Poland. Paper prepared for the PSA Annual Conference. University of Manchester. 10-12 April.

Millard, Frances. 1999. Polish Domestic Politics and Accession to the European Union. In *Back to Europe: Central and Eastern Europe and the European Union,* ed Karen Henderson, 203-219. London: UCL Press.

Polskie Stronnictwo Ludowe (PSL). 2001a. *Czas na zmianę ... Progam społeczno-gospodarczy PSL.* Warsaw: PSL.

Polskie Stronnictwo Ludowe (PSL). 2001b. *Blisko ludzkich spraw: Deklaracja wyborcza Polskiego Stronnictwa Ludowego.* Warsaw: PSL.

Prawo i Sprawiedliwość (PiS). 2001. *Prawo i Sprawiedliwość: Program.* Warsaw: PiS.

Reed, John. 2001. Election Result may Deal Blow to Poland's EU hope. *Financial Times.* 25 September.

Roguska, Beata and Jacek Kucharczyk. 2001. *Wybory 2001 a integracja Polski z Unią Europejską.* Warsaw: ISP.

Sabbat-Swidlicka, Anna. 1992. Poland Investigates Radical Farmers' Union. *RFE/RL Research Report.* 28 (September).

Samoobrona. 2001. Stanowisko w sprawie przystąpienia do Unii Europejskiej. www.samoobrona.org.pl.

Skotnicka-Illasiewicz, Elżbieta. 1998. Poland on its Way Towards Membership of the EU and NATO: Hopes and Anxieties in a View of Public Opinion Polls. In *Yearbook of Polish European Studies,* Warsaw University Centre for European Studies, 243-263. Warsaw: Warsaw University Centre for European Studies.

Strzeszewski, Michał. 2001. Adaptation to the European Union: Hopes, Fears and Costs. In *Before the Great Change*, ed. Lena Kolarska-Bobińska, 89-126. Warsaw: ISP.

Szczerbiak, Aleks. 2000. Spadek i stabilzacja. Zmieniające się wzorce poparcia dla członkostwa Polski w Unii Europejskiej. In *Konstytucja dla rozeszerzającej się Europy*, ed. Ewa Popławska, 405-428 Warsaw: ISP.

Szczerbiak, Aleks. 2001a. Polish Public Opinion: Explaining Declining Support for EU membership. *Journal of Common Market Studies* 39, no 1 (March): 107-124.

Szczerbiak, Aleks. 2001b. *Europe as a Re-aligning Issue in Polish Politics? Evidence from the October 2000 Polish Presidential Election.* Sussex European Institute Working Paper No 48 / Opposing Europe Research Network Working Paper No 3. Brighton: Sussex European Institute.

Szczerbiak, Aleks. 2002. Poland's Unexpected Political Earthquake: The September 2001 Parliamentary Election. *Journal of Communist Studies and Transition Politics* 18, no. 3 (September).

Szczerbiak, Aleks. 2003. *The Polish EU Accession Referendum, 7-8 June 2003.* Opposing Europe Research Network Referendum Briefing No 5. www.sussex.ac.uk/Units/SEI/oern/ElectionBriefings/Referendum/Poland5.pdf.

Taggart, Paul and Aleks Szczerbiak. 2002. *The Party Politics of Euroscepticism in EU Member and Candidate States.* Sussex European Institute Working Paper No. 51 / Opposing Europe Research Network Working Paper No. 6. Brighton: Sussex European Institute.

EUROPEAN STUDIES 20 (2004): 269-290

SWISS EUROSCEPTICISM:
LOCAL VARIATIONS ON WIDER THEMES

Clive H. Church

Abstract

Although the term is rarely used in Switzerland, the country is more involved in Euroscepticism than is often appreciated. It can be found, with a Swiss accent, in public opinion, in direct democratic votes and in day to day politics, if not in the press. If general attitudes to Europe are often nuanced there is also a fierce anti-European discourse. However, this is part of a wider Swiss creed of disengagement from international political involvement. Extreme anti-Europeanism is orchestrated less by the mainstream parties of the centre right than by small parties, by the Swiss Peoples' Party, and by special organisations like AUNS, often set up to fight referenda. It draws most of its support from the lower middle class, especially in German speaking Switzerland. Overall, it is a movement of the right, which it has helped to revitalise. In so doing it has further changed the party system in Switzerland. However, its roots go beyond the rise of the far right. Anti-Europeanism has helped to change policy inside Switzerland and is likely to go on doing this. It might influence European developments and our thinking about the nature of Euroscepticism.

Given its absence from the European Union and even from the European Economic Area (EEA), Switzerland might appear an odd candidate for inclusion in this collection. The country might be thought not to need a campaigning anti-EU force because, as Flood (2002) argues, the country has an anti-European consensus. This seems to be the implicit view of such outside political scientists in the field who deign to notice the country.

Surprisingly Euroscepticism has yet to become a major subject of study for Swiss political scientists. This is partly because the Swiss rarely talk of Euroscepticism as such. A search of the Swiss media's data bank shows that, over the last few years, the term is rarely used. Eurosceptic as an adjective relating to individuals does occur, at least after 1995, but normally in relation to politicians in other countries or to developments in the Union itself. When it is used about Switzerland, more by journalists than by politicians, it can signify simply the opposite of pro-European sympathies. Politicians sometimes use it in a more banal way. Thus the hostile journal *Schweizerzeit* can talk of scepticism about the EU developing a foreign policy, and Minister Pascal Couchepin could attribute Swiss scepticism about the Union to the latter's failure to decide on a clear division of responsibilities. This tendency to use 'sceptical' in a way more dispassionate than ideological was given its clearest expression in a parliamentary intervention by Radical MP Hans Mehr in March 2001 when he portrayed the country as divided between 'Euro-turbos', 'Eurosceptics' and 'Euro-gegners', thus clearly placing sceptics as middle of the road doubters and not as ideologically committed Euro-phobes.

Yet the country does deserve consideration both for what we actually find there and because it has something to tell us about attitudes to Europe. Swiss relations with the EU are more intense than is often appreciated and enjoy considerable public support. The country as a whole is not anti-EU, but is very divided on European issues. It can be seen as a case of a country with a contested consensus in favour of Europe. For some Europe has become the key cleavage in Swiss politics. This is because, alongside genuine doubts, there is a strong and significant opposition to Swiss involvement in European integration. This has showed itself in a range of ways, often typically Swiss, such as the frequent popular policy votes and the setting of anti-European attitudes in a wider context of resistance to Swiss involvement in world politics.

The organisational structure of Swiss Euroscepticism reflects the dominance of direct democracy, as anti-European activity is mobilised not just by political parties, but by broader campaigning movements. Although this opposition fits into the general pattern of anti-EU movements in Europe (reflecting a certain degree of Europeanisation), it does so with specifically Swiss accents. In other words, although the Swiss case supports Milner's (2000) observation that most explanations of Euroscepticism see domestic politics as a key factor, the nature and orientation of those politics are rather different in Switzerland. This *Euro-gegenerism*, or hard Euroscepticism, is an increasingly important force within Swiss politics. In fact, its impact often goes beyond those of other Eurosceptic movements, partly because the opposition can often mobilise broader popular uncertainties. It is a much wider phenomenon than is often suggested, going beyond the forces associated with Christoph Blocher, the leader of the *Schweizerische Volkspartei* (SVP), and questions of aggrieved identity, to Swiss policy concerns and social structures.

Given this evidence of *Euro-gegenerism*, the Swiss case repays detailed examination. This is done here by looking firstly at the prevailing patterns of public opinion, especially when expressed through direct democracy. The chapter then goes on to consider the political salience, ideas, organisation and social support of hard opposition to Europe. Taken together these demonstrate the existence of a varied and influential movement which does not deserve to be overlooked. This is especially so given that this movement is helping to change the domestic political balance. Having exerted a considerable influence on Swiss policy on Europe it now seems as though it will significantly change the party system. This could have implications outside the country.

Of course, this Swiss hard Euroscepticism, which operates within a broader context of pragmatism and doubt, did not emerge from out of the blue. It has it roots in earlier patterns of the country's relations with Europe. Up until the 1980s there was a general consensus that neutrality and other factors meant that the country could have close economic ties, but could not get involved in entangling political organisations. However, as the decade wore on, the government came to feel this was not enough. Hence it made an abortive attempt to join the UN and then associated itself with EFTA in an effort to negotiate a special relationship with the EU. This caused many to doubt, and some to oppose, the new line with vigour. Opposition developed in the 1990s, encouraged by external difficulties such as the 'Nazi Gold' affair, and became more extreme. Yet support for internationalisation remained, and much of the population also reacted pragmatically to European questions, thus encouraging the forceful emergence of hard Swiss opposition to Europe.

Polls and votations

The ambiguities of Swiss feelings on Europe show up both in polling evidence and in referenda. Opinion polls have very often showed a low level of support for EU entry, rarely getting above the 50 per cent threshold. This level was first achieved in the autumn of 1991, but proved to be a fragile and unreliable base for more purposive European policies, as the December 1992 referendum on joining the EEA showed. Support for entry then fell away very rapidly, with opposition rising to 55% in early 1993. However, once the trauma of the rejection of entry to the EEA faded, outright opposition in turn declined until mid-1995 when it more or less stabilised in the mid 30s until late 2000. Thereafter it again rose to virtually 50%. Nevertheless, on the occasions when actual opposition declined, the 'don't knows' tended to rise accordingly, showing the limited reservoir of support. By October 2001 only 39% were in favour of entry, compared to 16% who did not know and 45% who were against. Other polls showed an even lower level of support both for entry and for making this a long term objective. In fact only 19% agreed that entry should be a prime foreign policy objective, although 42% accepted it as a long term possibility (compared to 25% who were totally opposed). Yet over 50% declared themselves satisfied with the EU, albeit not with its levels of democracy (Graffenried 2001).

A recent poll (GfS 2001) shows further evidence of doubt about Swiss involvement in EU based integration. Some 46% of those surveyed professed themselves sceptical about the bilateral agreements with the EU, and a declining number saw them as being to the country's advantage. In October 2001 only 24% believed the deals were wholly advantageous, compared to 46% who saw them as a mixed blessing and 16% who saw them as disadvantageous. Other polls showed that neutrality remained more popular than European involvement. Thus doubts about European integration, together with elements of outright opposition, are a major factor in Swiss public opinion.

This is more significant than it might be in other states because the Swiss practice of direct democracy allows public opinion to make decisions on European policy through what are called *votations* or *abstimmung* – consultations of a wider character than that implied by the conventional English term referendum (Kobach 1993). Direct democracy embraces a range of policy voting, including what the Swiss call referenda. A referendum must be held as regards both changes to the constitution and the ratification of certain types of treaties. In the case of such obligatory referenda, a dual popular and cantonal majority is required for the adoption of the measure. Referenda may also be used to challenge federal legislation. The latter have to be called if opponents can collect 50,000 signatures within 90 days after the adoption of the law concerned. At the same time, the Swiss can launch initiatives, calling for constitutional changes (including those dealing with European issues), if they can collect 100,000 signatures.

Over the last few years all these facilities have been used in an anti-European way and have exercised a major influence on government policy, whether by blocking change or by forcing caution on the Federal Council by the threat of a referendum defeat. In fact over recent years there have been seven *votations* that touched directly on the country's European policy and involved all three types of referendum permitted by the Constitution.

The first, and most significant, of these was the obligatory 6 December 1992 *votation* on entry to the EEA. Despite the fact that the idea of entry was endorsed by most of the establishment, it was defeated by 50.3% to 49.7% (and by 14 1/2 cantons to 6 1/2) on a turnout of 78.3%, the fifth highest in Swiss history. Many habitual abstainers turned out to vote against the idea, encouraged by a skilful anti-EEA campaign which turned the establishment's earlier doubts about the EC against its new wish to join both the EEA and the EC. Although the referendum was lost by only 23,000 votes, the effect of the rejection was dramatic, humiliating and weakening for the government. Post-election analysis showed lack of confidence in the latter as the key factor (Kriesi et al. 1993). At the same time the defeat shifted the political balance towards the opposition leaders and hardened their approach.

The Federal Council was forced to put its application for entry on ice and eventually opted for bilateral negotiations to fill the gap left by being outside the Single Market. The government's position in these negotiations was then complicated by a second vote, this time on a successful popular initiative in 1994. This committed it to a timetable for shifting cross-Alpine transit from road to rail, complicating its transit understandings with the Union. It had to proceed very carefully in case such ecological Euroscepticism undermined the financing of the new rail tunnels. The legislation enacting this was twice challenged by opponents and, though it was easily approved in September and November 1998, fear of defeat had worried the government.

Before these approvals, a new anti-European initiative, encouraged by 6 December, had been tabled. This initiative sought to require that a popular vote be held before any negotiations were started, as well as at their conclusion. If passed, this fifth *votation* would have blocked the bilateral talks since it had retrospective effects. However, it was emphatically turned down, albeit on a low turn out, in June 1997.

The same fringe groups then launched a further initiative to challenge the bilateral agreements, even though the mainstream opposition groups chose not to do so. Despite difficulties, enough signatures were collected to put the matter to a vote of the people on 21 May 2000. In this sixth *votation*, the bilaterals were approved by a two to one majority, though on only a 48% turnout.

Initially, approval of the bilaterals was seen as removing a blockage in the country's relations with Europe. This proved not to be so, thanks to enthusiasts for membership who refused to withdraw their initiative for entry. This initiative had been launched after 6 December and had gained the requisite signatures in 1996. In March 2001 the idea went down to a catastrophic defeat by 76.8% to 23.2%, on a 55% turnout. Although the result was what the government wanted, this seventh vote was negatively assessed, forcing the Federal Council further on to the back foot. Any thoughts of re-applying for entry were consigned to the distant future, while the bar had also been raised for the initiation of any new round of bilateral negotiations.

The Federal Council also had to fight to win support for UN entry. Although not directly a *votation* on Europe, some opponents saw the UN issue in these terms. Thus, although the government sought to keep the 'E' word out of the UN debate, the issue did serve to galvanise the 'antis' into action, which might explain why the mainstream opposition groups had held their fire over the bilaterals. Deploying all their efforts to defeat UN membership when it came up for decision in March 2002, the 'antis' got within a few hundred votes of denying it the necessary cantonal majority. So direct democracy clearly shows continuing popular doubts about Europe, the influence of anti-European forces and the constraints thus placed on government policy.

Political debate

These campaigns further helped to generate an ongoing general debate on Europe. A whole raft of parliamentary questions and queries were tabled. The Parliament had major deliberations on government reports on European policy, while elements within it regularly but unsuccessfully demanded the complete withdrawal of the government's application for membership. In 2000-2001 an attempt was made to relaunch the EEA idea, a move typifying the limited enthusiasm amongst many MPs for going too far or too fast. In fact the Foreign Affairs Committee of the Upper House concluded unenthusiastically in April 2002 that there was no real alternative to going further down the bilateral road.

Parliament has a role in the direct democratic process. It has to pronounce on all initiatives and often adopted positions which were not those of the government. This was especially so when, in the spring of 2000, party aspirations helped to block compromise proposals which might have eased the government's difficulties with the 'Yes to Europe' initiative, which required it immediately to start entry negotiations and not at a time of its own choosing. At the same time the government came under pressure from anti-Europeans who felt that it enjoyed too much freedom of action during *votation* campaigns.

The government itself has been seen by some as having its own doubtful elements. Its policies prior to the 1990s have been described as 'Eurosceptic' and since then it has been seen as divided between pro and anti elements. However, the veil of secrecy which surrounds its collegial decision-making makes it hard to be sure. There was some reluctance to endorse the off the cuff decision of October 1991, made by the two ministers actually negotiating the European Economic Area agreement, to make membership the main aim when it became clear that the final EEA agreement did not give the country what it wanted. The decision to apply to the EU was the result of a majority vote, suggesting again a certain hesitancy. Even today there are different degrees of enthusiasm in the Federal Council. However, all Ministers endorse the official long term entry strategy, claiming that it is in line with popular wishes. Equally, they are united in resisting EU pressures for concessions on the exchange of banking and tax information. More generally, they are careful not to push things too far ahead of the public.

Where Europhobia and, indeed, scepticism do not show up in Switzerland is in the media. This is partly, as Stampfli (2002) suggests, a structural matter because, like the EU, Switzerland has no common media. This is due to a combination of linguistic diversity and, at least in the press, of local fragmentation. Generally speaking, however, the mainstream press tends to be sympathetic to Swiss engagement in international affairs, sometimes exuberantly so in the case of *Le Temps* and some other French language papers. The country does not have campaigning anti-European tabloids. Hence anti-European opinion can often treat the media as the enemy, lacking objectivity and purveying deception, lies and aggressive leftist partiality.

Blocher and some other anti-EU leaders have had brushes with the press, to do with such matters as advertising or unflattering portrayals. They have attacked the untoward influence which the press can yield, which is supposed to undermine grass roots democracy. Anti-Europeans, therefore, tend to rely on their own publications such as *SchweizerZeit*, *Europa-Magazin* and *Mattino della Domenica*. Since these do not have a wide circulation, anti-European forces often issue their own statements to the population at large and publish as much as they can. Thus, Swiss anti-Europeans have active communication strategies. They actively use the web and encourage advertising, pamphleting and letter writing. Indeed AUNS claims that at crucial moments, 40% of all references to Europe in the press come from them.

The anti-Europeans try to deny their opponents similar access to the public by using the rules on referendum spending, by attacking government information provision as 'propaganda', and through the launching of law suits. They also exploit the largely neutral broadcast media. The key example of this is the Friday 'Arena' show on German speaking TV, which is often used to debate European issues. Here *Euro-gegeners* tend to demonise their opponents and targets, while claiming to be the victims of a conspiracy.

Ideas

Although hard Swiss anti-Europeanism shares with other Euroscepticisms a clear dislike of the EU, it does so for reasons which are slightly different. Most importantly, the EU is seen as problematic not just in itself, but as part of a wider threat posed by interdependence to Swiss life and to the country's traditional world role. Anti-Europeanism, in other words, has a resonance in Switzerland because it fits into an older and well established political culture. Moreover, majority opinion seems to be less anti-EU as such than concerned about the costs to the country of various forms of relationship. This accounts for a pattern of pragmatic changes of opinion.

There appear to be five main elements underlying Swiss dislike of the EU (Martino and Pasquier 1995). Firstly, there is the absolute certainty about the virtues of the Swiss situation, what is known as the special case or *Sonderfall Schweiz* – the fact that since 1945 the country has enjoyed unparalleled prosperity and stability. This is attributed to the ultra-democratic political system with its federalism, direct democracy and consultation, all held in place by neutrality. To draw close to the EU is not necessary because the country, as a result of the *Sonderfall*, is not isolated.

Secondly, it is argued that drawing closer to the EU would jeopardise the *Sonderfall* economically because it would force harmful policy harmonisation. The country's recent history shows that prophecies of economic disaster outside the Rome treaty organisations are illusory. Much is made of the fact that the extreme prophecies of economic disaster if the country rejected the EEA have not come true.

Thirdly, the EU is seen as a political menace because entry would both impose constraints on the exercise of popular sovereignty through direct democracy and end the treasured freedom from law made by 'foreign judges', dating back to the thirteenth century. It would transfer decision making from communes and cantons to Berne and to Brussels, thus upsetting the federal balance. Such things are, moreover, seen not as the outcome of negotiations but as diktats. It is argued that the EU involves an authoritarian conception of the state, which is dominated by lobbies, by the *Brüsseler Bürokratie,* or by the big member states. There is particular dislike of the way that small states like Austria are treated, as well as of the push towards EU 'great powerism', something hard to reconcile with neutrality.

Fourthly, the fabric of Swiss society would be at risk. The all important peasantry would be at risk from the CAP, the mountains would suffer from increased traffic and environmental damage, and, most importantly, society in general would be under threat from immigration. This would pose a threat to wages, to social security and to property ownership, not to mention socio-cultural integrity, with talk of the Swiss becoming 'foreigners in their own country'.

Finally, most Swiss anti-Europeans accuse the national establishment of collaboration in the creation of the European threat. Rather than defending national interests, it has allowed itself to be bewitched by the huge salaries and excessive power of Brussels, showing itself *Heimatmüde,* or having given up on the fatherland. Those who think this way are Swiss centred, with few transnational links to other opposition movements and no great tendency to define themselves as 'Eurosceptic'. In fact they are more likely to see themselves as Swiss patriots defending the traditional rejection of entanglement in the outside world. As some anti-European publicity puts it 'Yes to Switzerland mean no to the EU, NATO and the UN'. This reflects the way that neutrality has moved from being a tool of policy to a defining and untouchable virtue linked, through the militia army, to national cohesion as well as to independence. Hence, following on the first UN vote, its main vehicle, the *Aktion für eine Unabhängige und Neutrale Schweiz* (AUNS/ASIN), campaigns, as its name suggests, for independence and neutrality. It calls for a foreign policy respectful of traditional neutrality and refraining from external activism and engagements. Such views have prevented Swiss Euroscepticism from going very far down the road which sees a wider Europe and other alliances as better than the EU.

In consequence, there has been strong opposition not just to NATO and the Partnership for Peace, but also to the UN and to bodies like the IMF and the World Bank (although the Swiss did join the latter in 1992). Equally, the US has been seen as something of a threat due to its support for pressure on Switzerland over its neutrality in the last war and its handling of Nazi gold. The Blocher view is that the country showed an unparalleled will to resist and, in so doing, upheld its neutrality. So it has nothing to apologise for, and there is no need to create a 'Solidarity Fund'. The opposition attacked the UN as a stepping stone to EU and NATO membership, and as something which would impose new costs on the country, financially, and in terms of identity, standing and sovereignty. NATO is seen as subjecting the country to the diktats of the 'veto' powers, and is often attacked as simply a tool of the US and as a vehicle for the pursuit of power politics at the expense of small state principles and rights. Surprisingly, even the OECD can be a problem when, as is now the case, it seeks to get the Swiss to give up on banking secrecy. This is seen as a cynical piece of great power manipulation to weaken the Swiss financial services industry. It will be clear, then, that Swiss Euroscepticism is less obsessive about the EU than other Euroscepticisms, but also less able to offer an alternative strategy of interdependence.

Party architecture

Whereas soft Euroscepticism in Switzerland is fluid and poorly organised, hard *Euro-gegenerism* has an impressive, if unusual organisational foundation. This rests not just on parties, but on pressure groups with a European focus and on loose coalitions and committees, as well as on campaigning bodies.

Despite – or because of – direct democracy, a range of parties are involved in opposition to the EU. To begin with, there are a number of very hostile small, mainly right wing parties. Prominent amongst these are the *Schweizer Democraten*, the remaining descendants of the xenophobic movements of the 1970s. Although they are now down to one seat in the Lower House, they are still active in out and out resistance to European integration. In alliance with the populist *Lega dei Ticinesi* they collected signatures for the challenge to the bilateral agreements. The *Lega* itself is a powerful force in Italian speaking Switzerland, based around the charismatic leadership of Biagnasca and Maspoli, backed up by the former's newspaper *Mattino della Domenica* and, sometimes, by street demonstrations. Its opposition to German Swiss 'colonisation', to the ruling political elite and to contamination from Italy helps to explain why the Ticino voted with with *Urschweiz* – as the founding German-speaking cantons of central Switzerland are known – in 1992, 2000 and 2002. Alongside this tandem is the *Freiheits Partei Schweiz*, formerly the *AutoPartei*. Although this is losing its parliamentary representation, its local branches allow it to support anti-European campaigns.

One unusual feature is the role played by religion in hard Euroscepticism. This is symbolised by the fundamentalist Protestant *Eidgenössisch-Demokratische Union* which is strongly anti-European because of its general defence of Swiss independence and neutrality. The *Evangelische Volkspartei*, the traditional Protestant party, can also lean this way at times, as in its resistance to a counter-project to the 'Yes for Europe' initiative. Traditionalist Catholic movements, the *Katholischen Volkspartei* in Luzern and Thurgau and the *Mouvement Chrétien Conservateur* in the Valais, also actively oppose EU links and helped in the collection of signatures to challenge the bilaterals. All of these oppositions are deeply rooted in Swiss history.

Most mainstream parties are, at least in principle, in favour of closer links with the EU, perhaps even of entry. However, there are many 'soft' doubts about the timetable and the conditions, while some elements take a more strongly critical line. The *Freisinnig-Demokratischen Partei* for instance is very divided on the issue. It holds together by agreeing to see how the bilaterals work first. The *Christlichdemokratische Volkspartei* (CVP) is somewhat schizophrenic on the issue, having expressed great enthusiasm for entry in 2000, but then cooling off as its core German speaking support showed it was doubtful. The Greens and the Old Liberals lean somewhat the other way although there are doubts as well. Even the Communist Party is now in favour of entering the EU, but only if the latter goes back on Maastricht and becomes more 'social'. Nevertheless, stances tend to be changeable and to reflect doubt more than root and branch opposition. Thus only one FDP MP voted against the bilaterals. In other words, the mainstream parties of the centre right on the whole exhibit soft Euroscepticism rather than hard Europhobia. As the main pro-European party, the Social Democrats show little hard scepticism, though there can be concern on specific EU policies and there are suggestions that the rank and file are less enthusiastic than their leaders.

The Swiss Peoples' Party and the party system

Things are very different when it comes to the *Schweizerische Volkspartei* (Ladner 2001). This has emerged as the main, and most dynamic, force in Switzerland under the leadership of Christoph Blocher and its Zurich wing. Thanks to a long march through regional parliaments it is now present in every canton, including in the Suisse Romande. This development drew in the old extreme right, more or less destroying the FPS in the process, and turned the party into a campaigning movement led not only by Blocher, but by a new cadre of often young lieutenants. Moreover, its new sections increasingly adopt the Zurich hard line and not the more moderate stances, dating back to earlier agrarian and liberal incarnations, in Bern and the Graubünden. So, although the latter hold the party's government seat, their objections to the party's new hard line external policies and style have largely been seen off.

This was partly because the SVP's cantonal expansion went hand in hand with national electoral victory, notably in late October 1999 when its share of the popular vote rose to an unprecedented 22.5% and its seats to 44 from its previous 29. In the context of Swiss political stability this was a far more significant rise than it might appear. The party's success has a number of explanations: a solid base in the lower middle classes of Zurich; its organisational and financial strength (in which Blocher is much involved); and its ability, so far, to combine its status as a party of government with its role as an activist opposition. It does not behave like a typical consensus party. Rather, it campaigns hard on a series of simple emotive issues: asylum abuse; taxation; and the defence of Swiss institutions, neutrality and sovereignty. Frequent use of referenda have been very helpful to its missionary zeal and to its ability to draw on traditionalist doubts about the direction in which the political class is leading the country. Its opposition to Europe serves as a surrogate for wider fears about globalisation. In fact its populist style is very effective and hard to counter, especially since the SVP is also involved in mainstream government policy-making.

The SVP is the only party consistently to reject EU membership and to call for the formal and definitive withdrawal of the 1992 entry application. However, it has also moved away from its old pro-agricultural stance because of concerns about the level of subsidy involved, since such expenditures conflict with its free market and small state policies. Paradoxically this has brought it into conflict with the Swiss business elite at times. The party has also taken a tough stance on migration and the size of the foreign population, which it sought, unsuccessfully, to cap. A Council of Europe parliamentary report (Gjellerod 1999) therefore denounced it as an extreme and, by implication, racist party. The SVP fiercely denied this and Blocher in particular has been careful not to say anything which could easily be construed as racist. Nevertheless, the charge has stuck (Gaffney 2002).

Not all anti-Europeans are convinced by the party's credentials on such issues. The *Lega* and other rejectionists have pointed out that the SVP's anti-Europeanism has its limits. The party did not actually object to the bilaterals, partly because these suited Blocher's own economic interests and partly because they were a way of satisfying pragmatic opinion which might otherwise have accepted entry. Hence, hardline critics can paint Blocher as part of the 'system'. Yet, despite such criticisms, the old political class has found the SVP to be a real thorn in its flesh. Because the former is consensual and managerial in approach, rather than demotic, it can be less effective in the use of the new media than the Blocherite SVP. Such weaknesses have been exacerbated by scandals such as the collapse of Swissair, as well as by the way that outside developments such as the EU's treatment of Austria have played into the SVP's hands.

In fact the rise of the SVP has dramatically changed the hitherto stable party balance in Switzerland. This is true both at cantonal and national levels. Nationally, there has been remarkable stability since 1959, with the three main parties each maintaining the support of about 20% of the electorate and the SVP about half that. This has won the big three two seats each on the Federal Council and the SVP one – the so called 'Magic Formula'. However, of late secularisation has consistently driven down CVP support so that it now enjoys the support of no more than 13% of the electorate. Yet it still controls two government seats. Given the corresponding rise of the SVP, the question of a second SVP seat on

the Federal Council arose. This was blocked in 1999 because of opposition to Blocherite extremism and the unwritten rule that serving ministers
themselves choose when to leave office. Nevertheless, the continued
disparity between the CVP and the SVP suggests that this may have to
change after the 2003 general elections. By consistently attacking Joseph
Deiss, the CVP Foreign Minister, for his pro-European and gauche
stances, the SVP is seeking to remind people of its claims. However, the
fact that the whole parliament choses members of the Federal Council
means that SVP candidates might well not come from the Blocherite
wing, as happened in 2000.

In any case, the way that the SVP has established itself as the dominant voice of insular right wing politics, leaving the Social Democrats as
the voice of progressive and pro-European opinion, means that Swiss
politics have become more polarised. This is being encouraged by the
whittling down, and sometimes the elimination, of several of the smaller
parties of the centre and right. However, this defragmentation is not
simply based on the European issue. It reflects wider divisions on
whether the country should be open or closed, issues which are themselves related to complicated domestic political disputes.

Campaigning organisations
Hard anti-Europeanism is not restricted to the SVP and the parliamentary arena. In fact Swiss proportional representation and direct democracy offer many opportunities for political involvement, which have
helped the anti-European cause in general and the Blocherite tendency in
particular by allowing the emergence of a number of campaigning pressure groups and committees (Aligiakis and Bellet 1998).

The most significant of these groups is AUNS, which allows the
Blocherite tendency to recruit outside the confines of the SVP. AUNS
started out life in 1986 with some 2,000 members and grew slowly until
1991. Profiting from public anxieties about the EEA, its membership
then shot up, adding 5,000 new members annually throughout the 1990s.
Although this has now slackened off, it still had over 42,000 members in
2002, far more than many parties. Given that it also had some 4 million
Swiss francs in capital, including a large fighting fund, it has been a very
successful organisation. It was, for example, able to raise 120,000 signatures against army reform in very short order (which was more than the
Lega and the Social Democrats could do). In 1992 it started campaigning

well ahead of the government, and put the latter, and the business community, to shame by its vigour.

Although clearly dominated by Blocher, AUNS is formally run by a committee which includes other anti-European MPs, not all of whom are from the SVP. Its grass roots membership also crosses party lines, although all are true believers. Hence they do not always do what they are told by Blocher, in 2000 voting to ignore Blocher's advice not to campaign against the bilaterals because these did not involve a challenge to independence, neutrality or security. Like other anti-Europeans, AUNS refused to see the accords as just economic and viscerally attacked them on grounds of political principle, ignoring their possible role as a barrier to EU membership. The failure of this abrasive policy meant that, when it came to the UN vote, AUNS felt it best to work behind the scenes, allowing ad hoc committees to lead the campaign. Conversely, Blocher himself, aided by his wife, campaigned vigorously, as did the SVP in general. The narrow failure to deny UN entry a cantonal majority means that AUNS remains a major factor in anti-European politics, notably at referenda.

However, it is not the only body of its kind. There are other smaller active forces. Again most of these are on the right of the political spectrum, although there is the Forum for Direct Democracy which publishes the *Europa Magazin*. This peasant and environmentalist movement apparently collected 2,500 signatures against the bilaterals. In the 1999 federal elections there were also several 'Solidarity Groups' in French speaking Switzerland which linked the bilaterals with threats to the welfare state.

More to the right, but also concerned with environmental and social issues, are bodies like the Basle-based *Presse Club Schweiz* of Ernest Indlekofer, which collected 3,500 signatures against the bilaterals and distributed a million hostile tracts, mainly because it saw them as a transmission belt to EU entry. Luc de Meuron and the Neuchâtel based *Lettre Politique* takes a similar view. The anti-European line is also upheld by the *EU-Nein* organisation, a youth movement set up after the bilaterals and also using the name of 'Young 4 FUN' (a word play from the German *Freiheit, Unabhängigkeit, Neutralität*). It maintains a vivid website and campaigned strongly against UN entry.

One very unusual movement is the *Verein zur Förderung der psychologischen Menshenkenntnis* (VPM, or the *St Michael Vereinigung*), a strange fundamentalist movement with roots in German speaking anti-alcohol Protestantism and beyond. With its considerable financial resources, its

many volunteers and an active secretariat the VPM is said to have collected the outstanding signatures necessary for the challenge to the bilaterals. Its political wing, *Schweizer Bürgervotum*, then campaigned against
the deal in the guise of the *Eidgenossische Komitee gegen den sektorielle EU
Beitritt* and *Eine Schweiz für unserer Kinder*. They often work with a whole
range of often transitory movements. Thus the EEA was resisted by the
'Swiss Action Committee against EEA and EC diktats and for a Switzerland Open to the World' and the bilaterals were fought by a whole raft of
Committees, such as the *Komitee gegen die Sektoralen* which brought together some twenty smaller groups. All this gives hard anti-Europeanism
an overlapping network of support at crucial moments.

Taken by themselves many of these are, no doubt, insignificant, but
collectively they show that hard anti-European stances have real roots in
Swiss society. To some extent this is territorially determined, being stronger in German speaking Switzerland than in French areas. Only 2,000 of
the 67,000 signatures challenging the bilaterals came from the latter.
Nonetheless, earlier claims that there was no support for such views in
the Suisse Romande have been belied by events. In fact about 12% of
AUNS members live there and possibly as many as a third of French
speaking voters are mildly Eurosceptic. The Ticino is also a stronghold of
anti-feeling thanks to its unease about its southern neighbour.

Age plays a part, as observers have often remarked on the elderly
nature of AUNS supporters and polling evidence backs this up. Nevertheless, there are many young anti-Europeans in the SVP and beyond.
Opposition to Europe also tends to correlate with lower levels of education and religious fervour amongst Catholics encourages scepticism on
European issues. The VPM example suggests that this would also be true
for extreme Protestantism. However, gender does not seem to be that
important a factor, although the majority of opponents are probably men.
Socially, anti-Europeanism tends to draw on farmers and small business-
men who are not plugged into wider circuits and fear competition. Craft
and trade bodies can also be cautious. Polls also consistently show a
considerable gap between the support for integration amongst business
and opinion leaders on the one hand and the doubts of ordinary Swiss on
the other. As the anti-European movement is increasingly urban, the
agricultural interest is decreasing. Even so, small towns and villages tend
to be more doubtful than big towns. Despite this a growing number of
workers are involved and many have moved from the Social Democrats
(SPS) to the SVP. In other words, although opposition to Europe tends

to be concentrated in the older parts of Swiss society, it is to varying degrees found everywhere. Soft Euroscepticism is equally widespread but is probably more representative socially.

Characterisations

Clearly then Switzerland, alongside many general doubts about EU entry, has a significant anti-European movement, based on traditional parties and campaigning organisations. This shows itself in *votations* and beyond, and it draws on a very critical view of European integration, albeit set within a wider ideology of resistance to a more active international political role for the country. Hence, whereas once the Federal Council tried to use the existence of internal doubts as a bargaining ploy, it now has to accept not merely that the Swiss people have to be convinced, but that it has to face down a strong opposition.

So how is such anti-Europeanism best characterised, why did it emerge and what are its implications? To begin with, it is rarely seen as Euroscepticism by those involved. They can see themselves as *EU-ge-geners*, but they rarely classify themselves in these terms. Implicitly they define themselves as much by what they are for, as by what they are against. They are patriotically concerned with a wide defence of Swiss political traditions and not just with the EU. Actually it is the supporters of integration who are seen as obsessed with the EU. In other words, *Euro-gegenerism* in Switzerland is not an ideological phobia based on Europe. It is broader and more Swiss centred than this.

Certainly it has to be located on the political right. It can often attack the Social Democrats and not only for their support for European integration. Blocher has tried to depict them as 'totalitarian' and linked to fascism. However, this view has not convinced the population at large in the way that traditional conservative opinions often do. This is perhaps why there is so little Euroscepticism of the left, despite Kitschelt's (1997, 148-149) assertion that neutrality based concerns would make the left an equally important foundation for Swiss opposition to Europe. Neutrality, in fact, is much more a right wing concern.

So why should there be these forms of Euroscepticism? One common explanation is that they derive from the anti-immigrant far right (Husband 2000). However, while this plays a part it is clearly subordinate to a wider and less reactive view of the country's place in the world. Nor is Milner's (2000) view, that relations between state and organised interest groups are the key factor, sustainable in the Swiss case. Equally, the

SVP's position, as both a government party and merely one part of a larger, overlapping alliance of anti-European forces, rather rules out Sitter's (2001) view that the real dynamic is a matter of making and breaking governments. Given the nature of the Federal Council and the importance of direct democracy this cannot be a full answer. If Swiss anti-Europeanism can be the politics of opposition, it is opposition of a different kind to that found elsewhere, more complex, but also potentially more far reaching (Taggart 1998).

Despite the ambiguous position of the SVP, Swiss anti-Europeanism can be seen as a form of anti-establishment politics. Opposition to the EU and to other perceived threats to national democratic identity are clearly used as a tool in the domestic power struggle unleashed by the government's change of external policy since the late 1980s. This opposition appeals to a specific social constituency and is also attractive to the sceptical pragmatism of the middle ground. So far, this has been brilliantly done, with all the opportunities provided by the political system being exploited. At the same time, Swiss anti-Europeanism has been helped by the weakness of the other side. Governmental failures in terms of information, of strategy and in its estimation of popular support have been compounded by the limited size, divisions and illusions of other pro-European forces. The fact that the lead is taken by the left leaning Social Democrats, who are often seen as the weak link in mainstream politics, has also been helpful.

So what impact has all this had? Internally feelings about Europe have contributed to the emergence of a new cleavage in Swiss politics. The cleavage line, however, actually goes beyond the European question, embracing a wider range of questions about the country's position in world society. Swiss political scientists talk of a division between an open, outward looking mainly urban Switzerland, aware of the country's similarities to its neighbours, and a closed, inward looking and mainly rural Switzerland, more conscious of Switzerland's particularities. This cleavage is complicated by the country's traditional plural fragmentation and the opposition is not dominant. Although people in the middle may line up with AUNS at particular *abstimmungen*, they are basically pragmatists and not faithful followers. So, hard anti-Europeanism often loses both arguments and *votations*.

Nonetheless, the European issue has helped to revitalise the right, probably more so than xenophobia. Thus it has increasingly dominated the SVP and has helped it to major election victories. In so doing it has challenged traditional Swiss party systems and balances. At the same time, it has helped to change the tone of Swiss politics, making them more strident and confrontational, calling into question *konkordanz* and compromise. Further gains for the SVP could lead to something closer to a two-party system, which would stand many aspects of Swiss politics on their head.

With the reservoir of doubt about entry, if not about integration *per se*, to draw on, anti-Europeanism has forced the government to moderate any enthusiasm for entry, at least in the short term. Constraints on government policy are one way in which the rise of such Euroscepticism affects the wider Europe. These, along with referendum defeats, have made many EU decision-makers doubtful about the ability of the Swiss authorities to embrace membership. Hence, there might be less willingness to make concessions in bilateral negotiations in the hope of encouraging entry. The EU sometimes seems to want the Swiss either to accept the *acquis* in the areas in which they are interested, or to go without. This means that Europe could become an increasingly important theme in Swiss political debate. With the UN question settled, opposition may well focus on this issue partly because the EU is the one organisation in which the country is not yet involved and partly because the bilateral route now threatens higher costs. On the one hand the original deals, notably that on free movement, have to be extended to Eastern Europe, which causes much alarm. On the other hand, the second round of bilateral negotiations has seemed to threaten both banking secrecy and interference with Swiss policing, assuming the country signs up to the Schengen Accord on the abolition of border controls between contracting states. Encouraged by recent successes, AUNS and the SVP, moreover, need new targets. Notably, a September 2002 *votation* saw the blocking of the Solidarity Fund proposal intended to quell international criticism over the so-called 'Nazi gold' affair, while an anti-asylum initiative failed by only the narrowest of margins in November 2002. In what Blocher termed a 'triumphant defeat', proposals for the harsher treatment of asylum seekers won a cantonal majority and failed by only 2374 votes to get a popular majority as well.

Even though banking secrecy now appears likely to escape unscathed, the bilateral approach still encourages concern about foreigners, and hence asylum. There is talk of new referenda on asylum and the bilateral deals. This means not merely that the EU may move further to centre stage but, with the bilateral approach coming under threat, the question could become a brutally simple matter of whether there should be any contact or whether the country should not embrace a more radical isolationism or *alleingang* strategy. With support for entry declining to little more than a third, and the SVP again rising in the polls, the willingness of more pragmatic opinion in the middle ground to reject this absolutist choice seems less certain than it has been. If general doubts about Europe continue to grow, this will further encourage the hardliners. It may even give them the chance of enticing pragmatist and true sceptics to join them. Because of such pressures, the government faces real difficulties. It may be forced into some kind of *alleingang* ('going it alone'), surviving on the first bilaterals and doing nothing to revive the application. However, this will leave it open to all kinds of pressure from the EU. The fact that the country could, in a passive way, be a destabilizing hole at the centre of the growing web of integration might intensify the influence of Swiss *Euro-gegeners*. Should the country take the plunge and successfully reapply, Swiss Euroscepticism could potentially, as Roberts-Thomson (2001) suggests, have even more influence through the leverage its referenda could give them. Whereas countries like Ireland and Denmark can query major constitutional issues, the Swiss could not merely do the same, and perhaps more often, but could conceivably also vote on policy matters. This could add a whole new dimension of uncertainty to ordinary policy making.

The Swiss case has implications for our understanding of Euroscepticism. European integration clearly helps to mobilise politics beyond the narrow confines of the EU and the candidate states. Alongside the hard Europhobes of the Blocherite camp there are many Euro-realists, as many supporters of closer integration sometimes describe themselves. The latter have roots in Swiss political culture, even if this is often denied by the opposition. In other words, the term is wider and harder to pin down than many British usages assume. In Switzerland, it often takes the form of honest doubt about the Union and relations with it and not root and branch opposition, a situation also found in Germany (Lees 2002). This suggests that Euroscepticism may not be, as Tiersky (2001) suggests, a serviceable term. Politically as well as intellectually, Swiss opposition to the EU matters now and may do more so in future. Despite the fact that it speaks in Swiss dialect, it deserves its place in this collection.

References

Aligiakis, Maximos and Marc de Bellet. 1998. Les acteurs non étatiques et la politique européenne de la Suisse. *Swiss Political Science Review* 4, no. 3: 33-52.

Dupont, Cédric and Pascal Sciarini. 2001. Switzerland and the European Integration Process: Engagement without Marriage. *West European Politics* 24, no. 2: 211-226.

Flood, Chris. 2002. The Challenge of Euro-scepticism. In *The EU Handbook* (second edition), 73-84, ed. Jackie Gower. Chicago: Fitzroy-Dearborn.

Gaffney, John. 2002. Right Turn in the Wrong Direction. *Times Higher Education Supplement* 10 May: 22.

GfS-Forschungsinstitut. 2001. *Europa-Barometer Winter 2001*. Bern: GfS-Forschungsinstitut. www.gfs.ch/europa.html

Gjellerod, Henning (rapporteur). 1999. *Threats Posed to Democracy by Extremist Parties and Movements in Europe*. Council of Europe Parliamentary Assembly Document 8517.

Graffenried, Valerie de, 2001 Euroscepticisme gagne du terrain. *Le Temps* 4 October, 11.

Husband, Christopher. 2000. Switzerland: Right-Wing and Xenophobic Parties, from Margin to Mainstream? *Parliamentary Affairs* 53, no. 3: 501-516

Kitschelt, Herbert. 1997. European Party Systems: Continuity and Change. In *Developments in West European Politics*, 131-150, eds. Martin Rhodes, Paul Heywood, and Vincent Wright. Basingstoke: MacMillan.

Kobach, Kris. 1993. *The Referendum: Direct Democracy in Switzerland*. Aldershot: Dartmouth.

Kriesi, Hanspeter et al. 1993. *Analyse des votations fédérales du 6 décembre 1992*. Geneva: GfS/Université de Genève (January).

Ladner, Andreas. 2001. Swiss Political Parties: Between Persistence and Change. *West European Politics* 24, no. 2: 121-144.

Lees, Charles. 2002. 'Dark Matter': Institutional Constraints and the Failure of Party-based Euro-scepticism in Germany. *Political Studies* 50, no. 2: 244-267.

de Martino, Luigi and Nadia Pasquier. 1995. De la confiance à la défiance: une analyse du courrier des lecteurs au sujet de la votation sur le traité EEE. *Swiss Political Science Review* 1, no. 1: 53-78.

Milner, Susan. 2000. Introduction: A Healthy Scepticism? *Journal of European Integration* 22, no. 1: 1-14.

Roberts-Thomson, Patricia. 2001. EU Treaty Referendums and the European Union. *Journal of European Integration* 23, no. 2: 105-137.

Sitter, Nick. 2001. The Politics of Opposition and European Integration in Scandinavia: Is Euro-scepticism a Government-Opposition Dynamic? *West European Politics* 24, no. 4: 22-35

Stampfli, Regula 2002. Political Communication in Switzerland and Europe Paper to Conference on Identity and representation, Centre for European Studies, Carlton University, Ottawa Canada, 9-10 May 2002.

Taggart, Paul. 1998. A Touchstone of Dissent: Euroscepticism in Contemporary West European Party Systems. *European Journal of Political Research* 33, no. 3: 363-388.

Tiersky, Ronald. 2001. *Euro-skepticism: A Reader.* Lanham, Md: Rowman & Littlefield.

AUTHORS IN THIS VOLUME

PETER ANDERSON has taught at the Universities of Southampton, Lancaster and Central Lancashire. Currently he is Research Co-ordinator in Journalism at the University of Central Lancashire. His research interests are focused on media and politics. Recent publications include: (co-author with Anthony Weymouth) *Insulting the Public? The British Press and the European Union* (Routledge, 2000) and (co-editor with Christopher Williams and Georg Wiessala) *New Europe in Transition* (Continuum, 2000).

KLAUS BUSCH is Vice-President and Director of the Institute of European Studies at the University of Osnabrück. His main research concerns the economic and monetary problems of European integration, the social policy of the EU and theories of integration. Recent publications include: Politikwissenschaftliche Integrationstheorien in Interaktion. In Wilfried Loth and Wolfgang Wessels (eds.), *Theorien europäischer Integration* (Leske + Budrich, 2001), and Economic Integration and the Welfare State: The Corridor Model as a Strategy for a European Social Policy. In Max Haller (ed.), *The Making of the European Union: Contributions of the Social Sciences* (Springer-Verlag Telos, 2001).

CLIVE CHURCH was, until his retirement in 2003, Jean Monnet Professor of European Studies at the University of Kent. He remains academically active and teaches both in Canterbury and Lille. His academic interests are in the European treaties and Swiss politics. On the first he is working on an update of the *Penguin Guide to the European Treaties* to take account of the work of the Convention on the Future of Europe. On the second he is the author, *inter alia*, of *The Politics and Government of Switzerland* (Palgrave, 2004).

KARIN GILLAND is a Researcher based at the Institute of Political Science of the University of Bern. Her research focuses on public opinion and party positions on European integration, and comparing voters' and parties' policy positions on the EU and other policy areas. Recent publications include: Euroscepticism among Irish Political Parties. In Aleks Szczerbiak and Paul Taggart (eds.), *The Comparative Party Politics of Euroscepticism* (Oxford University Press, 2004), and Ireland's (First) Referendum on the Treaty of Nice, *Journal of Common Market Studies* 40, no. 3 (2002).

PAUL HAINSWORTH is Senior Lecturer in Politics at the University of Ulster. He has published widely on French and European politics, and is a former editor and founder of the journal *Regional and Federal Studies* (formerly *Regional Politics and Policy*). Amongst his recent publications are: (editor) *The Politics of the Extreme Right: From the Margins to the Mainstream* (Pinter, 2000), and (editor) *Divided Society: Ethnic Minorities and Racism in Northern Ireland* (Pluto, 1998).

ROBERT HARMSEN is Senior Lecturer in European Studies in the School of Politics and International Studies at The Queen's University of Belfast. His recent research has focused on the Europeanisation of national political systems and on the development of the European human rights regime. Recent publications include: The European Convention on Human Rights after Enlargement, *The International Journal of Human Rights* 5, no. 4 (2001), and Les limites de l'européanisation: les administrations nationales face à la construction européenne. In Didier Georgakakis (ed.), *Les métiers de l'Europe politique: Acteurs et professionalisations de l'Union européenne* (Presses Universitaires de Strasbourg, 2002).

WILHELM KNELANGEN is Assistant Professor in the Institute of Political Science at the Christian-Albrechts-University of Kiel. His main research interests include the role of the EU in international affairs, the effects of Europeanisation on domestic politics and the EU politics of internal security. He has published widely on European issues and is the author of *Das Politikfeld innere Sicherheit im Integrationsprozess* (Leske + Budrich, 2001).

PETR KOPECKÝ is Senior Lecturer in the Department of Politics at the University of Sheffield, and, at the time of writing, was a Research Fellow in the Department of Political Science at the University of Leiden. His main research interests include East European politics, political parties, civil society and democratisation theory. He is the author of *Parliaments in the Czech and Slovak Republics: Party Competition and Parliamentary Institutionalization* (Ashgate, 2001), and the co-editor (with Cas Mudde) of *Uncivil Society?: Contentious Politics in Eastern Europe* (Routledge, 2003).

SUSAN MILNER is Reader in European Studies and Director of the European Research Institute at the University of Bath. Her research interests include 'social Europe' (social and employment policies), globalisation and labour, and attitudes towards European integration within the labour movement and the left, particularly in France. Amongst her recent publications are: Euroscepticism in France and Changing State-Society Relations, *Journal of European Integration* 22, no. 1 (2000), and (co-editor with Nick Parsons) *Reinventing France: State and Society in the 21st Century* (Palgrave, 2003).

PAUL MITCHELL has lectured at the University of Ulster at Jordanstown and Coleraine. His research interests are focused on the institutions of the European Union, Euroscepticism and the French far right. Recent publications include: Philippe de Villiers: A Valued Man?, *Modern and Contemporary France* 6, no. 1 (1998), and (with Paul Hainsworth) The Front National: From Crossroads to Crossroads, *Parliamentary Affairs* 53, no. 3 (2000).

CAROLYN O'BRIEN is a Research Fellow at the Contemporary Europe Research Centre of the University of Melbourne, and has taught European Studies at Melbourne and Monash Universities in Australia. Her research interests include French nationalism and the politics of the European Union. She is the co-editor, with Linda Hancock, of *Rewriting Rights in Europe* (Ashgate, 2000).

ANTON PELINKA is Professor of Political Science at the University of Innsbruck and Director of the Institute for Conflict Research, Vienna. He has published widely in the fields of Austrian politics, democratic theory and comparative politics, and is co-editor (with Günter Bischof) of *Contemporary Austrian Studies*. His recent publications include: *Austria: Out of the Shadow of the Past* (Westview, 1998), and (co-editor with Ruth Wodak) *The Haider Phenomenon in Austria* (Transaction, 2002).

MENNO SPIERING is Lecturer in European Studies at the University of Amsterdam and Director of the MA in European Studies at the International School of the University of Amsterdam. He has published on issues of national identity and Anglo-European relations. Recent publications include: The Imperial System of Weights and Measures: Traditional, Superior and Banned by Europe?, *Contemporary British History* 15, no. 4 (2001), and (co-editor with Michael Wintle) *Ideas of Europe: The Legacy of the First World War* (Palgrave, 2002).

MILENA SUNNUS studied and conducted research at the Universities of Frankfurt am Main, Bremen and Lund. Her main research interests are social movements, gender studies and political anthropology. She is the author of Öland. Lebenswelt und Konstruktion kultureller Identität auf einer schwedischen Ostseeinsel, *Frankfurt, Kulturanthropologie-Notizen* 61 (1998).

ALEKS SZCZERBIAK is Senior Lecturer in Contemporary European Studies at the Sussex European Institute, University of Sussex. His main research interests include political parties and electoral politics in Post-Communist Central and Eastern Europe and the impact of European issues, particularly Euroscepticism, on the domestic politics of EU member and candidate states. He is the author of *Poles Together? The Emergence and Development of Political Parties in Post-Communist Poland* (Central European University Press, 2001), and co-convenor of the European Parties, Elections and Referendums Network (EPERN).

European Studies

An Interdisciplinary Series in European Culture, History and Politics

New Zealand and Europe. Connections and Comparisons.
LUCIANO, Bernadette and David G MAYES (Eds.)
Amsterdam/New York, NY, 2005. 276 pp. (Vol.21)
Bound: 90-420-1904-2

Euroscepticism: Party Politics, National Identity and European
Integration. HARMSEN, Robert and Menno SPIERING (Eds.)
Amsterdam/New York, NY, 2004. 290 pp. (Vol.20)
Bound: 90-420-1168-8 Paper: 90-420-1946-8

Culture and Cooperation in Europeís Borderland.
ANDERSON, James, O'DOWD, Liam and Thomas M. WILSON (Eds.)
Amsterdam/New York, NY, 2003. 250 pp. (Vol.19)
Bound: 90-420-1085-1

The New Georgics.
Rural and Regional Motifs in the Contemporary European Novel.
KORTHALS ALTES, Liesbeth and Manet van MONTFRANS (Eds.)
Amsterdam/New York, NY, 2002. 244 pp. (Vol.18)
Bound: 90-420-1270-6 Paper: 90-420-1260-9

Morality and Justice: The Challenge of European Theatre.
BATLEY, Edward and David BRADBY (Eds.)
Amsterdam/New York, NY, 2001. 298 pp. (Vol.17)
Bound: 90-420-1398-2 Paper: 90-420-1388-5

Britain at the Turn of the Twenty-First Century.
BROICH, Ulrich and Susan BASSNETT (Eds.)
Amsterdam/New York, NY, 2001. 271 pp. (Vol.16)
Bound: 90-420-1536-5 Paper: 90-420-1526-8

Beyond Boundaries. Textual Representations of European Identity.
HOLLIS, Andy (Ed.) Amsterdam/Atlanta, 2000. XXII, 199 pp. (Vol.15)
Bound: 90-420-1543-8

Europeanization: Institutions, Identities and Citizenship.
HARMSEN, Robert and Thomas M. WILSON (Eds.)
Amsterdam/Atlanta, 2000. 274 pp. (Vol.14)
Bound: 90-420-1423-7 Paper: 90-420-1413-X

Germany and Eastern Europe.
Cultural Identities and Cultural Differences.
BULLIVANT, Keith, Geoffrey GILES and Walter PAPE (Eds.)
Amsterdam/Atlanta, GA, 1999. VI, 366 pp. (Vol.13)
Bound: 90-420-0688-9 Paper: 90-420-0678-1

Nation Building and Writing Literary History.
SPIERING, Menno (Ed.)
Amsterdam/Atlanta, GA, 1999. XV, 220 pp. (Vol.12)
Bound: 90-420-0627-7

Expanding European Unity - Central and Eastern Europe.
MARⱼ CZ, L· szlÛ (Ed.)
Amsterdam/Atlanta, GA, 1999. XVI, 170 pp. (Vol.11)
Paper: 90-420-0455-X
Europe - The Nordic Countries.
SWANSON, A. and B. T÷RNQVIST (Eds.)
Amsterdam/Atlanta, GA, 1998. X, 236 pp. (Vol.10)
Bound: 90-420-0326-X Paper: 90-420-0316-2
Robespierre -Figure Reputation.
JOURDAN, Annie (Ed.)
Amsterdam/Atlanta, GA, 1996. XIII, 236 pp. (Vol.9)
Bound: 90-420-0136-4 Paper: 90-420-0133-X
Machiavelli: Figure-Reputation.
LEERSSEN, Joep and Menno SPIERING (Eds.)
Amsterdam/Atlanta, GA, 1996. XII, 200 pp. (Vol.8)
Bound: 90-5183-987-1 Paper: 90-5183-996-0
Borders and Territories.
LEERSSEN, J.Th. & M.v.MONTFRANS (Eds.)
Amsterdam/Atlanta, GA, 1993. XII, 256 pp. (Vol.6)
Bound: 90-5183-506-X Paper: 90-5183-511-6
The Disintegration of Yugoslavia.
HEUVEL Martin van den and Jan G. SICCAMA (Eds.)
Amsterdam/Atlanta, GA, 1992. 218 pp. (Vol.5)
Bound: 90-5183-349-0 Paper: 90-5183-353-9
National Identity: Symbol and Representation.
LEERSSEN, J.TH. and M. SPIERING (Eds.)
Amsterdam/Atlanta, GA, 1991. VIII, 247 pp. (Vol.4)
Bound: 90-5183-253-2 Paper: 90-5183-254-0
Italy - Europe.
BRUYNING, L.F. and J.Th. LEERSSEN (Eds.)
Amsterdam/Atlanta, GA, 1990. 216 pp. (Vol.3)
Bound: 90-5183-194-3 Paper: 90-5183-195-1
France - Europe.
LEERSSEN, J.Th. and M. van MONTFRANS (Eds.)
Amsterdam/Atlanta, GA, 1989. 246 pp. (Vol.2)
Bound: 90-5183-098-X Paper: 90-5183-097-1
Britain in Europe.
BOXHOORN, A., J.Th. LEERSSEN and M. SPIERING (Eds.)
Amsterdam, 1988. 220 pp. (Vol.1)
Bound: 90-5183-013-0 Paper: 90-5183-013-0

info@rodopi.nl www.rodopi.nl

Lightning Source UK Ltd.
Milton Keynes UK
UKOW040659230613

212690UK00001B/98/A